STIR

IT

UP

STIR

Musical Mixes from Roots to Jazz

IT

G E N E   S A N T O R O

UP

New York Oxford

Oxford University Press / 1997

Oxford University Press

Oxford   New York

Athens   Auckland   Bangkok   Bogotá   Bombay
Buenos Aires   Calcutta   Cape Town   Dar es Salaam
Delhi   Florence   Hong Kong   Istanbul   Karachi
Kuala Lumpur   Madras   Madrid   Melbourne
Mexico City   Nairobi   Paris   Singapore
Taipei   Tokyo   Toronto
and associated companies in
Berlin   Ibadan

Library of Congress Cataloging-in-Publication Data

Santoro, Gene.
Stir it up : musical mixes from roots to jazz / Gene Santoro.
p. cm.   Includes index.
ISBN 0-19-509869-2
1. Popular music—History and criticism.
2. Jazz—History and criticism. I. Title.
ML3470.S28   1997   781.64'09—DC20   96-42930

1   3   5   7   9   8   6   4   2

Printed in the United States of America
on acid-free paper

Contents

PREFACE

M usic not only captures time; it mimics time. The ebb and flow that shapes the emotional tension between sound and space, spiked by dynamics and tonal colors, creates a rhythm analogous to the way we pass through history. Or can, anyway, when it's at its best. And when it does, music's language becomes an abstract mirror of human culture's passage at a given set of moments—a trail, sometimes of hope, sometimes of tears, but always in motion.

Hence these essays, all of which first appeared in some form elsewhere: *The Nation, The Atlantic Monthly, DoubleTake, The Village Voice, Fi,* and *Pulse.* If this book has a mission, it's to track some of the branches of that trail, uncover a few of the forks that got us where we seem to find ourselves. In that sense, *Stir It Up* is archeological, the kind of intellectual detective work that is part oral history and part informed intuition and part dissassembled teleology, part Studs Terkel and part Dashiell Hammett and part Michel Foucault.

But, above all, it's a reminder that if politics is what we do to each other, culture is the way we talk to each other. As the info age accelerates the fractionation of communities back into tribal groups with less and less allegiance to overarching traditions, languages, beliefs, or dreams, the importance of music's syncretic global interactions, its transformation of them into multiplying dialects that can function as something like common languages, and its role as a nexus for art and commerce will continue to help us plot, however roughly, where we are. That won't save us from each other, or ourselves. But along with post-Einsteinian physics and chaos theory, it may be one of our best shots at understanding the age we're leaving and the age we're entering.

Or, at least, enjoying the ride.

Shokan/New York City   Gene Santoro
October 1996

STIR

IT

UP

Me And Julio
Paul Simon

The Brill Building spreads atop the Colony Record Store on the corner of 49th and Broadway, one of the many pieces of architectural history that shape and resonate through New York's evershifting landscape. A monument to the hybrid glories of Art Deco, splashed through with gleaming brass doors and marble facings, its facade carved with pseudo-Egyptian reliefs, from the early years of the century until the 1960s it housed the songwriters and publishers who produced the pop music style called Tin Pan Alley. Everyone from Irving Berlin to Goffin/King churned 'em out here. It's ironic, then, that when Carole King (née Klein) was approached to work on Tin Pan Alley, her Forest Hills friend and sometime collaborator Paul Simon advised her against taking the job. It's ironic that Simon's own spacious and well-appointed offices nestle on the Brill Building's fifth floor. It's ironic, too, that the record we're discussing both extends and radically departs from the traditional Tin Pan Alley notion of what a pop song is—which has been his notion as well.

"I guess you could say that the preparation for this album goes all the way back to the sixties," he muses, "when I started doing things like 'El Condor Pasa' [a traditional Peruvian folk tune] on *Bridge Over Troubled Water*. I've always found it easy to travel to a place where there was good music and make music there. But this is the first time that I really immersed myself in a style, instead of trying to do a quick sketch of it, like I did with gospel ('Love Me Like a Rock' on *There Goes Rhymin' Simon*) or reggae ('Mother and Child Reunion,' inspired by Jimmy Cliff's 'The Harder They Come,' on *Paul Simon*). I tried to integrate my musical thinking with theirs, and let the synthesis be something that was neither mine nor theirs."

The catchy and provocative synthesis that is *Graceland,* Simon's bid to bring Afropop into American cultural awareness, is just that. It draws on a wide range of musical elements. There's American r&b and country and western, hybrids grown when rural acoustic sounds moved to the cities and plugged into electricity; South African styles like mbaqanga, many of them influenced by r&b and jazz; zydeco, where the blues met the accordion and Caribbean rhythms; Tex-Mex, born when Eastern European polkas collided with Mexican conjuntos; and, of course, that amalgam called rock and roll, the descendant of Tin Pan Alley tunesmithing, itself the first example of a mass-manufactured, mass-distributed pop music carefully attuned to marketing techniques. All dance to the infectious black South African grooves that power this album.

In the process, they demonstrate Simon's implicit vision of cultures and people entwining to grow, commingling to survive. Time and again, the lyrics articulate a sense of loss that leads to a yearning for transcendence and understanding, and the open eyes and ears that can further them. Take this verse from "You Can Call Me Al": "A man walks down the street/It's a street in a strange world/Maybe it's the Third World/Maybe it's his first time around/He doesn't speak the language/He holds no currency/He is a foreign man/He is surrounded by the sound/The sound/Cattle in the marketplace/Scatterlings and orphanages/He looks around, around/He sees angels in the architecture/Spinning in infinity/He says Amen! and Hallelujah!"

"I noticed," says Simon, "after I'd finished writing all the songs that a lot of them had a very similar theme: acceptance, aiming at some state of peace, looking for some state of redemption or grace. That was the theme of the album, although I didn't set out to write that theme." In fact, in the summer of 1984 Paul Simon wasn't setting out to write much of anything. Then came the catalyst that set off the explorations leading to *Graceland*: a friend gave him a cassette of black South African music called *Accordion Jive Hits Volume II*. "I've learned all this from a bootleg tape, which I'm sure the industry will be pleased to hear," he says with a wry smile. He was captivated by the instrumental music's jaunty dancebeats propelled by melodic, thudding bass, wheezy accordion, and chattering guitars, and found himself "playing the cassette on my car stereo constantly and scatting new melodies over the songs." He tracked the sound to its source, black South Africa, where the Soweto ghetto has nurtured a cross-pollination of indigenous forms with r&b and jazz called mbaqanga, or township jive. "At first I thought, it's too bad this isn't from Zimbabwe or Zaire or Nigeria, because life would be simpler," Simon admits. "But then I thought, It's beautiful, I like it, I want to see if I can interact with it musically. At that point, I didn't know much about the music, and I didn't know if it was even possible for me to interact with it."

So Simon enlisted Hilton Rosenthal, producer of South Africa's first integrated pop group, Juluka, for help. He listened and learned. Soon he was off to Johannesburg with longtime engineer Roy Halee to try to record with some of the black musicians whose work he found so energizing. Fearful of being politically misunderstood, he talked over his plans with musical activists like Harry Belafonte and Quincy Jones and got their votes of confidence. In the meantime, unbeknownst to him, the black South African musicians union held its own vote on whether or not to work with him, in view of the white regime's apartheid and the retaliatory UN-sponsored cultural embargo. As West Nkosi, producer of Ladysmith Black Mambazo (a singing group that appears on *Graceland*), puts it, "We felt that by promoting South African culture we were saying who we are."

As Simon recalls: "That first night I was in Johannesburg, there was a reception at Hilton's house, and most of the integrated music community was there. The discussion was open, mostly about music but also about politics. They asked about American policy toward South Africa; I told them that there was a unified sense of outrage but that the country was divided as to what to do about it. That's when they told me about the vote they'd taken. Basically, they saw me as a good vehicle for making their music better known. You see, they're experiencing a kind of double apartheid: by the South African government because they're black, and with their exported music because they're South African and therefore boycotted, which creates tremendous frustration. I support the cultural boycott because it's a statement of moral outrage, but I have to admit I'm not sure who we're boycotting."

Simon and various groups began working in the studio, groping toward a common musical ground. Reversing his usual recording procedures, Simon let the tape roll while the musicians laid down grooves; he had no material written. "I started with three groups whose records I knew," he explains. "We did overdubs on 'Gumboots,' the track I had heard on *Accordion Jive*, first. A track by Tao Ea Matsekha, a Sotho group, later became 'The Boy in the Bubble.' Another by General M. D. Shirinda and the Gaza Sisters became the basis for 'I Know What

I Know.' I started with those three tracks, which all existed—or a form of them existed—on other records. All the other collaborations were made up in the studio. The band would play riffs, going for a groove, then I would superimpose a structure."

To understand that superimposition, we have to delve a bit into the nature of African pop. Over the last generation, a vast range of pop-music styles have been imported into Africa, where they've linked up with existing forms. Rock and roll and the electric guitar hit everywhere on the continent. Latin dancebeats like rhumba and salsa spiced indigenous rhythms, yielding the high-powered grooves of Zairean pop, itself casting a huge shadow over western and central African genres. Other sounds, from country to reggae to funk, have filtered in as well. It's essential, though, to realize Afropop isn't a Western clone. Each style retains an identity, and a way of making music that's unique. Unlike Western pop, which tends to follow the Tin Pan Alley tune format of verse-chorus-bridge, Afropop tends to use repeating figures by each instrument to weave interlocking patterns over subtly shifting rhythms. For Simon, part of the challenge became keeping the key features of African sounds while reconciling them with familiar Western-pop forms.

His solution started in the studio, and extended into the editing process. "What I did was sit down in the studio with a microphone," he explains, "and improvise melodies and words, scatting into the mike over their playing—everybody was wearing headphones—just to make a form to start with. Then I'd take that form and erase my original scatsinging and write a song, a more thought-out musical idea and lyrics. Remember," he points out, "I'm not a musicologist. I didn't go to make an archival album of South African music, but an album of my music with musicians I could interact with. On all of the songs where I used music that was not from my own thoughts I considered that we were co-writers. It's the first album I've ever done with over half the songs co-written."

After three months in Jo'burg, Simon and Halee took a brief break, then resumed recording in New York, using a Shangaan rhythm section (guitarist Ray Phiri, fretless bass wizard Baghiti Kumalo, and drummer Isaac Mtshali), whom he paid triple-scale U.S. wages. Shaping the basic tracks as he had in South Africa, Simon began trying to fit lyrics to what he had in the can. "It took a while for me to fully understand what the tracks were doing," he explains. "I'd write something, and if it didn't work the reason would always turn out to be that I didn't listen to the tracks carefully enough. Some instrument was changing the chord and I hadn't heard it, or there was a drum pattern that made the phrasing of the lyrics awkward and I had to rewrite to allow that pattern to come out fully."

According to Simon, the title tune exemplifies his marriage of diverse elements: "The central image of Elvis's home, the Everly Brothers singing background harmonies, the evocation of the Civil War and the blues, are all American history. The pedal steel, even though it's by Sunny Ade's player, can sound like American country music. There are elements of 1950s rockabilly. But then in the choruses it's very South African, very influenced by blues and jazz: the bass is playing the flatted third and the guitar is playing the fifth, so I could always choose to sing a major or a minor depending on which instrument I wanted to follow. The syncopation of the choruses is also very much African. In fact, the whole thing is very African; it also just resonates, sounds to us like country. But the musicians were just playing what was natural and comfortable for them. On the other hand, that lick where the guitar is doubled by the pedal steel is my lick, so that's going to sound American, as is the use of the relative minor chord."

To guarantee empathy between American musicians doing overdubs and the basics, Simon used his standard approach: "I'd play the tracks for people and ask them to participate if they like it. It's not my intention to bring Adrian Belew in to put him in a musical straitjacket. So we just booked a couple of days in the studio with him and went over each track. Then he'd put different chips in his Roland guitar computer, and when we'd hear one that fit we'd throw up the 24-track tape and start to work. Same with Lenny Pickett and Tower of Power."

Working at home brought Simon's musical thoughts home, and he began casting for ways to unify the album's material. He used the kinship between the accordion sounds from *Accordion Jive* and the Louisiana zydeco of Clifton Chenier and Rockin' Dopsie (who appears on "That Was Your Mother") and the Tex-Mex-flavored rock of Los Lobos (who join on "All Around the World or the Myth of Fingerprints"). "Los Lobos, by its very nature, is a band that is doing constantly what I was doing on this record: taking two cultures and fusing them," Simon declares. "In their case, they're fusing traditional Mexican and Chicano music with rock and roll. But the motive behind my instinct to go to them was the accordion; it connected them, the zydeco track, and the African music. In addition, Los Lobos make their recordings sound very modern without undercutting the integrity of the music, which is something I wanted to do also. In fact, on that track we used Steve Gadd on gated drums with a touch of Simmons electronic drums triggered by his acoustic set. My intention from the beginning was to take the technology and apply it to a more raw, roots-type music, but keep the perspective that you're hearing the roots more than the technology."

The southern exposure of Simon's offices spills over with sunlight on this clear autumn day in the city that's served as the American gateway for millions. It's nearly time for his David Letterman rehearsal, so he wraps it up: "People tend to look at all aspects of South African life through the prism of politics, but really, this was primarily about music. That was a hard thing to explain sometimes. Not to deny the political implications, but they were implications: for me, music is the universal language through which we all connect. Art has a moral position, inevitably, and showing the life of the country through its music makes it easier to understand the humanity of the situation. I mean, I don't know anybody who is pro-apartheid except for Afrikaners. I have a tremendous fear of a civil war and bloodbath on a more personal level now, because I know people there, black and white, and their children. So I guess this album is meant to be a very small statement, an introduction to people we only know through newsreels. Now we'll know them on a more personal level." [1986]

Arc of a Diver
Steve Winwood

Something happened to Steve (then Stevie) Winwood around 1969. Maybe it started with the breakup of Traffic. That near-mythic and highly influential group (on The Band, among countless others that include the 1980s "downtown" New York scene) blended rock, pop, jazz, blues, folk, psychedelia, and Eastern and African and Native American music. Maybe it was distilled during the subsequent abortive months he spent with Eric Clapton and Ginger Baker. Refugees from the swashbuckling power trio Cream, they tried to breathe life into Blind Faith, that stillborn avatar of a stillborn concept, the supergroup, whose nostalgic appeal still casts its foolish shadow over rock. Maybe surrendering to the rampant elephantiasis of form that bloated 1970s rock after becoming a crafty tunesmith damaged his internal creative balance. Maybe he was caught, pure and simple, on the standard rocker curve: live fast, die young—and if you don't, outlive the thrust of your talent, except when you reprise or rework past triumphs. After all, in photographs of him what dominates his delicately handsome face, dramatically framed by draping hair, are his eyes: receding and wary, like a deer's caught in the headlights.

That's one way to hear *The Finer Things*, a four-CD retrospective of the Birmingham U.K.-born, 46-year-old multi-instrumentalist-vocalist's musical pursuits over the last 30 years. Beginning with his recording debut as a 15-year-old wunderkind anchoring the Spencer Davis Group, the box set traces Winwood's arc through Traffic, Blind Faith, Traffic redux, solo and group outings, and his 1980s comeback hit singles. The 63 cuts are revealing even as they make you lean on your remote control's fast-forward button for long stretches. For, like the career it recaps, the set presents several paradoxes. Well conceived and remixed, strikingly designed, saddled with an essay that, while it offers some pertinent info, mostly skates like an exercise in PR, exhaustively detailed about discographical and personnel info, *The Finer Things* serves up a telling picture of Winwood's wildly variegated, frequently meandering, sometimes brilliantly golden output.

When I hit high school, a few of my friends went on a mission to find *What's Shakin'*. The 1966 album was a precursor of the now-common compilation disc and featured the Lovin' Spoonful, the Paul Butterfield Blues Band, and a group called Eric Clapton and the Powerhouse. Clapton had already been immortalized in London graffitti ("Clapton Is God") because of his work with the Yardbirds, that seminally eclectic rock outfit, and John Mayall's decidedly uneclectic Bluesbreakers. He was a major draw, on the cusp of Cream. But what spiced the two tracks was that Stevie Winwood, the 18-year-old whose aged-in-cheap-red-wine vocals made the Spencer Davis Group kick with soul, joined Clapton for "I Want To Know" and Robert Johnson's "Crossroads," which became a Cream tour de force.

On *The Finer Things*, those two cuts land on the first (and most consistently listenable) CD, sandwiched chronologically between two phases of the Spencer Davis Group—the initial blues/soul cover sound that made it a U.K. presence, and the explosive, drum-driven hits that put it on the map in the U.S., "Gimme Some Lovin' " and "I'm a Man." Winwood, who grew up in a musical family that listened to (and played) American jazz, was doing like his Brit contemporaries Mick Jagger and Eric Burdon: more or less aping the vocals of American pioneers of blues and soul, reappropriating them into the reenergized rock that emerged following the music's early 1960s diffusion. In Winwood's case, the models he adapted included John Lee Hooker and, above all, Ray Charles, along with elements of Solomon Burke and Percy Sledge. But even on the first few tracks from 1965 you can hear the precocious youngster starting to literally find his own voice: the reedy, dryly yearning, cracking tone pierced by the trademark aching quaver, the fluid phrasing that deliberately, like Charles, toyed with the natural register breaks in his range to capitalize on their emotional impact.

Playing around Winwood's hometown of Birmingham, the Spencer Davis Group bumped into Chris Blackwell, then a young well-off entrepreneur who'd started a record label, Island, named after his Jamaican home. Blackwell would later become famous as the man who brought Bob Marley to the larger world, and already Jamaican sounds were his main passion. But in 1965 he wanted to manage the Birmingham band, and managed to get them recorded. In fact, their first hit, "Keep on Running," was a tune Blackwell brought to them from Jamaican singer Jackie Edwards, with the graceful lilt that powered the soul-music-derived Jamaican style of the time called lovers-rock. And more than that: guest vocalist on the cut was Jimmy Cliff, already a hitmaker on his home island. Thus began the string of sonic appropriations and reimaginings, the series of hybridized hyphenated forms, that would mark Winwood's best work. The fierce, dense percussion suffusing "I'm a Man" and "Gimme Some Loving," for instance, was clearly meant as an African-Latin homage.

In early 1967, Winwood left Spencer Davis with drummer Jim Capaldi and guitarist-singer Dave Mason, and, adding reedman Chris Wood, retired to a cottage on Berkshire Downs owned by one of Blackwell's pals, to give birth to Traffic. (Shades of The Band at Big Pink!) Released at the end of that year, *Mr. Fantasy* was a miraculous if uneven vista assembled from jigsawed pieces. That metaphor suits both the material's startling diversity and its method of recording. Like so many others of the era who were creatively energized by the then-new multitrack studio technology evolved from Les Paul's 1950s sound-on-sound wizardry, Winwood overdubbed like a mad one-man band, laying down guitar, organ, piano, bass, percussion, harmonica, and vocals while his comrades filled in and filigreed. By one of the coincidences that make cultural history a never-ending pleasure, Traffic's engineer was Eddie Kramer, who also happened to run the board for one James Marshall Hendrix and his Experience around the same time. So not only were Traffic's overdubs state of the art, they dovetailed with an air of inevitability—and often rehearsed the kind of psychedelic effects (distortion, panning, phase-shifting, and so on) that Hendrix was elevating to an art form while reimagining that very nature of recorded space in ways even the Beatles had only started to work out. Never a strong guitar soloist, Winwood nonetheless paid tribute to Jimi with the extended fretwork lacing "Dear Mr. Fantasy"—a five-minute-plus track that mirrored the move in rock toward longer forms and found an outlet on then-aborning FM radio. (Seven cuts from the album are on *The Finer Things.*)

But if Winwood was no Clapton, Beck, Page, or Hendrix, he was something else—a pop tunesmith for the psychedelic era who could fit together unlikely, cantilevered elements in flowing ways. The result: *Mr. Fantasy* and its followup, *Traffic*, were a bit like indexes of everything else floating around at the time. "Coloured Rain" combines soul music's stepwise riffs and harmonic movement with a sudden chromatic shift from major to minor for the bridge via a raga-ish lick, backing vocals that could've come from the Rolling Stones' *Her Satanic Majesties Request*, and a brief psychedelic sax solo over chugging rhythms. "Heaven Is in Your Mind" inverts the expected sonic mix, pushing drums and bass way up front for its funky verse, shifting to baroque-flavored piano in waltztime for the bridge. Following his outbreaks with the Spencer Davis Group, these moves paralleled stylistic experiments by everyone from the Beatles and Stones and Yardbirds to Procul Harum and Jethro Tull to the San Francisco psychedelic bands. Rockers in the 1960s toyed with unusual song forms, woke up to sounds from Africa to India, from jazz to Bach, and pilfered like kids in a toy store. World music—that pallidly amorphous rubric now hung indiscriminately from anything not recorded by U.S. or U.K. musicians—was being hatched, and people like Peter Gabriel (who might not exist at all except for Traffic tunes like "Withering Tree") and David Byrne and Sting being foretold.

One problem for Winwood's often clever music was the lyrics, at this point mostly supplied by Capaldi. They frequently lapsed, like those cited at this column's opening, into the sort of pastel bromides that still tint nostalgic images of the 1960s. Another was that, for all their alleged jazz background and influence, Traffic couldn't really improvise in any sustained or coherent way. Thanks to his collaboration with Kramer and producer Jimmy Miller, Winwood had evolved into a master studio technician. Live, he was less than dazzling. Blind Faith made that painfully apparent. Their only, eponymous album was a train wreck with some nice parts surviving, including sections of the two cuts ("Had To Cry Today" and "Sea of Joy") on *The Finer Things*. But the two live Blind Faith tracks on the set are—well, boring is a kind way to put it.

By no coincidence, that's the word I'd pick to describe most of the rest of Winwood's output between then and now, between Stevie and Steve—in other words, most of the other three CDs of *The Finer Things*. Whether he's attempting to stretch the reformed Traffic into ersatz jazz flights in the 1970s, noodling with other congregations, or locked into a studio full of synthesizers to dance with himself, Winwood's output over the last quarter-century has been spotty, at best. The peaks can be solid, like the catchiness of "Empty Pages," or sporadic and marred, as in "Low Spark of the High-Heeled Boys," where the slow-burning groove and stacked riffs would pack more punch at half the 11-minute length.

Winwood's apparent dependence on his co-workers, for all his vaunted multitalents, bedevils him to this day, as the vapid lyrics he draws from Will Jennings witness all too consistently. When he hooks up with the right people, he can still concoct musical excitement. Take "Higher Love," where he fronts Nile Rodgers' production team for a funky discoized hit. When he doesn't, or he's working in isolation, he tends to recycle moves over and over and over. Another partial, possible explanation for his career's arc, it also suggests that his basic strength lies in picking the right models—one reason his singles over the last decade-plus have been more interesting and fun than the tracks filling out their albums.

But when the singles are good—"Higher Love" or "Roll with It," for instance—they're very very good. In June 1988, I was working at the weekly 7 Days when an advance cassette of a new Steve Winwood record sparked this excerpted review from me: "There's good and bad and great news here. . . . The good news is that 'Roll with It' moves Winwood back to the soul-music regions that first launched him to stardom. The bad news is that less than half the tunes on this album live up to his potential. But the great news is that the title cut is a made-to-order, sure-fire Genuine Summer Hit—you know what I mean. From the moment its Funky Broadway beat swaggers out of your stereo, from the first second the Memphis Horns crease your skull, from the opening syllable of his deliberately garbled yowl of a vocal, you'll know you're gonna be hearing 'Roll with It' pouring out of beach radios and car windows and jukeboxes until September takes it all away again."

For as *The Finer Things* all too paradoxically demonstrates, when Winwood coalesces the shards of his undeniable talent, he can make you forget just how uneven his history has been, while he suspends time via the magic of a well-wrought tune. [1995]

Hippie Preacher
Jackson Browne

"I've been a compulsive sense-maker," says Jackson Browne of his songwriting. We're backstage at the Beacon Theater, squatting in one of the many rooms that amounts to a kind of vertical warren. "I've always wanted to have an impact immediately, so the song could be consciously digested and engage the listener's attention. You get a lot the first time, but like with a book or a movie, just by the nature of what music is there's always something you don't get until later. The more somebody can affix their own experience and imagery to a song, the better experience it's gonna be for them."

Browne and his feisty rock band are on the road behind *Looking East*, his first album since 1994, and only his eleventh album in 24 years. The stage show is tight, well-wrought. The audience thrills to the older material, like "Rock Me on the Water," and is polite or receptive to the new—a standard rock conundrum. As Browne himself sees it, "In the show now, 'Looking East' comes right after 'Rock Me on the Water.' It happened as an accident, but it's unmistakable for me in the course of doing a show what works, so there it stays. It's the album's title song, but I think it's one of the hardest songs for my audience to get into, and it's working because it's right next to another song with a kind of political context.

"'Rock Me on the Water' is about the '60s, the Watts riots and reading *Soul on Ice* and Bobby Seale's book. That whole idea of a city in flames and trying to find some sort of redemption in all of that has sort of come full circle with 'Looking East.' It has a political context but it's not really identifiable politically. It's not a specific political problem; it's the social context for a song. I guess whether I was consciously avoiding it or not, I didn't want to write a song that was a list, I don't want to catalog what's wrong with the world as much as refer to it and try to get to the heart of it. And so it winds up getting into spiritual territory, like 'Rock Me on the Water,' because the world is the way it is because we're the way we are. I'm sitting here, and I know it's not the Great Satan, it's just the Great Fuckup, the great snarl and tangle of commerce and people confusing commerce with progress, lifestyles with redemption."

The album's title track launches it to an ominous, snarling guitar-army that recalls the postpunk edge of singer-songwriters like James McMurtry, and lyrics that Browne delivers with just the right insinuating drama, a secular preacher's jeremiad that quavers with the tension between hope and fear: "Standing in the ocean with the sun burning low in the west/Like a fire in the cavernous darkness at the heart of the beast/With my beliefs and possessions, stopped at the frontier in my chest/At the edge of my country, my back to the sea, looking east. . . . There's a God-sized hunger underneath the questions of the age."

At 47, Jackson Browne is no longer the pretty boy who sat on Nico's lap in an Andy Warhol flick. But he's still a bardic voice for the boomers who fill his shows. Despite—or maybe because of—the lengthening string of ex-wives and lovers, the posse of kids, the critical attacks on his 1980s social activism, the scandal surrounding his relationship with actress Daryl Hannah, Browne keeps on keeping on.

Looking East is a beefy-sounding mix from the same band as 1994's *I'm Alive*, a more uneven effort focused largely on personal semi-revelations in the wake of the Hannah debacle. But the new disc combines the confessional, personalized storytelling the singer-songwriter first rode to fame and fortune with the metaphoric, prophetic jeremiads he's been drawn to increasingly since 1976's *The Pretender*—which, after all, predicted the yuppie phenomenon. But as that song implies, exactly what keeping on means seems a lot less clear than it did before the questions boomers like Browne faced had multiplied and the answers shrunk into tired mantras from right or left. At its best, which it is about 60-odd percent of the time—a solid average for any rock CD—*Looking East* finds Browne traversing symbolic ground, the staging area for his delvings into the visceral sense of hovering apocalypse that shadows his generation and so much of what he's written, whether on public or private themes.

Born in Heidelberg, Germany, but raised in California's Orange County, Browne was influenced by various folk musics, but especially the storytelling blues, early on. Not surprisingly, he soon fell under Dylan's sway. "Bob Dylan is a preacher; he's always been a preacher," he mused. "But the fact is that most of these songs—and especially Dylan's songs—exist on multiple levels. So it's possible to love a song for many years before you really hear what he might be doing with it. Look at 'Like a Rolling Stone.' I mean, what was I, 16 or 17 when that song first came out? I loved it. I took in every syllable, every inflection, and got so much from it. I really think you make more than you get. So much of what he was talking about, the references changed for me. The imagery of that song is so penetrating; it's so nonspecific, but it's exact. There's something really wondrous about it."

Trying out at hootenany nights and open-mike sets at the little clubs surrounding L.A., he met most of the folks who'd later coalesce around "The California Sound"—people who would cover his early songs and make him famous, not to mention rich. As he recalled, "Every club had a different night of the week when they had an open mike. So you could go from hoot to hoot, and get to know a whole bunch of music—folk music, even though it was happening in the middle of the Beatles and Stones. Ry Cooder and David Lindley came out of the folk scene at the Ash Grove, where they'd have Sonny Terry and Brownie McGhee, people like that. Ronstadt and me and guys in the Eagles like Bernie Leadon came out of the Troubadour on Monday nights. You see, you'd go hear the greats play at the Ash Grove, but the owner wasn't going to hire you. He'd send you up to the Troubadour, which was considered a bastion of commercial folk music—Hoyt Axton and the Smothers Brothers, which was not really folk. To me the Smothers Brothers were heroes: they were funny, and lost their show by criticizing the Vietnam War."

By the mid-1970s, Browne and his fellow Ash Grove rejectees were riding the waves of Hitsville. His first album, 1972's *Jackson Browne*, launched him in the period's singer-songwriter vein, with tunes that became staples of Browne's (and others') repertoire and the templates for his cult's empathy. Browne's confessional approach, enshrined during this period, stayed more linear than Dylan's, though it also grew in its insights: the conviction that choice is a zero-sum game that prices what you win at the expense of what you lose, and a grudging acceptance that you can't go home again. In

1973 came *For Everyman*, with its mini-morality-play title cut and its flashes of humor in "Redneck Friend," an early track shaped around the fuzzladen, surging guitar lines of David Lindley, whose obbligatos ran like a spine through most 1970s Browne songs. But albums like 1974's *Late for the Sky*, 1976's *The Pretender* (which followed his first wife's suicide), and 1977's *Running on Empty* that, with their vulnerability, wordplay, and (often overlooked by his fans) ironic humor, marked what Browne cultists still consider the artist's peak period. It was also his peak at the box office.

"*Running on Empty*," Browne says, "was about trying to demythify rock and roll, the experience. It's mythical stuff anyway." When I reply that demythologizing rock is usually as mythmaking as rock itself, he laughs, but adds, "It's slippery stuff, folks. But there's a certain point at which it would do people good to see whose life it is. For instance, you'd be talking to a journalist from the *Village Voice* about the MUSE concerts, 1979, somebody you'd hope would be a progressive or liberal type. But what you'd hear would be, This is really good of you; you don't have to do this. And you'd have to say, Hello, this is about the health and safety of people everywhere, and it is something I have to do, and you should feel that way also. People always want to set you off in the celebrity ghetto."

The outbreak of punk—something Browne, rather surprisingly at this late date, still seems to resent—thrived on trashing the existing state of rock. That included, naturally, headlong attacks on L.A. rock royalty like Browne and Ronstadt. The swirl of change, personal and public, helped lead Browne to more social themes and pronouncements. In the late 1970s he was a founding member of the anti-nuke MUSE movement, and helped organize the 1979 No Nukes concerts at Battery Park landfill and Madison Square Garden. But your heart being in the right place doesn't guarantee artistic quality: in 1986, Browne released *Lives in the Balance*, a shrill, strained disc that denounced U.S. intervention in Nicaragua in an attempt to cop the personal-meets-political vein mined by the likes of Panamanian salsa great Ruben Blades. That same year, he signed on with Amnesty International's Conspiracy of Hope Tour; two years later, he was the only white American artist asked to participate in a Wembley Stadium tribute to Nelson Mandela. Nevertheless, many of Browne's fans were disappointed by his apparent shift of emphasis; many critics scorched him for it—something else he still resents.

Maybe they'll be happier with the new album, though it has its peaks and valleys. That's been true of Browne's recordings from the beginning. He's written a couple of dozen gems, but like the vast majority of rockers he's rarely sustained that quality for an entire disc: *Late for the Sky* is an exception. *Looking East*'s above –.500 average is good for rock these days, where 70-plus-minute CDs force folks to come up with more stuff than creativity.

"Barricades of Heaven," a characteristic evocative Browne tune drawing from his Troubadour days, sets out one of the album's defining images. The chart-topping single "Some Bridges," which completes the symbolic dyad with an evocative meshing of public and private imagery, struts, fueled by David Lindley's instantly recognizable slashing growl of a lap steel. But while "Information Wars" rides a sonically interesting crosshatching of bass breaks, pealing harmonics, buzzing guitars, and so on, the outspoken lyrics flatten imagistically and emotionally—just what Browne's 1980s critics hated.

As you'd expect, Browne himself sees the arguments over the personal and political content of his music differently: "It's like Little Steven says: what's more personal than your political beliefs? Personal and political aren't poles, they aren't on opposite sides of anything. But personal and public are. So when people write stuff like that, what they mean really is songs about love or personal experiences that are not on sociological themes go over here, everything else goes over there. It's an inadequate description. That whole discussion is really framed by the writer's own grasp of the world. One critic who didn't like 'Lives in the Balance' wasn't that far off when he said that the song was more of a speech than a song. But it was a speech that needed to be made, so call it what you want.

"I think the real question is whether or not the song succeeds. I don't have to look too far into that argument to see that what it means is, (a) they're not interested in hearing about this stuff or (b) they're not interested in hearing about it from me. The politer version of that is, Why should we listen to a singer about nuclear power? Or, why should someone I'm used to hearing sing about love tell us about human rights? The answer is that all those things are part of life, and my job is to write about life.

"There are a number of models for successful political songs. One of my favorites is Sting's 'They Dance Alone.' It's an appropriated image: what he did was come upon a situation and transmitted this image of Chilean women dancing without their partners because they had disappeared. It was illegal for them to demonstrate; they could've been shot. So they did the national dance without their husbands, and that was a statement that was impossible to ignore in that country. So Sting did those women, that country, the cause of human rights a great service just by transmitting the image. So the criterion shouldn't be whether or not it's political; it should be whether or not it succeeds. Is 'Strange Fruit' less good because it's political?"

Some of Browne's songs on *Looking East* aren't any less good because they're not. Take the wry humor and loping beat of "The Cat," the groaners and metaphoric inversions of "Culver Me" ("I'm going to love you 'til the stars come down/'Til they park their limos and walk to town."). One shrewd colleague suggested that it feels like Browne is running on craft, not creativity. As a genre, rock is traditionally uncomfortable with that dichotomy—one reason it's still searching for ways to deal with its own history outside of recycling it. After all, one of the points of middle age is that you develop craft at whatever you do, that you learn to juggle and balance the demands that hurtle at you. The middle-aged Browne sure has developed an awful lot of craft to pull him through. [1996]

Every Breath You Take
Sting

"**Y**ou'd better put the tape machine closer to me; I speak very softly," says Sting, leaning back for a minute from the conference table at A&M's New York offices. We're surrounded by the tools of the trade: VCRs, cassette decks, turntables, TV monitors, huge Altec speaker towers, telephones. The view out the wall of 32nd-floor windows is hazy this late September midday, but even a quick look down sweeps in the hurly-burly mix of traffic and pedestrians and sounds from literally around the world that spills through midtown Manhattan during any typical week. Sting's running late, unusual for him, since he juggles his intense schedule with the ease born of organization. But today is a bit hectic even for him. He's just left his morning workout, is on his way to SIR studios, where he's holding auditions for his Brazilian tour. He's got a photo shoot to do. He's also got the inevitable and superficial MTV spot, though there are the equally inevitable snags there. But for an hour or so, over bagels and orange juice and coffee, he's parked his star status at the door to talk music, especially his new album, . . . *Nothing Like the Sun*; and the repercussions of some of what he says will reach a lot farther than his gentle speaking voice.

"My feeling is that with each piece of work I do I want to sketch out a new piece of territory for the future," he begins. "I want to be singing when I'm 40 or 50; I don't want to be doing Las Vegas singing 'Roxanne,' but I think it can be done with dignity and integrity. So I'm trying to expand what I do. I've been singing Mozart and Gershwin with my singing teacher, I think I'm a better singer than I used to be, I certainly have more range. And why not? I want to keep expanding, and hopefully people will accept that I can do more than just sing rock and roll."

. . . *Nothing Like the Sun* ought to convince a few more folks, if only because it ain't exactly *Second Dream of the Blue Turtles* or *Son of Synchronicity*. In fact, it's not exactly like anything else, even though it's an amalgam of all kinds of other things. There lies its beauty, its strength, its integrity, its diversity, and—not coincidentally—a great deal of its meaning. Like the Shakespearean sonnet from which that phrase is taken (and which appears as the lynchpin in the allusively structured song called "Sister Moon"), Sting's new release bundles together images and ideas received from all over, different poetic and musical traditions, and emerges as more than the sum of its parts. In their new hybridized contexts, the fragments have been energized into something more—a unified expression for the musicians Sting has tapped to collaborate. Drummer Manu Katche, percussionist Mino Cinelu, keyboardist Kenny Kirkland, saxman Branford Marsalis, and Sting himself on basses provide the nucleus, but along the way folks like Andy Summers, Eric Clapton, Mark Knopfler, Hiram Bullock, Mark Egan, Ruben Blades, Kenwood Dennard, Andy Newmark, Dolette McDonald, and Janice Pendarvis bring their unique talents to bear. As you can guess from the list, this is one ambitious project. Trained in music from early childhood, Sting became accustomed to making musical waves. When the Police hit the scene with their lean and crafted pop-reggae in 1977, the music industry was feeding off the bloated carcasses of dinosaurs like Journey. Punk had charged through, signaling that popular sympathies were moving to a different drummer, but it had small effect on the business side of the music biz. The Police purveyed a punkish sensibility and look, a stripped-back sound, and solid, catchy songs. The combination sold millions of records.

Sting, of course, scripted most of the trio's tunes, and that, coupled with his English-teacher background, has given him some controversial insights into writing music. "If I understood how a song is created, I'm not sure that I could do it," he says. "The closest analogy is, you start off with a seed idea that can be musical or lyrical. Once that seed idea is in the brain it then gestates. By a kind of process of almost DNA, the sort of code that's attached to this seed grows arms and legs: a bridge appears, a chorus appears, a B-section appears, a rhyme for line two appears. I'm not saying it's not hard work; there's a certain amount of grafting and fashioning. But ultimately it writes itself, it really does. Relaxing into that thing—that you're not actually doing much, that you're basically just monitoring the process—is how I've come to look at it now. For months I'll be writing, worrying, pulling my hair, saying I can't write any more songs. Then I'll relax, and realize I'm not writing them anyway; I'm basically collecting bits of information, putting them through me, and putting them down.

"There aren't any original ideas, you know. The most successful song that I ever wrote, 'Every Breath You Take,' is an aggregate of every rock song ever written, there's nothing original in it at all. It's a million songs, but it's archetypal; it doesn't sound like anybody else, it sounds like the Police. The originality comes through the band or the individual doing it, and you can get satisfaction from that. But the writing process is very mysterious, and belongs to everyone. Which is why I get so angry when I hear about court cases where people are saying, You ripped this off me. No one, no one wrote anything in that sense—you know? Even the great classic composers took folk music and fashioned it. The other idea is just bullshit, it's just lawyers making money. No one wrote anything. I mean, there've been a lot of my songs that I can see in other people's; I turn on MTV and say, Uh-huh, I remember that (*laughs*). But I wouldn't take the time to even telephone somebody to mention it, it'd be so embarrassing. It belongs to everyone. I'm just glad I can make a living at music, and I don't want to penalize anyone else who does the same. Copyright is a corporate function, people whose livelihoods depend heavily on the parasitic nature of taking copyright and making a living out of it. Musicians aren't like that."

For . . . *Nothing Like the Sun* Sting picked up "bits of information" from all over the globe—not that surprisingly, when you consider the Police's relationship to reggae and African rhythms, say, or Sting's own uses of jazz-tinged material in *Blue Turtles*. But what happens here goes beyond those models. . . . *Nothing Like the Sun* acts almost like a clearinghouse of musical ideas, but structures them around a musical biography. "In a way," he says, "the album is a reflection of my life in music. Having Andy (Summers) on the opening tracks, having other friends like Mark Knopfler and Clapton and Ruben Blades on there—if you read the liner notes, there's a list of people on there who've influenced me, from Shakespeare to Jimi Hendrix. I mean, why not? Why shouldn't an album be sort of biographical, in that sense? I'm not just interested in one kind of music, y'know: I don't listen just to rockabilly. I like rockabilly, but I want my albums to reflect a sort of catholic interest in the whole world of music. I don't feel it's limited to any one kind. I think pop music at its best essentially is whatever you throw in the soup; it shouldn't be precious about what it is. It can be anything. When I was growing up in England, pop music was this incredible mixture: you could hear Perry Como and the Rolling Stones, Connie Francis next to the Pretty Things, all on one radio station. You hated some things, but you were confronted with all this stuff. Some radio stations played popular classical pieces, like Beethoven's Fifth, and then pop things. So I was more fortunate than kids listening to the radio now, because what happens now is they turn on a radio station and hear one kind of music all day: heavy metal, jazz, country, classical."

The "stuff" surfaces everywhere. There are Branford Marsalis's sax and the chattering West African-style guitars chiming and twining over

Afro-Latin percussion on "Lazarus Heart," the whimsical music-hall lope interpolated with jazz and beat-box outbreaks called "Englishman in N.Y.," the opening ruminations (reminiscent of a Mark Knopfler soundtrack) of "Fragile," which quickly segues into a calypso-inflected beat coming off a talking drum. There's the 7/4 time and technology versus human love opposition driving "Straight to My Heart," the updated tale of Noah's ark done as a spoof on televangelists over the pre-reggae Jamaican feel that punningly helps name the track "Rock Steady," or the art-song-redone, "The Secret Marriage," that brings the album's personal and political sides together for a final statement.

Different tunes evoke different associations. Of "Lazarus Heart," for instance, he notes, "Andy and I have a long relationship; he knows how to please me, and I know the right things to say to him to get him going. It's a very easy, creative relationship: he just came in for one day, and we did those tracks ('Lazarus Heart' and 'Be Still My Beating Heart') like falling off a log. That solo spot in 'Be Still,' where he and Branford are sort of tossing the sounds back and forth, demonstrates the beauty of real musicians. You can't do everything on computers; computers are so linear, so . . . logical. The best thing about music is the accidents that happen. A note gets played somewhere else and you respond there; you don't really know what you're playing, but somehow the magic works."

Then there's the political aspect of Sting's music, more implicit up until his joining the Amnesty International tour. "History Will Teach Us Nothing," says Sting, "is a polemical statement to open a debate: history will teach us nothing, discuss. There are people in history who are obviously worth looking at, but there are situations in the world where history will not help, where it clouds the real issue of now." As the lyrics note, "Our written history is a catalogue of crime/The sordid and the powerful, the architects of time"; the words clearly echo the idea that history is the tool of the ruling classes, since it is they (and their academic instruments) who write the versions of history that we study, not the people they have conquered, oppressed, obliterated. But if "History" proposes a theoretical overview that shapes Sting's politics, "They Dance Alone" illustrates how that theory takes practical form among oppressed people he admires: the Chilean women whose male relatives are carted away to join the unnumbered desaparecidos in the jails, torture chambers, and unmarked graves of Chilean junta led by ex-president August Pinochet, installed by the U.S. and the Chilean armed forces after Marxist Salvador Allende won the presidential elections. "I hope he appreciates having his name in there," says Sting sardonically of the infamous subject of the English chorus, spoken by Ruben Blades, who is both a renowned musician and a potential candidate for president of Panama. "I met Ruben on the Amnesty tour," Sting explains, "and I think we share a lot of beliefs. He's very close to that situation, as a Central American, and I thought he'd help me give credence to the song." Closing with an uptempo dance-driven rideout, the tune holds out hope for a future that will banish the mournful, Andean-pipe-tinged dirge that is its body.

"The great thing about this type of protest is that when men protest, they go in cars and they throw bottles of petrol, tear gas, whatever, then they get taken into prison and beaten, or get killed—that's one kind of male response to oppression," is how he sees it. "But the female response is so much more pervasive and so much more powerful, because you can't attack it. In the song what I'm trying to do, basically, is magnify that power: the grief, the sorrow, certainly, but also the anger that is contained in this dance. I just see it as a victory every time the women do one of these dances, and it happens a lot. They will win, and not through violence." As "Fragile," which finishes off the overtly political tune-cluster, puts it, "Nothing comes from violence/and nothing ever could." Sting's liner notes for that track observe pointedly, "In the current climate it's becoming increasingly difficult to distinguish 'Democratic Freedom Fighters' from drug-dealing apolitcal gangsters or Peace Corps workers from Marxist revolutionaries. Ben Linder, an American engineer, was killed in 1987 by the contras as a result of this confusion."

The final track of this album is, like many of its neighbors, initially deceptive. A nostalgic-sounding evocation of art-songs past, "The Secret Marriage" is a multivalent, allusive tour de force. As Sting's liner notes point out, the tune's melody is adapted from one by Hans Eisler, a colleague of Bertolt Brecht who, like Brecht, barely escaped from Nazi Germany to America; once here, he, again like Brecht, was hounded by the McCarthyite right for Marxist views. So the implications of Sting's reshaping Eisler's melody are easily drawn. But if the music continues the allusive mode so fundamental to . . . *Nothing Like the Sun*, the lyrics reunite the album's alternating public political/private romantic motifs. Like the Shakespearean sonnet that gives the disc its title, "The Secret Marriage" defines its intentions negatively: "No earthly church has ever blessed our union/No state has ever granted us permission/No family bond has ever made us two/No company has ever earned commission." It juxtaposes the public and private spheres of every individual's life at a crucial point: marriage in our culture, after all, is not only a romantic statement but a social act. A fitting act that combines affirmation and defiance in a way that echoes, say, the dance of the Chilean women in terms of Sting's own life. [1988]

Buck Naked
David Byrne

About a third of the way through David Byrne's mid-June 1994 set at New York's Supper Club, the heavy metal-style spots kicked on, bathing his upturned face and flowing shoulder-length hair in relentless light. He was chipping his way through a minimalist, heavily distorted guitar solo, fronting a four-piece band that, as it moved from acoustic to electric instruments, worked more like a three-dimensional jukebox backdrop than an ensemble. All around me, the packed house chattered over the music, as they'd continue to do except when Byrne reprised by-the-numbers versions of classic Talking Heads tunes like "And She Was." At that point, I knew what bothered me about the show. He wasn't parodying being a rock star. He was getting into being one.

Slow dissolve, as the Supper Club, with its hints of poshness, gradually washes into a quite different setting. Two years before, Byrne showed up at CBGB, the haunt that launched a thousand punkers, including, of course, Talking Heads. He was armed with only a guitar and a collection of very sketchy prerecorded backing tracks, and the stripped-back results—the tunes that eventually became his latest album, *David Byrne*—were uneven but promising.

But as much as anything, Byrne's appearance was an Event. It seemed like the audience loved the fact that here was a guy who could afford to do whatever he wanted making this pilgrimage to his roots, standing buck naked, as one of his new song titles has it, before a crowd that, judging by the looks of them, could easily have been in the grungy venue when the Rhode Island School of Design refugees first showed up there during the mid-1970s. All the upbeat emotions floating around the historic room were enhanced by Byrne's touching gesture of returning to his roots in several senses—as it were, touching the ground before he made a new trip.

Unfortunately, the new trip has little liftoff. Musically, *David Byrne* feels like an attempt to refract familiar Talking Heads licks and grooves through a slightly altered prism. Some of the tunes are frighteningly recognizable, carbon copies of earlier work with a tweak here and there to "make it new" while keeping Byrne's Heads-acquired mass audience happy with the familiar. Lyrically, the disc is mostly limp and insipid and—that most common rock criticism—self-indulgent.

The same criticism could, and has been, leveled at some Talking Heads projects, too, with ample reason. But even though some of their work deservedly became rock classics, the Heads had the immeasurable advantage of wrapping themselves in irony. In their case—an example of this aspect, at least, of postmodernism at work—the wrap dissolved criticism in an eerily Reaganesque, Teflon-style fashion that owes more than anyone wants to think about (at least in terms of thinking through the troubling implications) to Andy Warhol's blank stare. If you thought, for instance, that Byrne's lyrics based on supermarket tabloid stories was reductive, or meanspirited, or condescending, or just pointy-headed, you got a knowing nod and a wink and a nudge from some fan or other who simply shrugged and said, "It's ironic, isn't it? Get it?" Maybe it was. At times it just seemed smug, especially toward the end of the Heads's deservedly long run.

But *David Byrne* makes the retrospective case that, in fact, in the case of the person David Byrne, the persona is what you get—and all you get. And, in fact, what you want. His new effort is meant to be somehow in a confessional mode, which the hype surrounding it makes plain. Kitschy statements by Byrne fill the press interviews he's done. When, for instance, the *LA Times*'s Robert Hilburn asked him what he meant by the lyrics to the new tune "Sad Song," which run, "But it's the truly sad people who get the most out of life," Byrne opines, "People want the world to be a Hallmark card place, but that's really disgusting. There's no richness to life without both sides." Of course, both the lyric and the pull quote represent sentiments that could easily be inscribed on a Hallmark card. So what's the point of personalized sincerity? In Byrne's elusive hands, the delicate confessional mode falls flat.

Life can be tough for a rock star whose moment has passed—as happens to nearly all rockers. Most, for instance, never last beyond a couple of discs at best, never mind getting a shot at something as tricky as navigating middle age. And if they get that far, their options are stark and appalling. They can opt for golden-oldies status, recycling their hit or hits endlessly, hoping to latch onto those lucrative cruise-ship gigs or to headline the package or revival tours that regularly visit big halls like New York's Radio City or Madison Square Garden. Or they can try for some redefinition, a refocusing of their sound and image that reworks the essential threads of their past into a newer, but congruent, form for their present. But since pop stardom is a demanding and limiting franchise—your fans want to hear what they already know, maybe with a slight twist—the second choice is loaded with potential missteps from the commercial, never mind creative, side.

These are the depressing horns the 42-year-old Byrne is clearly impaled on. The results: a remarkably weak album with lots of boffo press coverage, and an extended tour through North America.

At their best—albums like *Talking Heads '77, More Songs About Buildings and Food, Remain in Light*, and *Naked*—Byrne and Talking Heads surrounded themselves with two things: a supreme and attractive quirkiness enhanced by an indissoluble web of irony, and superb, innovative production values, often courtesy of producer Brian Eno. They were also remarkable students, quick and eager and apparently egoless as they scarfed down one lesson after another from nearly everything they bumped into, whether African chants or supermarket tabloids. (Not that their homework results were of uniformly high quality, but when they were good they were very very good.) Over the years, as he reached into areas like African and Brazilian and Latin music, Byrne developed a knack for appropriating and reworking the vicious rhythmic grooves that power those sounds into something that was recognizable for Heads fans.

He was, perhaps oddly but definitely tellingly, least successful at that when he stepped outside the Heads, in the mode of Paul Simon's

Graceland. Where earlier tunes like "I Zimbra" lifted sounds and beats and recontextualized them in a typical Heads sonic smorgasbord, the later solo album *Rei Momo* found Byrne fronting a high-powered Afro-Latin band. A revealing moment came when he toured with them, landing at New York's Roseland. For a couple of numbers mid-set, supercharged Brazilian vocalist Margareth Menezes came out for a star turn. With her at the microphone, the band suddenly cut in their hyperdrive afterburners, and the musical temperature went febrile. When her turn ended and Byrne returned, they settled back into idling—which still meant powerful rhythmic thrusts, given the aces who were onstage. But it was unsettling nonetheless to hear so clearly that Byrne couldn't inspire these crack players to put out their best.

Still, that rhythmic residue is the best part of the stripped-down, personalized new release that's supposed to introduce the new David Byrne. The question, though, is simple: Who wants or needs a new David Byrne? Especially since the new Byrne is quasi-intimate without being particularly revealing, groove-laden without being particularly compelling, doomed to repeat the handful of chord progressions that made him chief Talking Head and the anti-hero of a rapidly receding rock moment that even now is dissolving in the maw of the nostalgia machine.

Speaking of which, it may be helpful in understanding Byrne's new release to know that several years ago Warner Brothers gave Byrne his own label, Luaka Bop, which he used to showcase many fascinating international popsters from Tom Ze to Zap Mama to all manner of Cuban music. The record company lost money on the deal. Now they want it back. [1994]

This Year's Model
Elvis Costello

I stopped listening to Elvis Costello somewhere over a decade ago. It wasn't a cataclysmic breakup. I kept getting the records and playing them. But not a lot. After killer discs like *This Year's Model*, where every single track was deadly, even a pretty good Costello album (in rock terms, that's one with more than 50 percent solid material) like *Imperial Bedroom* just got to be . . . well, they got to be too much trouble to listen to, back in the days when you had to hop out of your seat to pick up a tone arm and reposition it on the next desirable cut.

So we drifted apart after a period of thrilling intensity that rivals any other fandom I've known. And by the time he broke off with his longtime band the Attractions in 1988, I barely noticed, mostly because I was only vaguely aware that they were still together.

In the late 1970s, Costello seemed—no, was—the epitome of what postpunk music (New Wave, it was quickly being labeled in that Adamic way of the music industry—if you can name it, you can control it) could be. Like P J Harvey, who is the nearest thing he has to a true disciple (as opposed to clone or wannabe), the self-renamed Declan MacManus was smart and smartass, savvy to the ways of hype and snide about niceties, cynical to the point of paranoia about what was really happening around him and ready to sneer at social and Tin Pan Alley verities. Of course, it helped as well that he rejected the dinosaur pomposity of arena-rockers but remained startlingly hyperaware of rock (and broader pop-cultural) history—not in a weighty way, but more as a collection of tools to be sharpened on the next target.

And his music, naturally, reflected all that. Beginning with and perhaps most transparently on his debut, *My Aim Is True*, his songs snatched beginnings, middles, endings, whole feelings from anywhere on the pop map. Here follows a brief, disorderly, and far from complete catalog: the Ronettes and Phil Spector ("No Dancing"); Motown and Stax-Volt; the Beatles and Stones and Who and Kinks; Buddy Holly and Eddie Cochran ("Mystery Dance"); the Seeds and Velvet Underground and garage rockers galore ("Waiting for the End of the World," and of course the cheesy Farfisa organ sound that runs through most of his early albums); the Byrds (the intro and guitar work for "[The Angels Wanna Wear My] Red Shoes"); Randy Newman (especially the eerie Newman of tunes like "The Dream I Had Last Night" and "Suzanne"); Bruce Springsteen (maybe because they're working-class contemporaries arisen on both sides of the Atlantic just in time to develop the same self-conscious sense of rock history that was also the sign of its Gotterdammerung); Hoagy Carmichael and Frank Loesser (by Costello's own admission—try running them past John Lydon); stylized British music-hall plotzi-ness; Bob Dylan (the surreal rocker's phase of, say, *Highway 61 Revisited*, with the same outrageous grabbing for rhymes and reasons but without the amphetamine logorrhea); Bob Marley and Alfred Hitchcock (the cinematic lyrics that course through dozens of tunes, but which are especially devastating over the pumping reggae of "Watching the Detectives").

You get the idea.

Musically, what was astonishing, subliminally or otherwise, was that Costello actually wrote songs, often with highly torqued and developed melodies, not a handful of chords glued together with hope and attitude and some shock value. This was just one of the ways he was starkly different from most of his confreres in punk and postpunk. Helped by his knock-kneed poses and his Buddy Holly nerd look, he managed to bring it off with just enough ferocity to undercut any potential criticisms of himself as pop wimp who'd walked out of the magic circle of three chords defined by the Ramones and Sex Pistols. Eventually, that liking—no, need—for musical complexity led him to collaborate with Paul McCartney, to perform an album of country tunes, and to venture into soundscapes few of his fans wanted to hear during the upheavals of the late 1970s.

As even the early demos from the Rykodisc CD reissues of his stuff demonstrate, Costello soon became a brilliant arranger who could evoke the models from music history he used for songwriting without simply mimicking them. More to the point, he was apparently fascinated by the way the parts in all the best rock probe the spaces around each other, only to interweave at staggered, if recurrent, intervals— plotting that, when it's good, suggests (and allows) a hurtling, raw spontaneity as it recalls the structural insinuations of Beethoven's late string quartets. (In 1993, Costello himself released an album of critically praised songs recorded with the Brodsky Quartet, *The Juliet Letters*.)

But it took a bit of time. *My Aim Is True* sounds a lot like the r&b-flavored point man who carried pub-rock into the postpunk Brit New Wave: Graham Parker. The album's arrangements sometimes hint at the sounds to come, as with the hovering reggae/mystery movie "Watching the Detectives." But by and large they're pretty conventional, slightly-left-of-mainstream 1970s rock ground out by Clover, a band from, of all unpunky places, California's Marin County. Produced by longtime fellow Stiff pal Nick Lowe (whose band with Dave Edmunds, Rockpile, would yield a great reading of Costello's "Girls Talk"), *My Aim Is True* put Costello on the map with a hit by, of all people, Linda Ronstadt ("Alison") who had already begun groping from some way to catch a new, post-L.A. Cowboys/Eagles wave.

Paradoxically, Costello's next album, *This Year's Model*, remains his most timeless and complete effort. It captures the fearsome combo of brilliance and rage, deep but easy pop-musical lore, the entwining of the personal and the political that marked Costello at his zenith. Oh, yeah, and punk's great weapon, its energy—the record shot out of the box like a streak, riding on wings of frustration and paranoid wit and sheer cheeky exuberance. Check out the way the drums keep sputtering on after the fadeout on the ferocious opening cut, "No Action" ("Every time I phone you I just want to put you down"), as if there's just too much afterburner cut in to be corralled by one song.

Key to the incredible multi-g-force impressions left by Costello's best work with the Attractions is how, like P J Harvey, he and the band lock together chart parts but avoid repetition, varying in at least subtle ways even choruses that recur. It's an explosion of creativity that leaves you gaping as it races by, forcing you to absorb its complete rationale and effects over time. With pounding rockers like "Pump It Up," rampantly aswirl with chromatic chords and wheezy organs and spi-raling bass lines, and gospel-soul punners like "Little Triggers," *This Year's Model* climbs right in your face, shredding your eardrums and your psyche.

Punk's energy was tinged with racism and misogyny—blue-collar rage, me buckos, is like that. But Costello was a misogynist for the thinking woman, as "This Year's Girl," a characteristically height-ened, dash-of-paranoia response to the Stones's long-before "Stupid Girl," shows: "Still you're hopin' that she's well-spoken 'cause she's this year's girl/You want her broken with her mouth wide open 'cause she's this year's girl/Never know what is the real attraction/All these promises of satisfaction/While she's being bored to distraction being this year's girl." Then there were "Lipstick Vogue" and *Armed Forces*' "Two Little Hitlers" to underline the metaphoric (and real) connections in Costello's work between the personal and the po-litical.

In fact, *Armed Forces*, his next disc, was first titled *Emotional Fas-cism*. Keeping the fierce sonics he'd developed on his second release, Costello primed the Attractions harder, though his songs were a bit more uneven. The good, however, were still great: "Green Shirt," with its skirling organ, Morse-code synth, and ominous 1984 lyrics; "Oliver's Army," a caustic tribute to the deft British handling of the 400-year-old Irish problem—and colonialism in general ("We could be in Palestine/Overrun by the Chinese line/With the boys from the Mersey and the Thames and the Thyme"); and the unusually direct plea, "What's So Funny 'Bout Peace, Love and Understanding."

By the time *Get Happy* appeared in 1980, a lot of Costello's strength seemed reduced to tics or gimmicks. The under-three-minute song lengths, for instance, were cut even more so that he could jam 20 tunes on a single LP—a move that also led to deteriorated sound quality. His lyrics became focused almost entirely on the ups and downs of male–female relations. (This is in inverse proportion to Springsteen's, which, with mixed success, increasingly sought self-conscious political metaphors in the bleak, postindustrial American landscape he chron-icled.) And even the chewy wordplay, which had often bordered dan-gerously on the rococo but had been redeemed by the pointed imagery and delvery, seemed rote, unreal, hermetic.

Trust, which tumbled out early the next year, was better. Musically based almost entirely on Southern-fried soul music of the late 1960s, it let loose prodigious bassist Bruce Thomas and his rhythm-section mates while managing some topical lyrics in "Clubland" and "Watch Your Step." But it was, for me, a relative blip. By *Imperial Bedroom,* I'd tuned out. And when Costello began incorporating people like McCartney into his act, I was not only sure I was right— I was gone.

So it's not surprising that, like lots of other folks, I was titillated when *Brutal Youth* landed in my hands. Reuniting Costello and the Attractions (and Lowe, who handles bass on more than half the cuts), recorded at an old-tech eight-track studio, the CD sounds dangerously close to a period piece—dangerously because, like sharks, like rockers in general but even more so, postpunkers are supposed to keep moving or die.

But in fact, more than half the CD—that number again, but the medium's changed—lives up to what Costello can deliver at his best. "Pony St.," a typically tautened and toned Springsteen-soundalike progression derived from their shared soul-music models (right down to the descending piano tinkles and stop-time bridge), serves up a picture of working-class British life with wonderfully sardonic twists: "If you're going out tonight, I won't wait up/Reading *Das Kapital,* watching Home Shopping Club/While you're flogging a dead horse all the way down Pony St."

In "Kinder Murder," crime—the premeditated yet casual, callous kind à la Hitchcock—will still out in classic Costello fashion, over a stark, tremoloed guitar moving back and forth on a couple of basic rock chords while the bass throttles hard into octave jumps and single-note bursts that are rhythmically subdivided à la McCartney. And there's evidence that his sense of shape and pacing has returned, when he follows with "13 Steps Lead Down." This incendiary parody of, among other things, 12-step psychoregimens begins over Holly-style acoustic strums, but soon gunfires into a pulsating bass and a psychedelic section that's largely quoted from, of all places, Steppenwolf's "Magic Carpet Ride." Cleanup hitter is "This Is Hell," which opens with a gong and portrays the place as a kind of Sartrean or Dylanesque banality, a disco on "Desolation Row": "Sorry to tell you it never gets better or worse . . . 'My Favorite Things' is playing again and again/ But it's by Julie Andrews and not by John Coltrane . . . All the passions of your youth are tranquilized and tamed."

It's intriguing to glimpse Costello at 40 trying to come to grips with age within rock's narrow confines. But it's comforting—actually, necessary—to feel that rage still underlies the best, most successful aspects of his musical thrust. And that he still interweaves the personal and the political in ways that are too recurrent to be chance, not ham-handed enough to make him a PC folkie in disguise. He is, after all, a punk with brains and direction and a gift he loves to flaunt—which already distinguishes him from the punkers per se, who meant to be as indistinguishable from their audiences as possible.

" 'What is your destiny?' the policewoman says. '20% Amnesia,' " responds the Greek chorus that names the tune, a raunchy but bouncy, herky-jerky genre piece that comes out of the music hall via the Kinks and The Who. It lists some of the surreal detritus of the 1980s that we—and Costello—have survived. "Mr. Gorbachev came hat in hand/ From a bankrupt land to a bankrupt land," he screams, torn and jagged, in one vignette.

It may only be fleeting, a single reunion's atom smashing, but *Brutal Youth* is worth the risk. [1994]

50-Foot Queenie
P J Harvey

A couple of times in every rocker generation—that's roughly every two or three years—somebody blows the lid off everybody's expectations and renews the possibilities of the idiom's lengthening history. This time, it's Polly Harvey and her fierce, feisty, voluptuous rhythm section, bassist Stephen Vaughan and drummer Rob Ellis. Between 1992's *Dry* and their 1993 album, *Rid of Me*, P J Harvey is resynthesizing—and in the process reimagining and redefining—the sound and shape of rock and roll. Just cock an ear toward her totally reworked notion of Bob Dylan's "Highway 61 Revisited" for a sample dose of how.

Twenty-three-year-old Polly Jean has all the ingredients of the perfect postpunk rocker. She's got attitude: she's pissed off, direct, articulate to the compacted point of imagist poetry, ironic, sarcastic, and bracing as salt sprayed into a wound with a fire hose. Listen, for example, when she sings, "I'm coming out man-size/Skinned alive/I want to fit/Got to get/Man-size . . . /I measure time/I measure height/I calculate/My birthright" through clenched teeth without dropping a single scooped note or melisma. She's also got the musical chops and smarts that mark her off from the pack: catch the subtlety of her intricate backing-guitar figures on "Missed" or the flatout way she wails a banshee solo on "50 Foot Queenie."

Rock is, perhaps above all, about two things: beat and overall sound. As for the first, this trio insinuates rhythms with a ferocious, walloping openness rare in any format, let alone rock. Like Trane's groups with Elvin Jones or Hendrix's with Mitch Mitchell, P J Harvey doesn't usually lean or land on beats in any straightforward way. Instead, they surround them until they pulsate, loom ever larger, become unavoidably definitive like a donut's hole. Even when all the parts the group is jigsawing and gyring around sound simple, they're not. During the first chorus of "Missed," for instance, they seamlessly drop half a bar in the midst of a sonic hurricane, and effortlessly, misleadingly (you'll find your foot tapping in the "wrong" place when the verse begins) turn the beat around with the customary panache of all those blues players young Polly grew up listening to. (Her parents, avid blues, folk, and rock fans, are also promoters in England.) What's maybe as telling is that they resist the temptation to repeat that move or any other. It's the kind of classic economy of means that speaks volumes while underlining for us just how many more moves they've got.

Their reveling in their own fertility bursts through everywhere on *Rid of Me.* The odd-meter patchwork of "Missed"; the barbed-wire licks and yodeling moans and Velvet Undergroundish violin-as-rude-noise running through "Legs"; the chunky-skidding-bass-chord-plus-intermittent-drum-slamdunks intro to "Rub 'til It Bleeds," and the chorus's punctuation by feedback that builds from wisps into a full-throated bellow; the buzzsaw guitar figures spiraling up from the drummer's offbeats on "Hook"—you get the idea. And they can do it all live with a vengeance, as they proved every time I saw them during 1992's two brief swings through the U.S.

On stage or on disc, the band doesn't miss a trick or a step. The million or so little touches, dabs of color and expressive rage or pain or sarcasm, musical twists and lurches and sidesteps that are the building blocks of their arrangements showcase a fabulous inventiveness and a precision-tooled interaction. But all that obviously well-honed grace never betrays the visceral kick of the music's aggressive rock slop. That's true even when Polly's singing "Man Size" in front of a string sextet that sounds like it's landing somewhere between late Beethoven and Bartok. So let's put it this way: P J Harvey is to garage bands what heavy water is to H_2O.

As far as its overall sound on disc, *Rid of Me*, like *Dry*, is what you might call radical-conservative. Despite the fact that the first album was recorded for a couple of thousand pounds—a pittance, in studio terms—and the second had a bigger budget, they clearly plot a sonic continuum. Along with their postpunk blurring of the normal mainstream rock distinctions—between vocals and instruments, frontline and backline—they inhabit a post-digital wall-of-grunge mix that's as filthy as a wrecked 78 and as precise as a laser. The sonic blear with its points of light deliberately echoes everything from the tautly driving postwar urban blues of Muddy Waters to the Sex Pistols' tortured, torturous unintelligibility.

With producer Steve Albini, a hardcore veteran, on board for *Rid of Me*, the trio laces their slash-and-burn attack with quotes and references as least as intense as on *Dry*. Only somebody who's been absorbing the music's history since birth the way a Ferrari gulps high octane could pull off so unselfconscious and effective and distinctive an effort. Distant fade-ins, sudden dramatic shifts in decibel levels, odd creaks and rumbles and billows of feedback feathering off at the edges of the dense, almost impacted, but still three-dimensional sonic imaging—the results are as visceral and immediate as a stomach pump.

And Polly's lyrics are ferociously scarifying, funny, polymorphously perverse, and metamorphically metaphoric as they survey and x-ray the scar tissue that covers human psyches and relationships. For a 23-year-old—for a 123-year-old—Polly Jean Harvey has a frightening grasp of the daunting and harrowing complexity beating at the heart of human emotion. As they've been for Elvis Costello, contradictions are her meat, and she likes serving them up raw and bloody.

On the title cut, there's the look at the kind of atavistic ferocity that surfaces as a relationship peters out: "I beg you/My darling/Don't leave me/I'm hurting . . . /I'll tie your legs/Keep you against my chest/'Cause you're not rid of me/Yeah you're not rid of me/I'll make you lick my injuries . . . /Till you say don't you wish you never never met her." There's the way "Missed" unfolds as a poetic thriller with homicidal results, brandishing the ominous refrain, "No, I missed him." There's the stunning way "Legs" opens: "Whoa-uh-ah-oh/Did I tell you you're divine?/Ah-uh-ah-oh/Did I ever/When you were alive?" There's the vicious emotional truth in the way it closes: "I might as well be dead/But I could kill you instead." There's the savagely ironic pivot by the narrator of "Rub 'til It Bleeds": "God's truth/I'm not lying" is how the verse finishes over a gently strummed accompaniment, which swells and pumps into the angry chorus that turns to crow, "And you/And you believed me." And, of course, there are the song titles themselves, things like "Me—Jane" and "Snake."

Those titles underline how Harvey's perspective translates consistently into metaphors and symbols that are uniquely female—one of the many things that could help make her a revolutionary figure in what looks more and more like rock's latter days. (Either of P J Harvey's first two albums would be a hiphopper's delight of samples.) She never lets you forget she's a woman, either. That's not because she's waving around some outsized rocker's ego or feminist posturing: shy in person, she's in command onstage but undramatically, understatedly. The power of her presence doesn't derive from flashy moves and costumes; it's the sheer irradiating force of her personality as the music represents it. This woman is no mouthpiece with a microphone singing one more time about the ache of being left behind. She's created a world that she dares you to enter while she's brandishing her volatile guitar and supple voice and poetic talents and dynamic leadership on every tune she cuts. So it's her blood all over the tracks that I find myself playing over and over and over again. [1993]

Polly Jean Harvey struck gold for the third time with her 1995 album, *To Bring You My Love*. As you'd expect from installments one and two in the turbulent, unpredictable psychodramas that are P J Harvey's pithy, pointed stocks-in-trade, nothing here is as straightforward as it seems.

Take the title track. A raunchy guitar lick adapted from Albert King's "Born Under a Bad Sign" is wreathed by the near-feedback drone of an E-bow guitar, then yields to recurrent organ-plus-overdriven-guitar explosions punctuating a chord progression from Traffic's "Dear Mr. Fantasy." Meanwhile, the lyrics, delivered in a voice that ranges from throaty grunge to ululating whoops, tumble *Rosemary's Baby* and the woman-as-witch trope in with John Bunyanesque rhetoric and the bluesman-meets-Satan-at-the-crossroads tradition. The volatile results turn the mix's ingredients 180 degrees: "I was born in the desert/Been down for years/Jesus come closer/I think my time is near/I've travelled over/Dry earth and floods/Falling high water/To bring you my love/Climbed over mountains/Travelled the sea/Cast out of heaven/Cast down on my knees/I've lain with the Devil/Cursed God above/Forsaken heaven/To bring you my love." In case you miss what's happening, the next track, a furious sonic squall called "Meet Ze Monsta," continues Harvey's bent for retelling fables from the alleged female victim's viewpoint, thus pulling them inside out: Fay Wray, as we all probably guessed or hoped, had a what sounds like a pretty great time with Kong after all.

In effect, *To Bring You My Love* is Polly Jean's first solo disc: she plays most of the instruments, does all the vocals, and is the dominant element here even more clearly than on *Dry* or *Rid of Me*, which were obviously her auteurial products. On the down side, that translates into less varied rhythms than her crackerjack ex-triomates fed into the creative musical storm with her. But she's also got such a deep bag of let's-get-this-music-physical ideas that that's less crucial than it might be. "Monsta," for instance, grinds out a techno-industrial feel beneath its oozing guitar spew. An almost subdued tune, "Working for the Man," matches techno-style organ bass with swamp-tremolo rhythm guitar and the eerie, disconcerting double-tracked octave vocals Harvey is so fond of using to create an offbalance sonic depth. "Long Snake Moan," continuing the bluesman-image reappropriation (the title, complete with sexual puns, is adapted from blues great Blind Lemon Jefferson's classic "Black Snake Moan"), takes its galeforce cues from breakthroughs like Jimi Hendrix's "Are You Experienced?" and "Voodoo Child"—and, in fact, it rides out to the fade asking, "Is my voodoo working?" [1995]

Who's The Boss
Bruce Springsteen

For me, the most irritating, wonderful thing about Bruce Springsteen is how he gets under my skin, whether I want him to or not. When I'm not listening to him, I can get plenty of distance. Maybe too much distance. Not listening means I can run all kind of riffs on him. You know, smartass schoolyard critic riffs like, How can you trust a working-class hero who calls himself The Boss? Or earnest varsity-level critic riffs like, How does a rich rock star who lives in Hollywood write songs about the blue-collar world's harsh and sentimental realities and fill arenas with the very people he's writing about from afar? Why do they believe in him? Or fancy pro-league critic riffs like, What are the levels of manipulation inherent in a best-selling pop star's release, especially when he's fired his longtime band, had a long layoff, and reappeared in bad economic times that threaten record industry profitability, which depends so much on major stars like him?

Duh. Yeah, I guess I don't really care either. So pop culture's mammoth tail—its distribution pipelines—can usually wag any young-dog artist it really wants to, just by the way it makes its demands up front. But the same machinery can be what slams a message home. Here's an analogy: Oliver Stone's *JFK*. I'm no Stone fan. I think he tackles big themes and reduces them to melodrama. I've squirmed through every movie of his I've seen. But think about it: *JFK*'s got mall-moviegoers who wouldn't otherwise know or care about the subtleties of the Warren Commission report and the Zapruder film asking intense questions. When I complained to one old-neighborhood buddy (who's currently devouring material about the Kennedy assassination) about Stone's reductionism in *JFK*, his puzzled comeback was, "But that's what I liked about it."

For my money, Bruce Springsteen is usually better—far better—at what he does than Oliver Stone. For one very important thing, he's not smug or self-satisfied or condescending. But his method's not unrelated.

He writes parables, too—in his case, parables of growing up and coming to terms with the bruised world that surrounds us. When he's doing it right, they resonate with a particularity that's haloed by implications.

When I played *Born to Run* not long after it came out for a California pal who didn't know from Bruce, his reaction startled me: "It sounds like *West Side Story* with a backbeat." Part of what he heard was the stylized street stories. Part was the big stagey voice soaring into exhilarated pain and strangulated hope. And maybe another part came from the nature of the music itself, Springsteen's personalized pastiche of r&b, rock, soul, folk, blues, country. It feels curiously static, reassuringly timeless, almost ahistorical—rock and roll translated to Broadway. The contrast with the sheer balls-to-the-wall dynamics of a Springsteen performance is enormous. Why the gap? Springsteen is a culmination, a summary. He's the product of so much that preceded him that he has, ironically, almost nowhere left to run. It's not like he can really change the way he sounds. It's not like he'd want to if he could.

When *Better Days* and *Human Touch* came out in 1992, I didn't know what to expect. I didn't even know if I really cared enough any more to write about them. I hadn't listened to a Springsteen record in literally years. But there was some kind of nagging loyalty in me. I mean, I feel like I grew up with the guy. We come from the same blue-collar ethnic places. I saw him playing in boomy high-school gyms and shithole clubs. And when I listened to him then I was ready—no, aching—to believe I could hop on a hog with some girl who had enough faith in herself and me so we could head once and for all out of Jungleland, even if it was only to crash and burn with a spectacular rage. And there were millions of me. I knew it. So did he. We gathered wherever he chewed up the stage with the sweat-soaked marathon shows that gradually made him a legend among us.

That was heading toward 20 years ago. Springsteen's career on disc grew more self-conscious and more sentimental and more uneven after the astringent, bleak *Darkness on the Edge of Town*, which followed a bitter lawsuit with his manager. He spawned a generation of more-or-less talented wannabes, like John Cougar Mellencamp and Steve Earle, who sang about Midwestern small towns and their clannish troubles in rock and roll accents taken mostly from, ironically, the Rolling Stones' *Exile on Main Street*. On *Nebraska*, a collection of home demos, he tried to be a sort of latter-day Woody Guthrie, with mixed results—

a batting average he'd pick up with 1996's *Tom Joad*, a biting parable of poverty and rage Guthrie would've been happier with.

But *Nebraska* marked a shift for the worse in Springsteen's songwriting, for a time. His lyrics got more direct and stripped-back; he mostly abandoned the heightened, slightly surreal sense of reality and overpacked lines that had gotten the New Bob Dylan tag hung from him in the early days. First *The River*, then *Born in the USA* felt bloated and diffuse and relentless, even monotonous; his sense of pain seemed to have devoured his sense of humor and watered down his urgency. His huge pipe-organ of a voice seemed to have all the stops pulled out all the time; no more veering from ragged-but-gentle intimacies to cathedral-sized caterwauls. If *The River* was overlong, however, it was still lit regularly with incandescent moments like "Cadillac Ranch" and "The Ties That Bind." *Born in the USA*, by contrast, simply reflected his stadium-rocker status. In its wake he took off on a prodigious world tour that apparently left him exhausted. He released a solid live greatest-hits-on-tour album and an inconsequential studio disc called *Tunnel of Love*, and retreated into silence.

A divorce, a marriage, and a child later, in 1992 he began trying to catch up with himself—and us. *Human Touch* and *Lucky Town* each have a fair amount of filler. Each will sound familiar in slightly different ways. Even though Springsteen fired the E Street Band, you couldn't tell by listening, except for maybe the missing sax. For most of *Lucky Town*, in fact, he plays all the instruments himself. Since he routinely taught the E Street boys their parts to his songs, it's not surprising how much like him they sounded. And as signposts, each album has a couple of instantly recognizable Springsteen anthems.

The two discs are obviously a bid for attention. But, at the same time, they're set up like complementary signals from two sides of his musical personality. The separation's artificial; traits leak back and forth. After all, Springsteen's personal pastiche of rock's history is the world of garage bands writ large with immense and loving skill. That's one reason he connects with us. One way or another, we've all been there. Yeah, the music feels oddly static as a result. But that also just underlines the fact that rock and roll stopped being the innovative engine of American pop-musical development around the time Springsteen appeared on the scene. (It's no accident anyone under the age of 21 usually keys into rap or techno faster than rock.)

So let's say *Human Touch* extends Springsteen's bar-band, urban, r&b-based self. Soulsters like Bobby King and Sam Moore match his vocals, and the progressions come mostly straight out of soul music. There are inevitable twists and exceptions, indicators of how deeply internal Springsteen's musical mix is, of his self-confident stylistic mastery. Take the title cut, which boasts a knife-edge guitar solo worthy of Television. Or "I Wish I Were Blind," a country-flavored lament whose grungy guitar rage could've come off Neil Young's *Ragged Glory*. Or the Credence Clearwater-type swamp fever of "Cross Your Heart," with its devastating guitar twanging in the sonic distance. Or "57 Channels," which describes every cable junkie's lament ("There's 57 channels and nothin' on") with a funny rock-legend spin.

And let's say that *Lucky Town* is his Heartland America side, the one rooted more in Woody Guthrie and the Stones that inspired the likes of Mellencamp. (The title track is so like a Mellencamp cut it's either a reverse tribute or a claim to take back what Springsteen codified—or both at once.) The rest, filler and all, is basic Bruce. "Leap of Faith" opens his characteristic escape hatch ("Oh heartbreak and despair got nothing but boring/So I grabbed you baby like a wild pitch/It takes a leap of faith to get things going") to echoes of the Stones' "Tumbling Dice." From a different perspective, "Big Muddy," a homage to the blues with all the puns intended, scorches lyrics like these with backing bottleneck guitar: "How beautiful the river flows and the birds they sing/But you and I we're messier things/There ain't no one leavin' this world buddy/Without their shirttail dirty/Or their hands bloody."

So the road from Jungleland doesn't lead to Eden. It only takes you out of town. As Springsteen told Mikal Gilmore in *Rolling Stone* a few years back, "Once you break those ties to whatever it is—your past— and you get a shot out of the community that you came up in, what are you going to do then? There is a certain frightening aspect to having things you dreamed were going to happen happen, because it's always more—and in some ways always less—than you expected. I think when people dream of things, they dream of them without the complications. And that doesn't exist."

So it's telling that both *Human Touch* and *Lucky Town* end on a gentle note of affirmation. For all its flaws, this is trying to be a grown-up brand of rock and roll that can tackle notions of responsibility. Like a few others—Neil Young, David Byrne, Jackson Browne, Sting, and

Richard Thompson among them—Springsteen is struggling. He's trying to reparse a musical language that has been aimed from its birth at a theoretically timeless and unambiguous "youth culture" into a method for describing a blurry reality. So yeah, rock's makers and listeners inevitably grow old and tired and compromised. Their dreams get tarnished. But the dreams are what remain.

On the morning after the 1989 Rolling Stones concert at Shea Stadium—a helluva blowout, much better than I would've dared hope—I shared a TV show's green room with author Stanley Booth. Booth, of course, wrote the classic *The True Adventures of the Rolling Stones.* We talked about the concert. Booth listened to my slightly hungover enthusiasm and agreed politely, then added devastatingly, "It was a really good show, but I can remember when rock and roll was supposed to change your life."

So does Bruce Springsteen. Despair and hope, rage and affirmation, the cycle of ambiguity that rides closer herd with age, are the central notions his songs circle back to. But his approach—his empathy with and power over his audiences, the way he allows them to connect the social issues he discusses in interviews and onstage with the vignettes he performs as their illustrations—makes him a kind of American pop-culture disciple of Bertolt Brecht. His parables, like Brecht's, outline key dilemmas. Catharsis doesn't have to end with dancing in the aisles; you can dance in the streets, too. For the last two decades, the left has insisted that the personal is the political, and vice versa. At their best, Springsteen's songs and performances demonstrate one way that axiom might work in rock and roll. [1992]

Punk Repunked
Television

The received wisdom on punk, that explosion of energy in 1970s rock, goes basically like this. Post-1960s rockers had become bloated and pretentious: so-called progressive-rock bands like Emerson Lake and Palmer, who flailed away at pastiches they titled suites or badly reroasted chestnuts like "Pictures at an Exhibition." Radio had already frozen into the prototypes of today's strict market segmentation after its free-format heyday. Corporate rock—a combination of bland, interchangable licks and sobbing vocals with a touch of inchoate rage about heartache—filled arenas via groups like Journey and Foreigner. It was the trough following the exploratory tidal wave of the preceding decade.

Punk, as the story goes, changed all that. The hippie subculture, personified by bands like The Grateful Dead, became an epithet. Pre-hippie dinosaurs like the Rolling Stones and The Who were dismissed as irrelevant old farts. Three-minutes-and-under tunes, blasting at neck-snapping speeds, became the order of the day. Solos were out. Technical polish disappeared in the firestorm of rock's rebirth, punk's deliberately amateur, I-just-picked-this-up-for-the-first-time thrashings that reflected the garage-band ethos at rock's roots. Politics reappeared in lyrics. What returned with it was attitude, the curled sneer and piss-off shrug that has fired the hearts of rockers since the 1950s.

All generalizations, including this one, are false, runs the old conundrum. It's no less true for the thumbnail sketch above. What's really interesting are the revaluations that hindsight and history's twists bring. Take Aerosmith. They started as a sort of downmarket Stones, pitching singles at the teenybop crowd. Because of that, early rappers Run-D.M.C., who grew up on their music, did a remake of "Walk This Way," one of Aerosmith's 1970s chart-toppers, that became an early hiphop crossover hit. That led to joint appearances and the reincarnation of a band that, frighteningly enough, probably sounds better today than it did the first time around.

Frighteningly, because things aren't supposed to work like that in rock. The mythology is still live fast, crash, burn, and along the way push the envelope. But as the mythology collides increasingly with the actual fact of rock's longevity, the music is beginning to consider on its history. As with the roots revivals of the early 1960s, bands are covering tunes that could be considered the rock equivalent of standards—songs by the likes of the Stones and the Velvet Underground. In some ways, that's because rock's history is closing, thanks to hiphop and acid jazz. With the pressure to be on the cutting edge lifted off it, rock can take the time to reflect. Or it can dwindle into the kind of timeless twilight that the big bands now inhabit.

Television has stepped out of that twilight, though you'd never know they'd been gone from *Television*. They sound like . . . well, Television, but they're not exactly a rerun. The band was one of the critics' darlings of mid-1970s CBGB-land, that Bowery dive with the flophouse overhead where protopunk and proto-New Wave were being birthed. The quartet featured the dueling guitars of Tom Verlaine and Richard Lloyd—a supposed punk anamoly. They refracted jazz influences (Verlaine adored Ornette Coleman and Albert Ayler) and sixties psychedelia (he loved the Dead and Jefferson Airplane). The guitarists strafed each other in the kind of stretched-out jams punkers love to hate, while bassist Fred Smith drove or floated and drummer Billy Ficca nailed the four-four into the audience's skulls.

That was live. On disc, the critics' darlings (who never even broke into six-figure sales—so much for the power of the press) edited things to a tighter-lipped ferocity. Television (which is to say Verlaine, who refused to share composing credits) made songs. Moody, raunchy, delicate, or hurtling, their tunes are such stuff as dreams are made of.

Their ellipses make them so. The best Television songs haunt because of their very unpunkish atmospheres, their hovering suggestiveness. (Verlaine, who changed his name after the Symbolist poet, is an apt student.) Glimpses of the underlying narrative flash, dart, disappear. Listening is like watching the lost-in-the-funhouse finale of Orson Welles's *Lady from Shanghai*, where killers stalk each other only by their misleading reflections in an endless series of facing mirrors.

The band has always insisted that Ficca's hi-hat is central to their sound, which underlines another curious aspect of Television's music. Like Verlaine's lyrics, the accompanying sounds are elliptical, shards. Now, rock's African roots, along with its American pop heritage, tend to make it riff-based. Short repeated phrases cycle around as tags, and create a call-and-response atmosphere that yields a forward thrust—what jazzers call swing. But Television creates its thrust in a characteristically odd fashion. Guitar riffs stuff each tune, gyring around each other in a series of dissolves and overlaps. But the underlying beats would seem flatfooted to a jazzer—slam, slam, slam, slam. There's no real bounce. Still, somehow the tense space between the two elements, the cast-in-stone foundations and the soaring, kaleidoscopic riffs, makes you feel like you're idling at 120 m.p.h.

What's fascinating about *Television*, made more than a decade after the group first dissolved, is how it picks up pretty much where they left off. It's almost as if the suspension of time that lurks between rock beats the way they play them magically reflects how history itself eddies around the band. On the one hand, aside from an expanded vocabulary of guitar sounds, there's little evidence on the disc that what's happened musically over the last decade has had any effect on what Television is or does. On the other hand, why should it? They foreshadowed much of what did happen, and the sound they evolved for themselves was so strong and defined, why shouldn't they just be themselves?

Rockers face this paradox more directly than most other musicians and artists because of the high premium rock puts on change. Here in the music's Gotterdammerung, change is often only a facade. One of Television's early CBGB cohabitors, Talking Heads, made a career out of transformation, but they could get away with it partly because their appeal hung from David Byrne's nerdy persona, which was a constant, and partly because their oddball videos helped fuel early MTV. It's not that rock's history has ended, exactly: Prince and P J Harvey refute that notion by themselves. But, as the pileup of reunions and reissues shows, the emphasis in rock culture has swung to a kind of nostalgia that embraces even those most committed of in-the-moment crusaders, the punks. Look: here come the resurrected Sex Pistols. What could be more incongruous, and more true to rock's schizophrenic notion of its history? [1993]

Bird on a Wire
Curlew

In the *OED,* curlew is defined as "a grallatorial bird . . . with a long slender curved bill." The entry explains that the name, which may originally have been derived from the bird's call, was probably crossed sometime in the eleventh century with corliu, which means messenger. In 1810, Sir Walter Scott used it in *Lady of the Lake*: "Wild as the scream of the curlieu." Taken out of eccentric Southern artist Walter

Anderson's journals by a fan who happened to be Curlew's founder, saxist George Cartwright, it's an odd but oddly apt name for a band that has pecked at the edges of the raggedy downtown-New York music scene for 14 years now. Like its namesake, Curlew feeds on whatever seems handy. What comes out of its scavenging is quite unlike anything else, though critics have inevitably hung labels like "art-rock" and "fusion" and "genre-busting" on it.

Labels can't be helped, of course, and Curlew could do worse than it has in that department. But notions like genre-busting imply an act of deliberate aggression (or artificial spacemaking) that seems entirely absent from what Curlew does. Its music feels more like mercury: it changes properties simply in response to what it needs to get done. Although it's clearly the result of worked artifice, it doesn't come across as cute or cribbed or cobbled together. It feels natural, integrated, inevitable—the sound of joy.

You could say Curlew is postmodernism without the ego, art-rock as long as you pronounce the first r and don't cock an eyebrow knowingly. For the quintet has almost nothing in common with, say, Emerson Lake & Palmer or King Crimson, though they've been compared to them. For one thing, Curlew isn't arch. They're never waving their arms or even winking at us to show how much cleverer than what they're doing they are. The rocker's sensibility that runs through nearly everything they do, no matter how far the elements may get from what we think of as rock, keeps them too plugged in to immediacy and physicality and play for that.

They share that with a major influence on the New York scene: John Cage. Cage's pieces for "prepared" instruments redefined the relation between sound and instrument by underlining the arbitrary and individualized nature of sound production. (This, not coincidentally, parallels the insistence by better jazzers and rockers on the need to create an unique voice.) And his famed emphasis on the role of chance in artistic creation opened the doors to a different realm of improvised music, one that potentially relied less on strictly defined forms (as jazz had done up through bop) and more on an instinctive or subliminal or emotional, rather than a formal, sense of development.

At the same time, Ornette Coleman had been working on installing the primacy of melody as improvisation's engine, and capitalizing on "chance" harmonic migrations rather than a regularly recurring cycle of chord changes. So by the late 1960s, rockers from the Yardbirds and Cream and Hendrix to the Byrds and the Butterfield Blues Band and the Grateful Dead were launching extended improvisations that owed more to Cage's sense of atmospheric unfolding and Ornette's mutating melodicism than they did to harmonic-based jazz.

That sense of open-endedness, the risk of the bird on the wire, reflects fractionated contemporary culture. Along with John Zorn, Tim Berne, and others who rose through the downtown-New York scene, Curlew captures the breakneck pace and self-conscious awareness of the late twentieth century, where information and noise proliferate faster than any pair of rabbits. As interesting as what they share, however, is what makes Curlew different. Zorn, for instance, reenacts our pin-wheeling Gotterdammerung by reducing sounds and formats to ever-smaller soundbytes that he then pelts us with. It's as if he's playing particle accelerator while he spins the imaginary radio dial, looking to strip out irreducible monads, then slamming them into juxtaposition. They're the pieces of a subatomic jigsaw puzzle whose Heisenbergian reality is connected by dots in the mind of the observer. By contrast, Curlew inhabits the blur itself, lives within the flux. In that sense, a tag like genre-busting or even fusion becomes irrelevant. They're more like a garage band with a hot-rodded sensibility. The elements threading their distinctive efforts are simply what's laying around and available for use.

Take Cartwright, the band's leader and mainstay composer. Born in Mississippi, he grew up on the psychedelic blues and extended jams of Cream, doubled back to the blues' local originators, learned to play sax along with Lester Young records, did his journeyman's stint in soul bands, studied in Woodstock with Anthony Braxton, and hit New York in time for the atoms-away No Wave ferment of the late '70s. With a background like that, Cartwright's compositional and playing palette would naturally, almost unavoidably, have to include the broad sweep of musics that regularly recombine within Curlew.

So you might be able to predict that he and his equally freewheeling comrades in arms might extract ideas from almost anywhere—Webern, Stockhausen, Muddy Waters, Illinois Jacquet, Miles, Ornette, Mingus, Albert Ayler, Otis Redding, James Brown, Jimi Hendrix, Bob Marley, The Mighty Sparrow. Maybe you'd even be able to guess that danceable grooves out of 1960s rock and soul or reggae or the Middle

East would drive free-jazz-meets-honking r&b sax and intoxicatingly rude hunks of sawtoothed guitar and a cello that skitters precariously, defiantly from Bach to Delta blues to Bartok and beyond. What the basic arithmetic of Cartwright's background wouldn't necessarily predict, though, is the band's quantum leap: the sly wit, the deft touch, the seamless and unique blend of the familiar and the outrageous that Curlew makes very much in its own image.

Initially conceived in 1979, Curlew didn't really stablize its lineup—Cartwright, Davey Williams on electric guitar, Tom Cora on cello, Ann Rupel on electric bass, Pippin Barnett on drums—until 1988. And Cartwright has never had enough time and money—he still holds down a day job as a custom house painter—or a record company big enough or interested enough to put out recordings more than every couple/three years. So 1981's *Curlew* was followed by *North America* in 1985.

Live in Berlin marked the debut of the current band, more or less: keyboardist Wayne Horvitz, another downtown mainstay, did the bass lines. Another three years passed before *Bee,* which finalized Rupel's place in the band. As a result, it also has a more organic feel of development—one of the puns in the title refers to bees "as in bumble," according to Cartwright, those crosspollinators par excellence; another refers to quilting bees and their process of producing art by collaboration. If anything, *Bee* also deepened the obvious sense of informed humor that inflects whatever Curlew does.

Look at how it opens and closes. "The March, or Ornette Went to Miles' House and They Didn't Get Along" kicks things off. Broken into two sections—slamming Ornette jazz-funk and a hazier Miles atmosphere—its two-something minutes are a pure parodic homage, a delightful Ivesian commingling that wittily echoes and deconstructs the two masters right down to the literal sound of their recordings. And, of course, it also reminds us that they didn't get along, personally or professionally, and that their "fusions" had two utterly distinct voices. A pretty straight tribute/remake of Cream's "As You Said"—a strange stepwise rock tune and one of the first to feature cello, an instrument that has lately proliferated across rock and jazz groups—finishes the disc up, with Rupel singing Jack Bruce's part. In between come goodies that stretch over musicland like a meadow of wildflowers. It's as if Curlew has packaged one possible set of their own open-ended tradition.

The group's internal chemistry from this album on borders on telepathic—a good and necessary thing when you work without a net like a repeating harmonic cycle and depend on your instincts to suddenly lunge as a group in this or that direction. Rupel and Barnett can either punch holes in the bottom or nail it down, depending on whether the music is floating like a butterfly or stinging like a Brazilian bee. Cora's solos regularly step out on the wild side, but his ensemble role is as a kind of glue, an internal voice that aligns the others. Cartwright is the band's usual melodist, though that doesn't stop him from frequently leaping into a kind of impacted rage that implodes Ayleresque excursions into the freewheeling Texas tenor tradition.

But within the hyperkinetic Curlew, Williams is the loose atoms-masher. His herky-jerky stage moves mirror his particle-physics unpredictability: you can never describe where he is and where he's heading simultaneously. Whether he's rattling eggbeaters against the strings or measuring tape against the pickups, hammering his tremolo bar to torque and grind a note into a scary vocal cry, or unwinding barbed-wire jags that corkscrew into expressive noise, he extends the Cage-meets-rock aesthetic of guitarists like Fred Frith (who's worked with Cartwright and Cora and Zorn) and Eugene Chadbourne. (An excellent Knitting Factory performance of much of *Bee*'s material is caught on a video called *The Hardwood*.)

During the late 1980s, Curlew was bypassed by record companies like Elektra/Nonesuch, who did their downtown turn to cherrypick heroes like Zorn or Bill Frisell. The band kept doing what it was doing without attracting much notice. But critical reaction heated up in the wake of their appearance at 1989's ten-day New Music America festival, which commandeered over a dozen New York venues, from BAM to the Knitting Factory, for a wild grabbag of sounds from around the globe.

Critical acclaim does not necessarily a commercial success make, however, as countless artists lining up for grants have discovered. Curlew isn't really "serious" enough to churn out sounds meant to attract right-thinking academic grants-bestowers. *A Beautiful Western Saddle*, the band's 1993 release, is better than almost anything likely to pop from, say, the NEA's bins, but it isn't likely to suddenly catapult Curlew into a major-label contract or land the band a fellowship. Still, it seems more approachable for new listeners, especially alternative-rock fans; it's both a logical extension of and a dramatic departure from their earlier work. Originally staged as part of New Music America, *Saddle* marries Curlew's recombinant joy with the unpredictably veering, darkly satiric poetry of Canadian Paul Haines.

It's a match made in heaven—if heaven has a healthy sense of irony. A friend once asked me why more downtown types didn't try to mix vocals into what they do; *Saddle* makes a real case that more should. Haines writes of endemic disconnectedness relieved by a gallows humor that can burst into guffaws, especially after being paired with Curlew's audacious but surprisingly hummable melodies, swerving songforms, and guest member Amy Denio's sleek-with-a-bite vocals. Check out "The Prince," a mock-dignified tango à la Astor Piazzolla that is shattered by spiraling chunks of noise-mongering and whose refrain is "To the amazement of/Even secret carnival/Workers/The prince continued/To shit three days/Past death/Little bay scallops." Or the delightful funky strut called "Peking Widow," with its closing line, "Chinese porcupines/Crying in the cold." If you're still doubtful, look over the song titles. Can you really afford to pass up any album with a tune called "All's Well That Ends"? [1993]

Voodoo Child
Jimi Hendrix

Pick up any of the three studio albums released during his all-too-short lifetime—*Are You Experienced?*, *Axis: Bold as Love*, or *Electric Ladyland*. Toss 'em into the CD player and get ready to explore a series of revolutionary sonic landscapes. Succored and seared by guitar virtuosity of previously unimaginable intensity, these are the musical legacies of that 1960s rock icon, Jimi Hendrix. Here legacy isn't a pro forma word: the sounds Hendrix pioneered course through today's rock of all varieties, from headbanger metal to ambient techno. What Hendrix left is as contemporary and timeless as the Sphinx.

Rock and roll's paradigm for its mythic heroes has always been simple: be a rebel, live fast, and die young. Hendrix was a classic case.

He lived as fast as anyone could imagine, even in the hippified 1960s, indulging apparently insatiable appetites for women and drugs. But he also directed his relentless energy at his music, kept pushing its envelope. That, plus his huge talent, made him a key catalyst for change, both musical and technological. In the breathtakingly short space of his three-year career as a composer and band leader, Jimi Hendrix changed the shape of rock and jazz forever.

Unable to read or write music, Hendrix ranks nonetheless with key 1960s sonic explorers: the Beatles and the Grateful Dead; Charles Mingus, Miles Davis, John Coltrane, and Ornette Coleman; and John Cage. Let's look at the short list for why. There's his unrivalled guitar virtuosity, a complex, ever-shifting compound of his blues idols like Robert Johnson and stringbending champ Albert King, the sweet soul-style broken chordings of Curtis Mayfield, the thick-toned raunch of Brit Invasion guitar heroes like Eric Clapton, Jeff Beck, and Pete Townsend; his unprecedented control of feedback; and his adaptations of contemporary free-jazz approaches, especially the exchanges between Coltrane and drummer Elvin Jones. There's his pioneering of then-prototypical electronic effects, usually manufactured to his demands by pal Roger Mayer, who managed to bundle everything from phase shifters to compression and other distortion devices into a flying saucer-shaped set of foot-pedals. There's his dual approach to the recording studio, inspired and made possible by guitarist Les Paul's invention of sound-on-sound recording in the 1950s. Like his great predecessor, Hendrix saw the studio—and he spent prodigious amounts of time in studios, finally building his own, Electric Lady, on West 8th St. and Sixth Avenue in New York City—as both a cradle for sketches of tunes and arrangements, a sort of composer's palette, and as a workshop for refashioning finished pieces via overdubbing echo, phase-shifting. And last but not least is an aspect of Hendrix overlooked by guitar-clone wannabes: his songwriting, which at its best combined sci-fi verbal and sonic vistas with Dylanesque surrealism and soul stylings in a cohesive, taut framework—the opposite pole of his documented tendency to lapse into meandering jam sessions.

Adored as a voodoo-child bluesman for the Aquarian Age, Hendrix was one of the very few black Americans participating in the period's overwhelmingly white hippie culture. That certainly gave him a racially tinged authenticity at his career's outset in England, and allowed him to synthesize elements from America's ethnic subcultures. But being in between cultures also created problems. His manager apparently looked down on him; certainly a couple of his roadies and sidemen did. His music was disdained by black radio outlets, by many black contemporary performers, and by most black audiences, who preferred blues or soul or nascent funk. His white handlers and audiences expected him to be a trained monkey who should produce on demand. And there he was, stuck in the middle and more and more frustrated, hurt, angry, and baffled.

Born on November 27, 1942, young Johnny Allen Hendrix—his name was later legally changed to James Marshall Hendrix—was raised in poor sections of Seattle by his father Al. His mother left them early, and his younger brother Leon was sent to a succession of foster homes. The shy boy fantasized guitar heroics with a broom at the foot of his bed when Al left him to work at odd jobs. Al tried to provide for him—bought him a ukelele, his first guitars. But maybe it's not surprising that the quiet youth found himself involved with drugs— popping Benzedrine and guzzling cough syrup—and petty crimes, as well as playing in bands. After he quit school and got picked up for his second joyride in a stolen car in 1961, the judge suggested he go army, and young Hendrix enlisted in the paratroopers—101st Airborne, the Screaming Eagles.

Stationed at Fort Campbell, Kentucky, he slept with his treasured Stratocaster guitar—an imitation of some great bluesmen that inevitably brought derision from his fellow grunts. But there he hooked up with lifelong buddy Billy Cox, with whom he jammed continually during off-duty hours (Cox later replaced Experience bassist Noel Redding, and stayed in Hendrix's bands until the end). But most important about Hendrix's airborne experience was the aural input. It was during this time that he began reimagining the sound of the electric guitar, inspired by truck doors slamming, shells bursting, machine guns ackacking, and the howling rush that swept his ears during jumps themselves, the Doppler-shifted frequencies that he'd later replicate with a guitar, a tremolo bar, and distortion.

When Hendrix got his discharge in the fall of 1962, he headed with Cox for Nashville, but after scuffling he hooked into the r&b chitlin' circuit. For nearly a year, he toured with anonymous bands around the country. Then, for two years on and off, he worked for Little Richard, who was, at that point, back out of the church and into rock and roll. Here, sideman to a master, Hendrix got an education in the outrageous rock showmanship that permeated his early stage shows. Richard Penniman was a combination of gospel possession and sexual suggestion that forged the mold—although he has, ever since, tried to overstate the duo's relationship. Playing safely anonymous sideman guitar, Hendrix moved around the scene. One of the few gigs where he got to exhibit his growing stagecraft was with the Isley Brothers in 1964. Living for a while in their house, Hendrix met young Ernie Isley, later one of his more interesting disciples, who watched the guitarist practice in his family's living room, where he slept on the sofa. After stints with local New York groups, where he began selling speed to make his meager ends meet, Hendrix decided to stop being a sideman and make his own way.

In *Jimi Hendrix*, the solid video that collects footage of Hendrix with interviews of friends, co-workers, and musicians, his then-girlfriend Fayne Pridgeon recalls when and why Hendrix left the difficult-to-break-into Harlem scene for the friendlier folk-rock cauldron of Greenwich Village. He'd discovered Bob Dylan, whose lyrics would deeply affect his notion of songwriting. Soon Hendrix, pockmarked and rail-thin from a period-piece mix of amphetamines and no food, was playing at the Cafe Wha?, home to the Fugs and jam sessions and poetry readings. Here Jimmy James—his nom de guitar at the time—and his Blue Flames held forth as the proto-psychedelic house band in 1966, until John Hammond dropped in from his gig down the block at the Gaslight, got hit with Hendrix's wizardry, and brought him into the Cafe Au Go Go as his sideman, in time for a batch of English rock stars to see and hear him.

Among them was bassist Chas Chandler of The Animals, who was circulating through New York on tour, taking in everything from Cassavetes to Mingus to the Village folk scene. Chandler saw Hendrix and, as Jon Landau said later of Bruce Springsteen, the future of rock and roll. So he convinced the young black ace to come back to the U.K., to put together a group and record. They ran around town, buying up as many of the recording and management contracts Hendrix had signed as they could find, getting passports and papers in order. Bye-bye Jimmy James.

In London, Hendrix quickly became a cause celebre—not least be-

cause U.K. guitar heroess like Eric Clapton, Jeff Beck, and Pete Townsend realized they were looking at the full culmination of musical and
dramatic ingredients they'd copped from the U.S. blues tradition. Beck
saw Hendrix as stealing his and Townsend's stage show—the wind-
milling and leaping and splits and other guitar acrobatics. Clapton and
Townsend went to the movies together one afternoon to discuss their
shared awe. The London "birds," from Mick Jagger's then-girlfriend
Marianne Faithful on down, swooned and fought over him. But it took
some doing to land him a U.K. record contract, and even then Chandler had to sell five of his six guitars to finance a launch party for his
new trio, the Jimi Hendrix Experience. The party, flush with celebs,
yielded one job offer—for $65.

But the Experience had cut its first single, an explosive remake of
the Seeds' "Hey Joe," which began racing up the U.K. charts when it
was released in December 1966. Suddenly the trio had all the work
they could get—club dates, TV and radio, the gamut. Festooned with
velvet Edwardian jackets and colorful scarves, Jimi Hendrix began to
rip up stages around Europe, squatting on his haunches to pick his
guitar like a phallus while flicking his tongue, burning his guitars and
ramming amplifiers. With the release of *Are You Experienced?*, he rapidly became the guitar hero of the guitar-hero generation—and another
of countless Americans who've had to launch their artistic careers overseas, in order to return home in triumph.

By 1967, the Experience had an American label deal and was ready
to hit the U.S. Unlike in the U.K., the group's singles didn't top the
U.S. charts, but rode the airwaves on nascent "underground" FM radio, which played album cuts not on AM-radio's top-40 playlists, pro-
pelling *Experienced* onto the charts for a breathtaking 100-plus weeks.
It was the beginning of "The Summer of Love," and what brought
Hendrix home after his seven-month exile was the event that kicked
off that summer: June's Monterey Pop Festival, where the Experience
shared the bill with, among others, the Who, the Grateful Dead, Big
Brother and the Holding Company, Otis Redding. The Experience
blew them all away. After years of scuffling, Hendrix was an overnight
star in his native land.

Against sage advice, the Experience was booked by Chandler's partner, Mike Jeffery, to open a tour for the Monkees—a deal that collapsed, for obvious reasons, after the first few shows. It was the

beginning of a long misunderstanding and mishandling of Hendrix, driven by Jeffery's old-style notions of what was good exposure and how to work an audience. He treated Hendrix like a trained seal, booking him incessantly even when he begged for rest, insisting that he perform hits even when he was tired of them. Worse, it seems that Jeffery diverted funds from Hendrix's earnings to a Bahamian bank account for himself. Thus began antagonisms and crossed interests that, exacerbated once Chandler exited in 1968, distorted Hendrix's career trajectory.

But in late 1967, everything seemed cool. The Experience was back in Europe and touring to raves. In the studio Hendrix was under the tutelage of the veteran Chandler, who as producer was a strict and masterful organizer of material and time. The guitarist was more than holding up his end, unleashing a barrage of ideas at the little four-track machine manned by engineer Eddie Kramer. Kramer would remain on the board with Hendrix until his death, with some ellipses, and became his technological translator. When Hendrix, for instance, talked about wanting to get an "underwater" sound, Kramer obligingly submerged a waterproof speaker in a bucket of water and tried to create the desired effect. That ploy didn't work, but others did—brilliantly. To take just one example: Kramer devised a way to phase in stereo, which had never been done before, in order to capture Hendrix's sonic memories of parachuting.

Hendrix made his first two albums with this team. But by *Ladyland* in 1968, he took control himself—which is why the credits read "produced and directed by Jimi Hendrix," even though Chandler was involved for the initial recordings. By now Hendrix was thoroughly weary of repeating his hits onstage, and had begun reaching out for something quite different, via long jams that recalled the flights of contemporary idols like Coltrane. Between gigs, he holed up in studios around New York, like the Record Plant, for weeks, jamming with different people without an apparent agenda. Or he'd head over to the Scene, a small club in the West 40s that hosted the likes of Tiny Tim, Buddy Guy, Johnny Winter, and the Blues Project, lugging his tape recorder so he could capture the jams he'd push to often incendiary heights. And, of course, there was always a bevy of girls bearing drug offerings who wanted nothing more than a moment of their idol's time, fracturing his concentration. The shy Hendrix apparently never figured out how to say no.

The pressure of success, and the hangers-on draping themselves around him in escalating crowds, created more problems. In early 1968, Hendrix was busted in Stockholm on drunk and disorderly charges. Later that year, he threw a groupie down a flight of stairs, buying her silence for $10,000. Still, he managed to keep the chaotic swirl sufficiently in check to yield *Electric Ladyland*, a double album of astonishing, almost preternatural musical depth, range, and passion. The Experience had blown apart due to internal friction—a lot of complaints, for example, about Hendrix's apparently slapdash working methods in the studio. But Jeffery harangued them back together temporarily, to fulfill their summer 1969 commitments. One big carrot: their concert fees were up to between $50,000 and $100,000.

By the time he got to Woodstock, two months before the August 1969 festival that would give the era its defining symbolism, Hendrix was as dissipated as he would ever get. He had been busted at the Toronto airport for heroin possession. Jeffery, worried about losing his star, persuaded him to rent a house in the village of Shokan near Woodstock. There Hendrix took the summer to try out different musical concepts, musicians, and groups. Most of the time was passed noodling—a release from endlessly cranking out hits like "Foxey Lady" and "Purple Haze" for his fans, but not in itself musically coherent. That showed when he hit the festival stage, where his new, expanded band was ragged, well below the intensity of the Experience at its best. The only unarguable artistic success was Hendrix's now-mythic "The Star-Spangled Banner," heard by the estimated 60,000 fans left of 500,000 festival attendees.

With the Experience at an end, Hendrix continued his club-and-studio jam routine, starting work on some 40 new songs, until a long-simmering contractual dispute forced him to make an album. To minimize the time and money necessary, he recorded it live on New Year's Eve, 1969, at the Fillmore East. *Band of Gypsys*, with Cox and drummer Buddy Miles, is rightly best known for "Machine Gun," Hendrix's hellacious guitar recreation of a warscape. Brilliant and scarifying, a bleaker mood than his national-anthem satire, it was the most overt political statement Hendrix would ever make—and a defiant, stunning virtuoso exposition.

After a debacle concert at Madison Square Garden a month later, Jeffery, never subtle, insisted that Hendrix drop his black sidemen, claiming white audiences couldn't deal with an all-black rock band, and demand that he reform the Experience. A compromise was reached, thanks to the financial pressure Jeffery could turn on his star: Hendrix was overdue on two albums for Reprise, owed back taxes and legal fees, needed money to finish his state-of-the-art recording studio, Electric Lady, and had an acute, understandable fear of winding up down-and-out like Joe Louis. He talked with black lawyers and other potential managers, including Chandler, about leaving Jeffery, but never followed up. So with Mitch Mitchell back in the drum chair and Cox on bass, boosted by just-released films of *Monterey Pop* and *Woodstock* that revived his dormant star power, Hendrix made lucrative concert forays in 1970. Though at times he felt forced to revert to the flashy stage show and early hits he'd grown to detest, he also continued to try the longer-form musical flights he was drawn to—one of the key reasons he recorded with John McLaughlin and talked about recording with other jazzers like Miles Davis and Dizzy Gillespie.

Hendrix's last months were a deepening haze of compromise and chaos. He'd begun an ambitious double album, tentatively titled *First Rays of the New Rising Sun.* His drug and alcohol use steepened, as this onstage dervish, so gentle offstage, was increasingly torn between Jeffery's incessant demands, his fans' desire for the same old Hendrix, and his own need for new directions. Leaving the U.S., he played the Isle of Wight Festival in late August, with mediocre results. In Denmark he walked offstage after two tunes, saying, "I've been dead a long time." In Germany, the unsuspecting Cox, one of Hendrix's closest friends but no drug head, was fed punch laced with LSD, and collapsed into catatonia.

Back in London, Hendrix went on a few-day tear, then stayed at a girlfriend's apartment. After a night of intense talk, she left the morning of September 18 to buy cigarettes. She returned to find him sleeping— and nine of her sleeping pills missing. She tried to wake him but couldn't, and called an ambulance. The attendants strapped the still-living guitar hero down on a stretcher and, in the process, may have unintentionally killed him. The coroner ruled he suffocated on his own vomit due to barbituate intoxication. And with that, Jimi Hendrix passed into legend. [1996]

Mr. Soul
Sam Cooke

On March 1, 1951, 20-year-old Sam Cook—the "e" would be added later—joined the famed Soul Stirrers in an L.A. recording studio, replacing Rebert H. Harris, their fabled tenor lead. By that point in time, the Soul Stirrers were one of gospel's foremost quartets, prime exponents of the twin-lead-voices format that contrasted a liquidy tenor with a gruff, bluesy baritone in alternating sections of each song, backed by barbershop quartet-derived harmonies that pumped driving crossrhythms. Harris's tenor had been the pride of the Soul Stirrers, with its elastic melismas and invigorating presence. Specialty Records founder Art Rupe watched the tapes roll while the young man tackled "Peace in the Valley," a venerable and mighty piece by Thomas A. Dorsey. Dorsey was a former bluesman turned prolific gospel composer whose tunes had helped pave the gospel highway—the concert circuit of churches and so on that sacred performers like the Stirrers and the Clara Ward Singers traveled around the country.

Cooke was undoubtedly nervous—he was, after all, stepping into a pair of gospel's largest shoes. But he already had plenty of experience. Beginning as a kid with his family's gospel group, he graduated to the Highway QC's during high school. They became a sort of Stirrers' farm team, when the older men took the talented youngsters on for tutelage. So daunting as the day may have been, Cooke had talent and training, and was ready to bear down. You can hear it during the first half of "Peace," which he, as lead vocalist, fills full of floating melismas.

One verse of that section holds a revealing moment I've always treasured. "You know the bear will be gentle," Cooke sings in a high, just-a-bit-tentative voice, slurring "gentle" in a way that hints at his Clarksdale, Mississippi, birthplace, as he surfs over the tightly harmonized, wavelike a cappella background the Stirrers hypnotically unwind behind him. "You know the wolf will be so tame/The lion will lie down with the lamb (this last line shot through with bluesy thirds and fifths)/I know the host from the wild/Will be led by a little child/ And I'll be changed from this creature that I am." During the last line, Cooke's youthful voice breaks on the word "changed." It's a wondrous coincidence that that word marks the transition between the earthly and the spiritual, the fault line between the secular and the sacred, that Sam Cooke would spend the rest of his creative life, like so many others before and after him, traversing.

By the time Cooke died on December 11, 1964, he had long been the focus of the fierce antagonisms between the sacred world of gospel music and the secular world of popular culture—worlds that he, more than anyone else except Ray Charles, had successfully bridged with his artistic hybrids. The story of his death was widely reported in the media, usually with huge headlines—itself a testament to Cooke's pop-star status. As Peter Guralnick explains in his excellent *Sweet Soul Music: Rhythm and Blues and the Southern Dream of Freedom*: "The details were so sordid that many refused to believe the story as it was reported."

Cooke's death was reported like this: Earlier that night, at a restaurant with friends, he picked up a young Eurasian model named Elisa Boyer. After a few drinks, Cooke took her to the Hacienda Motel. There, she later testified, he dragged her into a room after registering, and tried to rape her. He ripped some of her clothes off, and then went into the bathroom—and Boyer made off with his pants. Cooke, wearing only an overcoat, pounded on night manager Bertha Lee Franklin's door, shouting, "Is the girl there?" Eventually he broke it down. Franklin, frightened, grabbed a pistol and fired three bullets into his body—but he lunged at her one last time, saying, "Lady, you shot me." She fended him off with a stick until the 33-year-old star, holder of 29 top-40 Billboard hits with a seemingly unlimited future in his music, collapsed.

More than 200,000 fans came to see his body in Chicago and L.A., moved to pay tribute by Cooke's light-with-a-touch-of-throat, arresting vocal lilt over the style he'd helped create and popularize—soul music, the hybrid offspring of gospel music and rock and roll. But on the gospel side of the aisle, many true believers pointed fingers of retribution: this, they wagged, was the wages of sin. It was rather ironic, then, that the profound sense of loss in the pop world at Cooke's death mirrored the gospellers' reaction seven years earlier when the young vocalist began, as they saw it, to betray his heritage by trifling with pop seductions that appropriated, trivialized, and even blasphemed the music meant to uplift and heal the soul.

Like Aretha Franklin, whom he knew well and with whom he performed as both a young gospeller and a pop artist, Sam Cooke was one of the keenest embodiments of the tension between the sacred and the secular that continues to define the American political and cultural landscapes. In sheerly musical terms, the Reverend Al Green, one of Cooke's outstanding artistic heirs who still straddles that divide uncomfortably, can attest to its border's near-impassibility. (The largely lily-white Christian-rock movement of the last decade is another matter: an attempt to reclaim and use the devil's music to reach new disciples for its right-wing cultural politics.) That tension was not strictly limited to battles between ideological fiefdoms, however. The way Anthony Heilbut, in his essential *The Gospel Sound* describes it, the gospel highway was paved with hymns, but the fuel for the male and female wayfarers alike came from earthly furnaces. A stunningly beautiful youngster, Cooke apparently developed a taste for gospel groupies at an early age—and, not coincidentally, brought young, especially young female, audiences into the churches where he appeared.

Recording for Specialty, the group left a rich legacy now reissued on CD, including *Sam Cooke with the Soul Stirrers*, which boasts "Peace in the Valley." But Rupe wasn't willing to follow Cooke when he began to get the idea, in the mid-1950s, that there was a crossover audience possible for the gospel-influenced pop he was hatching. Ray Charles, of course, was already chasing a similarly inspired mix of the sacred and profane from his own unique angles at Atlantic, with hits like "I Got a Woman," a revamped gospel shout for secular ears, and "What'd I Say," an orgasmic use of gospel's call-and-response format. Doo-woppers like the Orioles, descendants of groups like the Mills Brothers and the Ink Spots, also made Cooke aware that reaching a mass white audience with gospel-inflected pop was not only possible but the next logical step for the music (and his career).

And so, Rupe notwithstanding, Cook and his then-manager Bumps Blackwell (who'd been Rupe's general factotum until he, too, was fired when he and Cook started recording pop material under the transparent pseudonym Dale Cook) found a small, recently formed L.A. record label called Keen. (Its producer, Bob Keene, would later form another

label and record early Latino rocker Ritchie Valens.) There he trans-
ferred his gracefully wafting attack with its trademark modified yodel
from the sacred realm to the profane, and Sam Cooke was launched
with "You Send Me" in 1957.

After three years of hit singles, Cooke signed with one of the major
labels, RCA. There he went on to have a string of hits. Some, like
"Bring It on Home to Me" and "Chain Gang," were a bit grittier.
Most, though, were middle-of-the-road pop confections, turning gracefully catchy hooks and Cooke's limpid phrasing into cash. Virtually all
sported big backing orchestras—novelty-dance tunes, recycled standards, rearranged blues and ballads, teenaged love songs, whatever.
While some had more rhythmic subtleties than others, almost all were
drenched with the hovering strings and whitebread backup vocals that
were the staples of pop music at the time, from the postwar crooners
headlining in Vegas to Jackie Wilson, the mad stage acrobat with the
humongous voice whose act inspired both James Brown and Elvis Presley.

In his recently published biography of Cooke, *You Send Me*, Daniel
Wolff represents the singer as forced into this nongospel mode by
racism. Now, it's true that most of 1950s white middle America wasn't
in the mood to be moved by raucous black gospel-derived vocals and
churchy falling-out. But if you look at the historical situation three-
rather than two-dimensionally, emphasis shifts a bit.

Nat King Cole and Sammy Davis, Jr., were two among many African
Americans who had already reached across the musical color bar for a
mass audience in pop. Just looking at nascent rock, Chuck Berry had
blended rockabilly and blues to attract white teenagers across the country. Yes, Fats Domino and Little Richard had their hits covered by
Wonder Breadites like Pat Boone, but they also had their own versions
aired. Meanwhile, Ray Charles was succeeding—as he always succeeded—on his own terms. In fact, while Cooke was crafting his frothy
pop hits like "Everybody Likes to Cha-Cha-Cha," Brother Ray was
singing rockabilly raveups like "I'm Moving on" and string-laden classics like "Georgia on My Mind." Charles and Cooke shared a target:
to reach the broadest audience with what they did. That audience was
white—in Cooke's terms, white teenage girls.

Cooke's emphasis on diction and demeanor, his deliberate approach
to the crafts of songwriting and arranging—to his whole career—

shows that he knew exactly how to get where he wanted to go. And as Wolff himself notes, he didn't take orders if they conflicted with what he wanted to do. His use of strings on his records, rather than being an artistic sellout to achieve commercial goals, a diminishing of his talents, was a choice. It's akin to what Charlie Parker felt about his often maligned recording with strings: it was state of the art, it meant respect. Whether or not you prefer Cooke's somewhat rawer gospel sound, his pop approach was a statement of value, human and artistic, not a forced compromise that's somehow degrading.

It follows that there wasn't a rigid split between "authentic" and "phony" Cooke, one performing at the glitzy Copacabana for the white folks (*Sam Cooke Live at the Copa*) and the other (*Live at the Harlem Square Club*) for the other folks, as Wolff and others would have it. There was a continuum, defined and integrated by Cooke himself. He'd spent nearly all his life, don't forget, as an entertainer, one who succeeded by sizing up audiences and delivering the goods that would make them "fall out," whether in church or out. That was his overriding goal. His various facets coexisted to create a complex, compelling artist who searched for as many outlets as his undeniably large talent could supply.

Cooke was an ambitious man, with enormous drive, which brings us to the recently released two-CD set that's been in the works since 1987, *Sam Cooke's SAR Records Story*. SAR was the label Cooke started with his old gospel-highway mates J. W. Alexander and S. Roy Crain in 1959. It became his laboratory—which is only one of the things that makes the box so fascinating. As producer and owner—probably the first rocker to start his own label, and one of the few African Americans, aside from Motown's Berry Gordy, to do so—Cooke took the opportunity to record the likes of his old cohorts the Soul Stirrers, young organist Billy Preston (playing in a Booker T and the MGs vein), gospel vets-going-pop like the Simms Twins (whose call-and-response lead vocals influenced the later hitmakers Sam and Dave), and young protégés like the Womack brothers. (As the Valentinos, they cut a tune for SAR called "It's All Over Now" that became a massive hit for the Rolling Stones, who covered it as soon as they heard it.) In a real sense, many SAR cuts were Cooke's demos, fodder for his own career: "Meet Me at the Twisting Place," for instance, which he produced for blues screamer Johnny Morisette on SAR, was slightly altered to become

"Meet Me at Mary's Place" for Cooke on RCA—complete with his usual ripe orchestral backing. (The set also, a bit incongruously but nicely, has the guitar-plus-vocals demo Cooke did for "You Send Me" back in 1957, two years before SAR started.)

SAR was a rare example of a black man—and, for that matter at this stage of rock history, any artist—taking over his art and career on his own terms. (Later, Ray Charles, Charles Mingus, and Betty Carter would launch their own labels.) The 57 tracks selected from some 200 SAR masters to compile this box demonstrate the extent of his control, including studio chatter between producer Cooke and his artists, as he directs their approach to the material, most of which he wrote. (In the accompanying essay to the set, Guralnick and the SAR artists he interviewed repeatedly make the point that they sang how and what Cooke wanted them to—which usually meant they sounded as much like him as possible.) Cooke had begun taking charge of his life at RCA as well, thanks to help from Allen Klein—Abkco's owner, and a justly well-known, if often disliked, artist's rep who had taken on the industry for everyone from Bobby Darin and Cooke to the Beatles and Rolling Stones, straightening out their royalty accounts, setting up publishing deals for them, and so on. In fact, it was Klein who, from 1963 on, managed KAGS and SAR, and renegotiated Cooke's 1960 RCA contract so that the major label became merely the distributor for Cooke's material, which would be recorded for Tracey Records—Abkco's predecessor. That allowed Cooke both to solidify his artistic control and to reap the major financial rewards of his success.

Cooke had learned from his mentor, J. W. Alexander of the Pilgrim Travelers, that publishing—owning the rights to your material—in the record industry is where the long-term money is. In 1958, after the singer had miraculously survived a severe auto crash that put his pal Lou Rawls (then lead vocalist with the Pilgrim Travelers) into a long coma, he became partners in Alexander's KAGS Music, using it as his publishing company, thus assuring him a steady stream of royalties from the songs he wrote. A prolific writer, Cooke used that money, along with the pop-hit dollars he was bringing in, to fund SAR, which initially didn't pay for itself—and never made a lot of money. It was a going concern, and a statement, but it was also a one-man show in many ways, and it died with its guiding light.

Thirty years on, Cooke's death is still surrounded by questions. Elisa

Boyer had a record as a prostitute. Bertha Franklin had been arrested several times. And practically right after his death, his childhood sweetheart and widow Barbara began dating, and soon married, the much-younger Bobby Womack, even giving him Sam's clothes to wear to her husband's funeral. (Later, Womack's brother Cecil married Cooke's daughter Linda.) Fierce disputes over ownership of Cooke's estate broke out, since he left no will. Barbara Cooke, as the estate's administrator, moved in on Alexander's office, announcing that Bobby Womack would be taking over Sam's desk; she soon filed suit to dissolve the company. (She wound up selling her half of it to Cooke's nominal RCA producers, Hugo and Luigi. Eventually, it came to Klein.) Lawsuits flew: between RCA and Klein, between Barbara and KAGS, between Barbara and Klein. The legal furor foreshadowed the similar wrangling that would follow the death of reggae great Bob Marley—who, like many Jamaican vocalists, was profoundly influenced by the soul mix of gospel and pop that Cooke helped shape.

Several months before Cooke died, he premiered a song on the *Tonight Show* that lyrically was a dramatic departure from anything he'd ever done before. "A Change Is Gonna Come" was inspired by his listening to Bob Dylan, especially "Blowin' in the Wind"—a song Cooke himself recorded before his death. Ironically, "Change" only hit the charts after its maker's death, and then peaked out at Billboard's number 31 slot. Shot through with gospel phrasings, its gentle but insistent references to the civil-rights struggle, which had by then culminated in the Civil Rights Act that Congress passed in the wake of the Kennedy assassination, rode a characteristically full-blown orchestral arrangement. At Cooke's funeral, his friend Muhammed Ali arrived with one of Elijah Muhammed's sons, his gospel pals and protégés showed up, Lou Rawls and Bobby Blue Bland sang, and Ray Charles, his comrade in musical arms, did an impromptu version of "Angels Keep Watching Over Me." For a moment, the sacred and secular sides of African-American culture—of Cooke's own life, with its Duboisian double consciousness—joined hands for a great native son. [1995]

R-E-S-P-E-C-T
Aretha Franklin

The four-CD boxed set called *Queen of Soul: The Atlantic Recordings* is a pretty posh affair, a high-powered, top-of-the-line packaging effort. There's the cardboard slipcase for the 6-by-12-inch clothbound book that holds both the CDs and the elaborate 80-page booklet. There's the booklet itself, which serves up essays by famed producer Jerry Wexler, Thulani Davis, critic Dave Marsh, arranger Arif Mardin, engineer Tom Dowd, quotes from Franklin interviews compiled by David Nathan, and even a few paragraphs from the notoriously history-shy co-founder of Atlantic, Ahmet Ertegun. There's the discographical and session info. There's its beautiful sound—clear, precise, yet not digitally inhuman or untrue to the originals. And naturally there are all the classic, heartstopping cuts that made Aretha Franklin a household name.

So why, after listening to it on and off for three weeks, in the background and cranked past subway-level decibels, do I find this set so unsettling, even annoying? The short answer is the glaring, grating unevenness it spans. Take this example. When I got to disc 3 and heard those unmistakable pipes crank up for "Son of a Preacher Man," I shuddered. When they started rooting around the melody, then broke the bridge down into a rubato section that transformed the gently singsong melody into a nursery-rhyme parody, I started digging around the joint to find the original Dusty Springfield version. To my simultaneous surprise and relief, I relaxed as soon as I heard the English singer's take. Recorded in Memphis, the place where country music, blues, and gospel came together to make it the true and natural home of 1960s soul (and the place where Aretha herself was born to her famed preacher father and the mother who later fled the family, leaving never-fully-healed scars), Dusty's "Preacher Man" mixes control and shape with passion to create a narrative tension. So despite her relatively wispy voice, despite all the biased instincts that scream blue men can't really sing the whites (apologies to the Bonzo Dog Doo-Dah Band), Dusty's relatively straightforward, classical reading took me where I needed to go.

Now, one song out of 83 ain't bad. And the songs you know are all here, they all sound great, and they'll all give you a fine time, not to mention a musical education. Vintage soul music is close to jazz in the value it places on the individual voice and its improvising. If the standard comparison critics from Peter Guralnick to Dave Marsh invoke for Aretha's fearsome flights is Ray Charles, it's with that point in mind. Few other vocal instruments in the history of pop match hers. With an apocalyptic vengeance, her sly, seductive rhythmic displacements and soaring, otherworldly filigrees and shouts and scoops and melismas infused the secular moans of soul with the wall-shaking power of the gospel church she'd been born into.

But we're talking here about this boxed set, not Aretha's unassailable place in the music pantheon, and the set still bothers me. Partly, I think, because so much of it is so unriveting. It's dispersed. It doesn't really cohere. And the portrait of the artist it unfolds, especially as it progresses through its third and fourth discs, is hardly flattering, though it is revealing. Sometimes—too many times—it sounds like an elephant straining to give birth to a mouse. Sometimes—also too many times—it sounds like Aretha doesn't really notice or care which song she's singing, as long as she gets to pack in as many of her patented gospel flourishes as possible. But what worked brilliantly for "Think" or "Dr. Feelgood" or "Baby Baby Baby" sounds either like it's missed the point or just gone plain out-of-control on material like "Eleanor Rigby" or "The Weight."

From that perspective, Aretha's high-octane virtuosic verve reminds me of Art Tatum's. After all, Tatum—God to all jazz pianists, with good reason—also apparently lacked the skill to curb his ever-flowering expansiveness even when it was leaving skid marks all over the tune at hand. It's uncomfortable to slot Aretha Franklin as an artist whose almost overabundant talent all too rapidly transformed itself into mannerism, but this set rightly paints that picture. As another longtime Aretha lover sagely commented when I was trying to make my own complaints coherent: "I don't even own her last three Atlantic albums. Who needs to hear her sing 'That's Life'?" It's not a question of some misguided sense of purity—that the lady should have stuck to her area of stylistic expertise. Judging by her sheer talent, she should have no limits. Ray Charles, after all, conquered everything from Hoagy Carmichael to country music, and did it with fewer missteps and without losing an iota of his own inimitable vocal thrust. It's a question of whether the pleasure of her jabbing and feinting would be even more pleasurable, more aesthetic, if it had been anchored more firmly in a less solipsistic sense of craft.

Ironically, one thing that's got me thinking along these lines is the recent release of *Jazz to Soul*, a two-CD set that selects some of the reams of stuff she recorded for Columbia between 1960 and 1966, before she went to Atlantic and ascended to near-instant superstardom with "I Never Loved a Man (The Way I Love You)." During the six years after John Hammond, talent scout extraordinaire, signed her, she hit the pop charts once, in 1961, with a hardly earth-shattering version of "Rock-A-Bye Your Baby with a Dixie Melody"—not a tune to start or further a music revolution with.

But what's intriguing about this Columbia set is that, despite its relative slimness and lack of dynamite hits, even despite its frequent mismatch of singer and approach, it presents a portrait of the artist as working girl, trying on different styles and learning to work within them. The set itself, like most of the songs within it, has a narrative shape. The vocalist's attempts at everything from Dinah Washington-type pop to Billie Holidayesque jazz are far from uniformly successful, though there are some blues and early soul stylings that tantalize and please. In fact, the now-traditional lament about Aretha's Columbia tenure—that the label didn't have a clear idea what to do with her, and noodled around looking for a way to break her obviously unique voice—is reaffirmed even by this extremely choosy compilation. All it takes is one listen to a horror like "If Ever I Would Leave You," complete with wraparound string glop.

Still, the most interesting thing about *Jazz to Soul* is how it places this young and obviously talented and trained singer whose preacher-father stage-managed her (and her sisters) from toddlerhood. The beneficiary of all that previous live and recording performing experience had, as a teenager, cut an album released during the 1960s as *The Gospel Soul of Aretha Franklin*. The Columbia sides show her trying to come to grips with the discipline of making many kinds of music, emerging from her religious chrysalis, prodded by her handlers to test her wings on different, not-always-congenial flights. The Atlantic compilation, by contrast, frames a picture of a mature woman whose prodigious talent gradually dissipates into a series of gestures as she finds herself increasingly in the driver's seat of her own burgeoning career. While not exactly perfunctory—in fact, they're frequently dazzling in and of themselves—those gestures just don't seem to play any necessary musical role on an awful lot of what she sings. They fracture rather than enhance the tale she's allegedly telling.

That's consistent with what came after. From the late 1970s, when she wasn't in self-imposed retirement because of the deep personal tensions between the sacred and the secular that haunted so many soul singers from Sam Cooke to Al Green (and that in her case were exacerbated by her relationship with her father), Aretha's musical quality has steadily dwindled. That's due less to a diminishing of her voice's awesome impact, which remains largely intact, than to its surroundings, which grew more sterile in the post-disco, post-synthesizer era. It's almost painful to hear that beautifully free voice straitjacketed into such narrow, machine-driven rhythms. The essence of her vocal art, even when it goes bad, is its extraordinarily human elasticity, which seems cordoned off by digital rigidity on most of her output from the last decade.

Now soul, reflecting its gospel roots, was fundamentally about the art of vocal testifying. The music was there to push and prod and hoist and buttress. Each of the key soul studios—Atlantic in New York, Criteria in Miami, Stax and FAME and Hi in Memphis—had a key group of players who jammed out head arrangements, which mirrored that studio's particular sound, during sessions. The beauty inherent in the dialogic tensions between the vocals and the music, and the vivid particularity of how the charts were hand-tailored, at least for the best-selling singers, to their strengths, is what made superstars out of Aretha and Otis Redding and Wilson Pickett, who knew better than most how to exploit them. Disco's metronomic pulse flattened the chug-a-lug pull of soul music's bumps and grinds—its breathing spaces. Cramped by the beat and the strings or synth washes hovering airlessly nearly everywhere, it's no wonder that even the best of soul's descendants, like Ashford & Simpson, Freddy Jackson, Whitney Houston, and Anita

Baker, have been reduced to either brandishing their vocal bravura in a stifling near-vacuum or fitting themselves into increasingly mechanistic productions.

Unfortunately, Aretha's output has followed that same curve. The last two and a half discs of the Rhino/Atlantic set go farther than the later discs of the nine-CD *The Complete Stax/Volt Singles 1959–1968* in tracing the early paths of that development. That's probably why I find them just as hard to listen to now as then. There's a growing anonymity, for instance, to the musical backing as time progresses. Still, even at its nadir *Queen of Soul* usually comes up with something every three or four tunes that hooks you back in, snares your attention after the cloying or annoying. As boxed sets go, this is a well-made one; it does, after all, portray the artist's career fairly. The question is whether you really want more Aretha if you've got, say, the *30 Greatest Hits* (Atlantic), even if its sound is nowhere near as good as *Queen of Soul*.

See, the same smart record company exec who reminded me how sub-par Aretha's late Atlantic stuff had always seemed also reminded me that black vocalists more often than not had their albums stuffed with filler to surround a hit. And as Marsh points out in his characteristically bristling essay, Franklin has always studded her (usually awful) stage act with pop-diva yearnings, as if she really wanted to be Barbra Streisand. So *Queen of Soul* is doing its job when it reflects that. But since it offers no alternate or previously unreleased takes—in other words, it's got nothing on it you shouldn't be able to get somewhere else—the question shifts to whether you can or want to pay the freight for the portrait.

And after two years of Christmas-related boxed-set releases, saturation may be setting into the market. Too many exist for a simple reason. Following decades of neglect, the major labels rediscovered that the gold in their vaults was a way to lure the over-18 crowd, who'd abandoned record stores, back into buying via the artists who had been soundtracks for their lives. (Rhino, like Fantasy and a couple of other smaller labels, had done excellent work in the reissue business before CDs, when the majors were still indifferent.) Factor in the bottom-line: that digitally remixing and/or remastering old tracks costs a fraction of recording new ones, that CDs themselves have a higher profit margin than LPs or tapes, that you don't really have to market a tried-and-true self-seller like Aretha Franklin as hard as you would a new band.

Add how the current economic, uh, recovery has eaten into the music biz's retail sales, how even artists who usually sell out tours are having trouble moving tickets, how risks are being even more avoided or spread around than usual. You don't have to be a CPA to figure the impetus behind celebratory, high-ticket boxed sets.

But their sales figures, reflecting their pricey appeal, have been too uneven, made them too much of a financial gamble. Now many of the smarter record execs are beginning to make noises about backing away from more blockbuster-type sets for next year. Instead of so much time and energy spent on big-ticket multiple-CD repackagings, some combination of one-or two-CD greatest-hits compilations and individual album reissues seems more likely to tempt already-pinched buyers. And in many cases, like Aretha Franklin's, they also might just be a more accurate reflection of what the artists actually did. [1993]

Blues Walkin' Like a Man
Willie Dixon

Toward the end of his informative and characteristically immodest biography, *I Am the Blues*, bassist-composer Willie Dixon says, "Most blues artists haven't been able to get their rightful dues. They do the songs and lose 'em and get lost in the copyrights and publishing. That is why so many youngsters today don't really know about the blues until they hear about them from some other source. They hear 'em after they've been doctored and rearranged by somebody else. A lot of times, these other people get the biggest of royalties and everything."

The man who penned songs for the likes of Muddy Waters and Howlin' Wolf is setting us up for his triumphant lawsuit against Led Zeppelin. When he (and manager Scott Cameron) brought the suit in 1985, Dixon claimed that "Whole Lotta Love," Zeppelin's 1970 smash, was actually a song he wrote for Muddy, a 1962 single called "You Need Love" that was released only in the U.K. Two years later, the Zeppelin folks settled out of court.

Maybe blues ain't nothin' but a feelin', but the ways that feeling's been shaped in musical terms offers a revealing look into the nature and notion of composition itself, as well as improvisation within an oral tradition. The methods and materials of prewar blues composition hail from a place on the cultural timespace-line that doesn't necessarily match what we've been taught to think of as composing or writing.

In the post-Romantic terms we're used to, composition is (or, at least, should be) an act of supreme originality. The poet is seen as an analog of an absolute God. All our legal understandings of that vague abstraction awkwardly labeled intellectual property flow from this set of assumptions. And the copyright laws codify them.

Which leads, inevitably, to lawsuits about originality. The tunes usually under suit over the last couple of decades have been rockers, those latter-day descendants of the blues. Now rock is a music defined relatively strictly in terms of syntax and formula. And so, given its deliberately circumscribed vocabulary, it's no great wonder to find many building blocks repeated almost infinitely throughout its history.

Take the nearly two-decade-long case brought against George Harrison for "My Sweet Lord" by Allen Klein, who held the copyright for the Chiffons' 1963 hit "He's So Fine." The similarities of the two tunes' overall sound were enough to warrant the protracted case, which finally led to an out-of-court settlement last year.

Fair enough, given the terms we use to understand that slippery notion of intellectual property. But the ironic kick came with what Harrison admitted. Like many (if not most) rockers, like many (if not most) songwriters in general, he said he routinely starts composing by working around a familiar song's melody and/or chord progression. For "My Sweet Lord," his template was, in fact, "O Happy Day," a 1969 gospel hit by the Edwin Hawkins Singers. The ex-Beatle had deliberately changed the melody of his evolving song to avoid duplicating the gospel tune, but in the process he inadvertently veered onto the familiar turf of the girl group's smash. And he paid the copyright price.

Money, Cyndi Lauper sang a decade ago, changes everything. If the potential stakes weren't so high, it'd be easy to imagine literary/linguistic scholars like Milman Parry and Albert Lord chortling at the whole idea of legalistic tangles like these. Their studies of Yugoslav bards would've explained the whole notion of originality we apply in quite a different, and equally relevant, light.

What they found was that these roving bards—the living descendants of earlier figures like the Homeridae, who wandered ancient Greece singing Homer's songs, or the troubadours of medieval Provence—worked from certain basic sets of structures and lines that they'd memorized and then used for templates. From there, they'd fill in what they couldn't remember, or wanted to change, or needed to change because of the audience's prejudices, expectations, focus, or inattention.

In many ways, the rural bluesman of the prewar South and West were forged in the same mold. Many of them, of course, traveled around the ad-hoc circuit of juke joints and streetcorners and parks that sustained them. For they were entertainers. They wanted to keep the crowd and the dancers happy enough so they'd drop some cash, offer a place to stay and some food and women. (Relatively late in blues history as he was, Texan Lightnin' Hopkins was famous for his habit during shows of dropping verses into tunes that reflected whatever was happening in the club around him.)

Keeping audiences happy is never quite as easy as detractors of "entertainment" in art make out. Audiences for popular art forms (and for the so-called high art forms too), from the Homeridae on down, have two sets of expectations that can clash, although they don't necessarily have to.

One set deals with the familiar. Kids aren't the only human beings who love to hear the same story told over and over and over again. At the same time, kids of all ages also tend to like some spice—the shock of the new—stirred into their expectations. So the bluesmen (and with rare exceptions they were men) had to straddle that fine and eternal and eternally difficult line between giving people enough of what they already know they want and giving them something unique enough to make their own mark and pique and sustain audience interest.

They reconciled those demands in ways that recall the oral art of the Homeridae. Looked at from this perspective, blues lyrics are, more often than not, a series of prescribed, almost predetermined building blocks in stanza form that can be dropped in (or edited out) as needed.

Say a performance is going well—folks are on their feet, drinking and eating, spending money, whooping it up. No performer in his right mind wants to waste or lose that momentum. And so stanzas are simply piled on until the momentum finally dribbles away or can be rechanneled. Think of the lyrics as sets of changes and the singer's riffing as an improvised solo, and you're close to what the blues performance ethos probably was.

Not surprisingly, the phonograph changed that—though slowly. Some bluesmen tumbled quickly to the fact that the three-minute time limit enforced by 78-rpm discs could be used as more than just a limitation, that its discipline could foster a tauter narrative than was possible in the midst of streetcorner shuffles or dancefloor hurly-burly.

Charley Patton, widely acknowledged as one of the form's fathers, demonstrated that shift toward greater cohesiveness on tunes like his famed "Pony Blues." Judging by the couple of alternate takes available on Patton, he began formatting his songs for the recording sessions, and varied little from the mold from take to take.

Skip James wasn't your typical itinerant blues musician. Mostly he stayed at home and played locally, until the conflicts—recurrent in blues history—between his religious and secular sides forced him to retreat from blues into complete silence for decades. But James was also a rarity for the 1920s and 1930s: he obviously thought of himself as a serious composer, and the phonograph is what gave him currency via his recordings.

James's tunes generally avoid obvious blues devices like double entendres and innuendos in favor of scarifying directness. Whether it's brokenhearted love ("I'm So Glad," made famous by Cream in the late 1960s) or the terrifying threat of revenge ("22-20 Blues"), James clearly wasn't improvising lyrics or even guitar parts. (Interestingly, his guitar work featured odd tunings to eerie effect, but his piano accompaniments are far looser, spur-of-the-moment variations on backing licks.)

Robert Johnson is the greatest example of the impact of recording on the blues, from composition to sound. When he recorded "Phonograph Blues" in November 1936, it was one of the first blues references to the technology. Recording hadn't yet transformed the blues from a hodgepodge of widely variant regional styles into a more homogeneous approach that, by the 1960s, had become virtually generic.

Although an essential part of his myth (and life) was rambling, Johnson's blues were shaped by more than his travels. They also reflected what he heard on records. And, as blues historians have pointed out, Johnson's compact, crafted songs differed from most of his contemporaries (with rare exceptions like James's or Leroy Carr's) because they were clearly shaped (or could be) for 78s.

But the phonograph did more than redefine the nature of the blues song and push the ever-accelerating process of musical synthesis several notches faster. It also inserted a fourth term into the relationship between tradition, the blues musician, and the audience. That term, of course, was the recording, and with its appearance in the picture the other three relationships inevitably changed as well. Gradually, what had been a relatively freewheeling oral tradition of people plucking long-standing riffs and verses from wherever they could master them became more static. Materials became property.

Enter Willie Dixon. Cast as a giantslayer, he commands a lot of sympathy. But flip his looking glass and the 300-pound-plus great looks like he's holding the slingshot in questionable hands.

Yes, he has a unique way with the simple but hard-rocking riffs that he'd use to structure his distinctive tunes. Yes, he is obviously a more self-conscious blues artist à la Johnson than he is a mindlessly spewing collection of refried tropes. And everyone knows he's responsible for some great songs. But over and over, Dixon's tunes rip whole patches out of the woven cloth of the blues tradition with no acknowledgment or shared credit.

It's not his fault. In a sense, he just embodies a tangled historical moment when the blues stopped walking the crossroads like a man from an oral tradition and settled down to an urban-industrial existence on a piece of intellectual property. [1993]

The Black Liberace
James Booker

Years ago, I went to New Orleans' fabled Thirteenth Ward—"uptown," in local parlance—to hang with and interview the Neville Brothers on their turf. They weren't exactly hot then. In fact, they'd been relegated one more time to relative obscurity. Like most top-flight New Orleans musicians, and indeed like the Crescent City itself, they'd cycled through ups and downs of popularity so many times they must've thought they were on a loop-de-loop. And after 20 or 30 years of the biz, they'd done so many interviews that heralded them as The Great Undiscovered Next Big Rediscovery that they must have been more than a little bored with the whole process. Still, they were polite at first, then gradually warmed up with an increasing tumble of anecdotes and asides the more they realized I knew something about their music and its history and the teemingly fruitful environment that is New Orleans, the only truly Caribbean city (with the possible exception of very different Miami) somehow nestled on the North American mainland.

So we talked about what Art Neville kept calling the "gumbo" of the place, the spicy cultural ingredients that gave birth first to some of jazz's most vibrant idioms, then to some of the most influential strains of rhythm and blues and early rock and roll. There are the traditions of local Indian cultures that still show through at Mardi Gras, with its tribes and street fests and sturdy sense of community and communal creation of culture, and the stories about Indians hiding runaway slaves; the "Spanish tinge" that Jelly Roll Morton so famously pointed to in his (and the city's) music, derived from a combination of Mexican marching bands and the ongoing infiltration of Cuban rhythms via local composers like Louis Moreau Gottschalk; the calypso and other Caribbean elements that journeyed across the short seas via sailors, immigrants, radio, and records; the opulent European high-culture support systems for classical formats and dances, which were rapidly annexed to popular culture as musicians moved between playing high-society functions and less posh bashes; and so on.

Inevitably, James Booker, a high-school pal of Art's who'd shared a band with him called the Rhythmaires, came up. From the Nevilles' mix of reverence, disappointment, and humor as they unfolded tales of his preternatural musical insights and recurrent bouts of mental instability, far-reaching talent and self-destructiveness, it was clear that for them, as for so many New Orleans types, Booker represented one of the fullest flowerings of the prodigally lush garden of delights that grows in the Big Easy. (Ironically, as far as I can tell—there's no index, and I haven't read it cover to cover—he's barely mentioned in the recently published, seemingly solid *Musical Gumbo: The Music of New Orleans* by Grace Lichtenstein and Laura Dankner.)

James Carroll Booker III was a both a wonder and an enigma even to the people who knew him best. His parents, both pianists themselves, made sure he took lessons until he was 12, and he interpolated classical pieces into his music all his life. The year before he stopped his studies, he'd started playing blues and gospel organ over a local radio station; two years later, he cut his first single. He studied music for a while at Southern University, and was famous among musicians for being able to hear any piece of music and play it back instantly—backwards or forwards. He contributed uncredited piano on recording dates for the likes of Fats Domino, Little Richard, Wilson Pickett, Bobby "Blue" Bland, and the Coasters. (Many local pianists, including Art Neville and Allen Toussaint, did the honors in the studio for New Orleans hitmakers like Fats or Larry Williams when they were on the road—or, better still, impersonated them on tour, as Booker did for Huey "Piano" Smith.)

This man who dubbed himself "The Black Liberace," who refused to record his first album unless his piano sprouted a candelabra, toured with chitlin'-circuit stars like B. B. King and Joe Tex. He was also a drunk and a drug abuser who was busted more than a couple of times, who served a year for heroin possession, who never let his employers rest easy about whether he'd show up for a gig or what he'd do if he did. He wore an eyepatch, often with a gold star, and a set of false teeth whose front left tooth sported a gold star too. But ten years ago, when he ended his 43 years in a physical collapse of intestinal bleeding and heart and lung failure, he was working for the city of New Orleans as a three-piece-suit-and-tied computer jockey. Typing, he told guitar great (his former boss) Earl King, helped keep his fingers in shape.

As a performer Booker was as unpredictable as his hometown's weather. He could go from flamboyantly free-associative outpourings to catatonia, sometimes within a single session. Which is one reason his two studio albums that have been in circulation here, *Classified* and *Junco Partner*, can only suggest the startling, shifting visions that drove him. On his good nights—and the anecdotes that surround him so unflaggingly make it sound like there were many—he thrived on the theatrical thrill of dazzling his hearers with the sound of surprise—one definition of jazz.

For Booker's mode was jazzlike: the open-ended musical quest. His restlessness in life was inseparable from his obviously insatiable musical curiosity. So a melody opened up vistas for him rather than existing in some clipped-off, sealed state. The scary thing about his segues is that they don't feel like segues: they feel inevitable as water flowing downhill, because they're coming from so far inside what he's doing with his material. There's no question of something as artificial as a bridge, however well constructed. Everything is happening so in-the-moment that simultaneity triumphs over sequentiality. For the possessed Booker, time seems to have stopped while he played.

And now come two new CDs lovingly culled from 60 hours of tapes made at his old stomping grounds, the Maple Leaf. *Resurrection of the Bayou Maharajah*, which has vocals, and the all-instrumental *Spiders on the Keys* have made live Booker available in the kind of thoughtful, organized way that, oddly enough, only serves to underscore his intrinsic and restless fluidity, brilliant flair, phenomenal range, and possibly unmatched technique. After listening to them, it's hard not to think of him as the Art Tatum of New Orleans, the immortal nexus through which the varied currents wafting around that city's glorious history merged, then passed into the future.

For, as producer Scott Billington rightly points out in the nicely reminiscent notes, "Many people, especially those exposed only to the live European albums, might think of James Booker as a blues or rhythm and blues pianist, but he was this and more." Yes, indeed. He was a throwback to the era of the songster, where anything that pleased a crowd was grist for the performer's mill.

Booker was an improviser who had worlds at his fingertips, from

Chopin's "Minute Waltz" (which he once recorded under the title "Black Minute Waltz") to Ernesto Lecuona's "Gitanarias" to "Besame Mucho" to his own truly frightening arrangement of "Malagueña," where in just one of the utterly breathtaking sections his right hand trills a tinkly circular pattern on the extreme treble keys while his left plays chords and melody at once. His touch was so varied and his pedal work so assured he could cascade glissandos, choke a bass line until it sounded like a damped bass guitar, mimic a harpsichord, downshift from precision-drill ragtime to lush grand-piano Romanticism to boozy blues upright to thundering gospel chords without a hiccup. His left hand was a marvel that moved seamlessly between block chords and lightning runs, boogie rolls and mutant stride leaps and trills. But usually underlying whatever he was up to, whether "St. James Infirmary" or "Sunny Side of the Street," "A Taste of Honey" or "Eleanor Rigby," was that New Orleans bump-and-grind rhythm that's had such an impact on every style of pop music from r&b and rock and roll to reggae. And its interaction with his right—remember "Malagueña"—could redefine polymorphous perversity.

He was a caustic, slyly subversive wit. His version of "Knock on Wood" on *Resurrection* has him singing, "Think I'm gonna knock on my piano," which he then follows with what amounts to a fistfight— but a harmonically true, musically engaging fistfight—across the keys. And there's "Papa Was a Rascal," his version of "St Louis Woman," which begins, "There was a sweet white woman down in Savannah GA/She made love to my daddy in front of the KKK," and ends, "We all got to watch out for the CIA." He could sing in a stretched-out, parched tenor or a fluent falsetto, both streaked with blues, but he was also a crazed yodeller who could outdistance any alpine Swiss or forest Pygmy or movie cowpoke. In fact, his only rival in that department (as in others) was his contemporary, the better-known Professor Longhair.

And in all of what he did, there was a headlong rush of deep emotion, a damburst of feeling that fuelled the techniques and buoyed them into art like no one else made.

There are a lot of Rabelaisian catalogs strewn throughout this piece. That's because there's no simple way—at least for me, and I only saw him live one unforgettable time—to draw a bead on Booker and his music. Almost entirely unknown to the public outside New Orleans, uncredited veteran of countless recording sessions, he was a giant underground, whose seismic shifts are still measurable in the history of his friends and students and admirers, from the Nevilles to Allen Toussaint to the far less talented Harry Connick, Jr. These two CDs are as close as aluminum, plastic, and glue can get to to his boundlessly freewheeling spirit. [1993]

Master of Space
Thelonious Monk

Like a motif, the scene recurs during the course of *Straight No Chaser*—one of the most compelling, poignant, and informative films ever made about a jazz musician. Thelonious Sphere Monk, wearing some kind of outré hat as always, gets up off his piano stool and begins to spin around, like a kid playing the old schoolyard game "I'm Busy Getting Dizzy." He does this for indeterminate, variable lengths of time. Meanwhile, his quartet carries on, pianoless but led by his twirling figure. The rhythms of his spins have no necessary or apparent correlation with the rhythms of the music being played. And yet it's clear that to Monk, at least, some deep syntax of the beat is what's driving him round and round.

Meet Thelonious Monk, Master of Space.

Over the last few years, Monk has come increasingly into his own again, as reissues of his music have come tumbling out. His reputation as a composer has grown, and more and more jazzers have scrambled to record versions of his classic tunes. So it's worth remembering that Monk, whether as a composer or as a player had no easy time of it for much of his performing life, especially in his earlier days. What he wrote, like his highly eccentric piano attack, was considered by kindlier critics to be at best refreshingly primitive, and by nastier types to be an oddball if not unfathomable byway along jazz's main superhighway of historical development. (Much later, after he'd been accepted into the jazz pantheon, folks complained that he and his touring quartet just played the same pieces over and over again. Sometimes you just can't win.)

His contemporaries in the 1940s and 1950s were right to be confused by Monk—although they weren't right, by and large, about why. (The exceptions—which, according to Monk's longtime producer Orrin Keepnews, included Coleman Hawkins, Duke Ellington, Nat King Cole—were musically big enough themselves to have room for the not immediately explicable.) Monk's tunes and improvising attack both differ drastically from those of his bebopper peers like Charlie Parker and Bud Powell.

It's a difference that doesn't require a degree in musicology to hear. As the late jazz historian Martin Williams put it, in his influential essay on Monk included in *The Jazz Tradition*: "Perhaps the highest tribute I have ever heard paid to Monk's music was offered by a novice who said, after first hearing recordings by Bud Powell, Parker, and Monk, 'Monk seems to finish things, to get them all said. I feel satisfied and sort of full when one of his things is over.' "

The key reason for this is Monk's veering and gyring and utterly unique sense of rhythm. As Williams also pointed out, "In all the stylistic developments of jazz a capacity for rhythmic growth has been fundamental."

Let's over-schematize history's inevitable slips and slides, glitches and sidesteps and tentative probes to make the point clearer. Early New Orleans jazz was largely organized around its inheritance from marching bands, the two-beat bar. (So were Harlem's stride piano stylings, which derived from ragtime's similar beat.) With its increased emphasis on a different format for dancing—the ragtime period's cakewalk doesn't have much in common with the foxtrot, rumba, or lindy—the Swing Era smoothed those somewhat herky-jerky two-beat measures out to a more easily flowing four-beat bar. Bebop, rhythmically as well as harmonically, upped the ante: eighth notes became the common currency of riffs and solos, with triplets and dotted eighths appearing as frequent spikes to break up the rhythmic flow, prevent it from becoming too mechanical—although in the hands of the many Little Birds, it often did.

Monk's sense of rhythm was like no one else's, in his writing or his execution. Partly that's due to his roots, which ran deep in Harlem stride piano, filtered through later influences like the spare, crisp keyboard work of Count Basie. It was from these influences that Monk began to develop what would become one key aspect of his sonic signature: the jagged, floating spaces that erupt and spread between his angular phrases and crushed chords. It was almost as if his notion of harmonic space (especially his favorite intervals, the flatted seconds and ninths) was collapsing into ever tinier increments, while the space between runs and even individual note choices was becoming ever more unpredictable. In that sense, listening to Monk's music is like having the burgeoning notion of entropy in the universe enacted in sound.

So you could say that space defined Monk, especially vis-à-vis his bebop contemporaries. Like Miles Davis, Monk was grouped with the beboppers but was not really of them. They frantically sought to over-power space with sound, to filigree it with a latticework of harmonically structured ideas—an attempt to control the inevitable. Monk and Miles, on the other hand, both sought to incorporate space into the essence of what they did. Space created relief, texture, definition—even humor. This discovery parallels the moment when physicists and chemists realized that space was one of life's essences, that each mo-lecular building-block (and whatever results from their bonding) is made up far more of space than it is of the mass and particles that space defines.

As John Litweiler puts in his invaluable book *The Freedom Princi-ple*, "This tension of space and sound is an ancient mystery of the spirit in solitude, a mystery that was always immediate to Monk." Now Monk, introspective as he and his music no doubt were and are, may have often been oblivious to the outside world's most mundane de-mands. One of the touching scenes in *Straight No Chaser* comes when his wife Nellie is trying to get him dressed, and one of the funniest is when an officious bellboy tries to take his order for dinner, with Monk steadfastly refusing to yield what he wants to the limits of the hotel's menu. But even if he didn't always seem aware of the reality of his immediate surroundings, Monk's musical vision saw through the ac-cidents of day-to-day life and projected a penetrating topography of the postwar world.

"Space is the place," as Sun Ra, a contemporary of Monk's (one of the few far-out enough in his own terms to seriously grasp what Monk was up to), and his Arkestra used to chant on their way to and from the stage. And indeed, in the twentieth century, the concept of space in music, especially in American music, became an idea and technique whose importance would be hard to overestimate. In that sense, Monk was tapping into a mental shift that was occurring across especially the post-World War II American musical landscape regardless of stylistic faultlines.

Space in America was changing dramatically. Once the soldiers came home in 1945, suburban sprawl began in earnest. Cities, for millennia the hubs of civilization, gradually began to erode, not just in physical terms but in more intangible ones. Power flowed out from urban to suburban areas, following the flow of money. People no longer lived where they worked, where they shopped, where they sent their kids to school. The pace of life itself, which had been picking up relentlessly since the Roaring 20s, accelerated yet again. Ironically, that undercut one of the main points of suburbia, which was to regularize life, to use the larger sense of individual space that suburbs could offer and cities couldn't in order to make life safe and predictable.

It was an idea that, not surprisingly, many of America's best artists reacted against at the time, implicitly or explicitly. Monk was among them. All it takes is one hearing for any listener to realize that Monk's music rides the irony and accumulated knowledge that has traditionally been the mark of the urban sophisticate.

Like all his most important contemporaries, Monk had clearly listened to all kinds of music, including classical music from both the U.S. and Europe. Jazzers from at least Gershwin and Ellington onward had been lured and fascinated by the shimmering, suggestive harmonies of Impressionists like Debussy. But there are few overt signs of a direct classical influence on Monk's work. What there is, however, is the sense of a confluence, a feeling that often happens during the evolution of a culture at key points: that more than one person or group is confronting a particular problem from different angles, and that their ideas, however couched in their individual idioms, have an overlapping set of concerns.

Thus it is with Monk and his American cousins in the barbaric yawp, composers like Harry Partch and Henry Cowell and, of course, John Cage. Among Cage's most famous works is 4' 33", which amounts to a challenge to the audience as well as to notions of composition itself. Basically, for slightly over four minutes of silence, listeners are forced to contemplate the meaning of the space that surrounds sound. In the process, they come to understand that sound is like the old pictorial conundrums cited by art historians like E. H. Gombrich that outline either a duck or a bunny depending on which way you look at them. In short, silence and sound are two sides of the same coin, mutually defining terms.

Now, dynamics are no news in music, and dynamics are, from one angle, simply relative indexes of sound and silence. But the absolute nature of Cage's *I Ching*-inspired experiment revealed some other aspects to the relationship. What if, for instance, you became fascinated with the rhythm of your own pulse during the piece? Or were gradually alerted to the random pockets of noise that burst into our lives in more or less erratic ways during a typical day simply because there was no other dominant noise (or music) to mask it? In that way, listening to Cage becomes a reflection on the random nature of the universe and its building blocks, the intrusive and affective nature of creation and observation itself—a kind of representation of Heisenberg's uncertainty principle at work.

Like Cage's, the jagged humor of Monk's musical concept reflects a playful but informed sense of just how chance becomes irony—the irony of, say, the unexpected, the uncertain, the unpredictable. (The unpredictable is, of course, one of the key ingredients of jazz at its best anyway.) In his music Monk, like Cage, was building implicit social satires that undercut the postwar American Dream via his prickly eccentricities—especially his playful, satiric concept of space. [1994]

Chasin' the Answer
John Coltrane

Divisions in the jazz world are always with us. They're classic tempests in a teapot, these recurrent theological disputes about who is betraying the music's fundamental nature: 1940s moldy figs vs. the boppers, 1960s boppers vs. free jazzers vs. fusioneers, 1980s neoboppers vs. nearly everyone else.

Suspended over significant parts of these last two arguments is the titanic figure of John Coltrane. On the one hand, he probably didn't think jazz had a fundamental nature, aside from improvisation and assimilation. Certainly his post-1960 plunge from bebop's syntax, the recurrent cycle of chords it finessed from rhythm changes and Tin Pan Alley, into open-ended flights on modal, Indian, and African material points that way. And he put his money where his ideas were. Certainly no comparable jazz star today would, at the height of his popularity, drop the style that brought him fame and wealth to embark on an uncertain journey into the vanguard. Only death at age 40 cut off Trane's futuristic forays.

On the other hand, for all his lunging and sprinting and perseverance, for a long time and in many ways Trane never really left bebop behind. Legendary as one of the most dogged students and prodigious technicians jazz has ever produced—his daily practice sessions of scales from theory books are a bedrock jazz legend—he brought that perceptual grid with him everywhere, as Kenneth Burke might say. The frantically lengthy, anguished solos Trane squalled through pieces with names like "Om" may seem a contradiction, but from at least one angle they're something else: frustration, raised to an exquisite, excruciating musical level, the sounds of a traditional formalist slamming head-on into jazz's variant of the indeterminacy principle. Like Einstein faced with Heisenberg, Trane understood how his own past had helped create the possible futures younger men, like Ornette Coleman and Albert Ayler, were envisioning. Unlike Einstein, who spent the last years of his life trying to undo his past's implications, Trane struggled heroically to adapt to what he saw coming. In the end, he had to remain himself—and, as a result, found himself. His recurrent odyssey into his own contradictions—one mark of a truly great and persistent artist—has left us an energizing, terrifying, uneven, and invaluable legacy.

Trane's dilemma embodies a basic tension that still exists: what is jazz, anyway? The question is unresolved, largely because it's unresolvable—though that isn't gonna stop anyone, as usual. Theologians don't like compromise, and each jazz faction, from mainstream neocons to jazz's status quo, traditionally accuses the vanguardists of the moment of not being able to play. What that really means, naturally, is that they can't or won't play the day's dominant idiom—swing or dixieland for boppers, bop for free jazzers, and so on. I suspect that this is what avantjazzers mean when they counterattack by claiming that what they play reflects their time, and that their sectarian opponents are whistling into the past.

But jazz is actually just an umbrella term for a collection of idioms that have developed, been annexed, and diverged over the last century. What if the only attribute they all share is improvisation? Then there's no right or wrong way to play jazz any more than there is to paint. There's just what works and what doesn't. Each idiom can and should be judged within its own parameters. And we may discover that, even beyond the rhetoricians' scope, some styles are fundamentally aesthetically inimical to others.

Take it farther. What if, after a century, jazz's idioms have reached a point of mutual incomprehension? What if being able to play some well means not being able to play others at all, because the mindsets and skills demanded are less and less compatible? The jazz musician's primary goal is to create a personal improvising voice within the community of a band. What if the all-around jazz musician, who can master all of the music's divergent material is, like Castiglione's perfect Renaissance courtier, an idealized fiction, a fanciful, not necessarily useful projection that's rarely attainable in an age oversaturated with data, where the center not only doesn't hold but doesn't even exist?

Trane's own herculean struggles imply these paradoxes. His love for harmonic density contrasted with the melody-oriented avant-garde he became a de facto leader of, opening a fault line in his music that extended throughout the rest of his life. That's what makes *The Avant-Garde* one of his most interesting, provocative recordings. Cut not long after he met Ornette in 1960, the disc unites him with the altoist's then-band for one tune by cornetist Don Cherry, three by Ornette, and one by Trane's onetime boss, Thelonious Monk. Aside from its obvious historical value, the album has always fascinated me. It works and it doesn't.

In his insightful essay on Trane in *The Jazz Tradition*, Martin Williams shrewdly suggests that he owed a lot to Coleman Hawkins and Don Byas. Separated by a generation, that pair shared two concerns that shaped Trane: they favored vertical arpeggios over linear melodies, and they depended on heavy, regularly accented beats. The first led Trane to what Ira Gitler famously dubbed "sheets of sound," notes piling up to suggest stacked harmonies. The second meant his sense of rhythm was closer to rock's (via its r&b roots) than bop's.

Following Ornette's music is like trying to ride unpredictable ocean tides: you have to stay loose and easy, ready to float when you can't fight the currents, quick to seize on imperceptible shifts that will carry you closer to where you want to go. Already ambiguous key centers dissolve in the elastic rhythms. In this context, Trane is like an Olympic gold-medallist whose pool suddenly disappears, leaving him literally at sea. He limns some otherwise nonexistent harmonies in "Focus on Sanity," he starts to follow the lead of Cherry's lilting, key-shifting solo with double-time breakouts on "The Blessing," but winds up thrashing his soprano sax into scalar curlicues. Only on "Bemsha Swing," one of Monk's idiosyncratic blues, does he sound sure of where he is.

His impatience was a key part of his makeup—and his genius. Check out the earlier work compiled on *John Coltrane: The Complete Prestige Recordings*. Once he joined Miles Davis's group in 1955, Trane began recording for the same label as his boss, with and without him. This mammoth 16-CD set collects all the sessions without. (Those with are gathered on *Miles Davis: Chronicle*.) Taken together, these two compilations gather Trane's documented work between 1955, when he left Johnny Hodges's band, and 1959, when he went on his own as a leader.

Compared to the solid Miles set, the Trane is more scattershot. The material doesn't help—too many blues and rhythm changes that sound tossed off on leaderless sessions. Not surprisingly, much of Trane's best, most focused playing is found on dates led by Mal Waldron and Tadd Dameron. Dameron's late-bop ideas offer a sturdy framework for the barrelling young tenor to push against; he sounds more relaxed when he wrestles with them. On the jams he tends to double-time routinely—a virtuoso technical achievement, but not necessarily a musical one. Take the set's leadoff cut, a basic blues called "Tenor Madness" that's the only track he ever recorded with one of his key influences, Sonny Rollins. Trane revs through implied harmonies piled up to skyscraper height; the unflappable Rollins unlooses his broad, easy-rolling lyricism in response.

Two key discs from the late 1950s illustrate both Trane's own development and his reactions to different settings. The suggestive *The-*

lonious Monk with John Coltrane hems him in reassuringly with the eccentric pianist's typically tight-knit tunes. But then on Miles's pivotal *Kind of Blue*, Trane finds himself outside bop. He faces the modal energy. His fierce and inevitably lengthy solos build largely around repeated motives, which he uses almost as African-style touchstones— an organizing principle quite different from Ornette's, say, which would have modulated or altered the phrases on each pass.

The sly Carl Woideck points out in his notes to the Prestige set that once Trane began to record as a leader elsewhere he also started to use his own compositions. (Only three tunes on those 16 CDs are his.) *Giant Steps*, his debut, was recorded two weeks after he cut *Kind of Blue* with Miles—and in many ways, sounds like it. As John Litweiler puts it in *The Freedom Principle: Jazz After 1958*: "Coltrane's achievement overshadows his quest for a change. Now that he is not obsessed, melody flows in a stream, his phrases are rhythmically dispersed, and his music acquires new power. . . . The sound sheets, downbeat accents, repetitions, great speed, and other features of his most single-minded works are part of his *Giant Steps* solos; but now they are distributed throughout his solos, and the variety of his phrase shapes is unique in all Coltrane's career."

My Favorite Things marks a different kind of watershed. The album features Trane on soprano sax, an instrument that had fallen out of jazz favor long before, with Sidney Bechet. Via Steve Lacy, another young saxist who got his push to maturity with Monk, Trane discovered the soprano as another voice. He started when a hitchhiking musician left one in his car. The results he got were astounding. As Litweiler notes, "With the soprano's piping sound, the ideas that sounded so dark and brooding . . . now acquire a feeling of giddy fantasy." Commercially, the soprano made Trane a star: "My Favorite Things" was a crossover hit, and carried a perennial paycheck. But it also, ironically, cemented another aspect of his enormous influence. In her passionate if flawed *As Serious as Your Life*, Val Wilmer explains how multi-instrumentalists were prevalent in jazz's earlier days, but later were disdained. Many jazzers increasingly felt that session players, who often had to "double" on instruments, weren't serious musicians. How do you develop a unique and characteristic voice on more than one ax? They didn't want to be tarred with that brush. But, says Wilmer, "After the example set by Coltrane it became a matter of pride for a musician to add to his or her armoury."

Trane recorded more for Atlantic: a pleasant album with Duke Ellington, for instance. Then he moved to Impulse!, where he gave his most adventurous sides free rein. What emerged were some of the most turbulent, controversial, and pivotal sounds of an already turbulent, controversial, and pivotal period. Neocon attacks on the 1960s just serve to underscore that they're still at the cultural heart of whatever epoch we're living out, even in—maybe especially in—our disputes over who we ought to be. This was the Trane rockers turned on to. His sax lines had a congenially predictable rhythmic bounce, his music was fervent, raucous, lyrical, personal, in your face. His influence among rockers, as a result, was huge. He introduced them to the extended solo, complete with chromatic tinges and modal feel. The Byrds' "Eight Miles High" famously had Roger McGuinn mimicking Trane on electric twelve-string guitar. The Grateful Dead's "Dark Star" directly echoes themes from Trane's "Your Lady" and "India." And the saxist's brooding Eastern modalities—he'd met Ravi Shankar in the 1950s, before Beatle George Harrison annexed Shankar to the Woodstock generation—and furious multiphonics filtered into rock groups like the Yardbirds, where guitarist Jeff Beck used soundshapers and feedback to similar ends.

But the rocker most impacted by Trane, and with a comparable impact of his own, was James Marshall Hendrix. Following Trane, Hendrix raised the long solo built around repeated phrases into a rock art form. He spent most of his career working with Mitch Mitchell, whose circular drumming buttressed Hendrix's searing, soaring guitar in much the way Jones did Trane's sax. And like Trane's, his example spawned innumerable wannabes who farted through long, pointless solos. (In a poignant historical irony, before Hendrix died, Trane's old boss Miles Davis was planning to record with him.)

By the Impulse! years, Trane was furiously chasing his own influences: Ornette, Ayler, Eric Dolphy, John Gilmore. Dolphy's rediscovery of the bass clarinet paralleled Trane's of the soprano sax, and the younger man pushed himself and his mentor/follower on spectacular classics like *Impressions*. Gilmore, Sun Ra's longtime tenor mainstay, impressed Trane in the 1950s with his scalar facility, unyielding tone, and manipulation of harmonics. Ayler's ecstatic, blues-laced screaming and spiritual abandon led Trane to probe deeper into multiphonics as well as his own growing spirituality. And group improvisation—the kind of Cubist Dixieland update practiced by Ayler and Ornette—found its Coltranesque expression on albums like *Acension* and *Meditations*.

Characteristically, the lineups Trane put together for those extended experiments were larger and denser than those of his compatriots. Critical mass, after all, was essential to his methodology as soloist or leader. Litweiler, for instance, says of *Ascension*: "The modal substructure and theme material are hardly important in the face of the masses of players gathering in simultaneous lines, parting for brief solos, and rejoining in heavy wailing."

With these discs, John Coltrane moved further toward the incantatory, the shamanistic. After Jones and McCoy Tyner left his band, he kept Rashied Ali and hired his wife Alice, then added Pharoah Sanders. Sanders's enduring preoccupation with split tones, overtones, bent tones, microtones, and drones manifested itself in chanting, vocalizing sax lines that ululated with the fervor of transcendental possession. Coupled with Alice's and Ali's shimmering drones and additive rhythmic concepts borrowed from India and Africa, Sanders framed Trane dramatically differently. It feels as if his magical powers of repetition, set against this backdrop, finally let him fully open the door and find his way forever out of bop's maze. Maybe chant proved a key for Trane because its method is mesmerism, so it's at once rigidly structured and open-ended. That apparent dichotomy let him satisfy both his aesthetic urges, channeling his epic sheets of sound into a different form of duration, one with a dramatically refocused psychological value. Now it's not technique he's searching for; it's life.

At least, that's how a lot of the four-CD reissue of two 1966 concerts, *Live in Japan*, sounds to me: Trane is acknowledging catharsis. A year later, he was dead of liver cancer. At his request, Ayler and Ornette played at his funeral. The worlds that had trapped him in their retrograde motion sped further and perhaps irrevocably apart. [1992]

Harmolodic Philosopher
Ornette Coleman

"Music is all made out of the same notes; it shouldn't have a caste system dividing it up," says Ornette Coleman in his soft-spoken, nasal drawl. It's early October, and we're sitting in the offices of his new company, Harmolodic Inc. The suite is still little more than sparsely furnished rooms sprawling around one floor of an aging Harlem building, but it marks the outset of an exciting experiment for the 65-year-old godfather of the postwar avant-garde.

After seven years of near-silence, the famed saxist-composer, winner of a 1994 MacArthur "genius" award, has a fine new album, *Tone Dialing*, released by his own label. Coleman has total creative control, though he's funded by PolyGram—a rare business deal. And so he's ready to talk—the sort of talk that's stirred up the fractious jazz world since he hit the scene in the 1950s. Hierarchies, limits, linear development—Coleman jettisons these notions in the way he lives and talks, and the music he makes, which thrives on democracy, open-ended inquiry, concentric circling that examines from all angles. Take one surreal segment: we discuss his upcoming multimedia performance-art plans, and he grills me about French deconstructionist philosopher Jacques Derrida, whose ideas overlap some of his, though from a more arid, academic perspective. Turns out, he and Coleman may share a Paris stage.

The studio abutting the offices is state-of-the art, all gleaming wood and banks of new hardware. Here Denardo, Ornette's son, drummer, and manager, spent months mixing Coleman's electro-jazz octet Prime Time on *Tone Dialing*. It's a brilliant, beautifully conceived and re-corded disc. Thanks to the best mix of Coleman's post-1970s electric period, the new album vividly illustrates the playful yet challenging paradoxes that power Coleman's music, which he calls harmolodics. Dense and multidimensional, with individual lines jigsawing across the 3-D audio image, it somehow stays gentle despite climbing in your face to shake your assumptions. *Tone Dialing* is Prime Time at its best: crying and whinnying alto, floating or gritty electric guitars, thumping tablas, burbling basses, haunting melodies streaked with dissonant flashes, and rhythms from Africa, India, the Caribbean, Funkland. There's a jazzy rap track and even a hilarious, earopening take on Bach's "Prelude."

Harmolodics—a contraction of harmony and melody—is almost Zen. Disassembling the recurring chord sequences mainstream jazz and pop rely on, Coleman explodes them like you would a schematic diagram. Each bandmember must find his own way to connect the pieces. The result: polyphonic, democratic improvisation that's a kind of post-bop cubist Dixieland. He explains: "It isn't just a musical idea; it's David Copperfield on Broadway. During his show, at one point he had it snowing, because where he grew up it used to snow a lot, he had his head and torso on one side of the stage, and his legs on the other. That's harmolodic."

Coleman's impact is audible over the postwar music spectrum. The Modern Jazz Quartet were early champions. John Coltrane studied with him, tried to persuade him to join his own quartet, and recorded and performed with Coleman's band. Two key groups of post-1960s jazz explorers, the Chicago-based Association for the Advancement of Creative Musicians (AACM) and the St. Louis-based Black Arts Group (BAG), took their cues from him, as does New York's Knitting Factory scene. Pat Metheny recorded and toured with him. The Grateful Dead had Prime Time open for them. The Velvet Underground studied Coleman pieces like "Ramblin'." His trademark alto wound through the soundtracks for *Naked Lunch* and *Philadelphia*. *Tone Dialing* had a multimedia (video art, poetry, and body piercing plus Prime Time) premiere at the 1994 San Francisco Jazz Festival, to mixed reactions. But, whatever the verdict on individual projects (which often changes with time), Ornette Coleman's stature is not in doubt.

Despite his influence, Coleman has been living on the margins for 40 years. For one thing, though he's often made a lot of money, he either gives it away, or plows it back into his music. Then, too, for a gentle man whose alto's trademark whinnies and bluesy cries display a remarkable lack of aggressiveness, Coleman has borne numberless attacks on his ideas—and himself. Baffled by his music, nonconverts claimed he couldn't play. Music-biz types have never known what to make of him—or he of them. They've seen him as a cult act; he's determined to find a larger audience for his work. And his financial demands on labels and promoters are always far above the norm. Factor in America's background noise—racism. "I've always told people that I consider myself a composer who performs," he says. Even though he copped the first Guggenheim awarded for jazz composition in 1967, Coleman's classically oriented works, like *Skies of America*, have never been accepted by the classical community.

Born in Fort Worth on March 19, 1930, Randolph Denardo Ornette Coleman picked up the sax early, in a way that left him convinced about the fundamental nature of musical expression. "In my hometown," he says, "kids were always playing imaginary music. I just thought it was fun until one day a band appeared at my elementary school and played for us, and I saw this guy get up and take a solo on saxophone. I had no idea how it was happening, but I thought it sounded so nice I wanted to try it. I asked my mother, could I have a horn? She said if I went out and worked and saved my money that I could buy one; I was about 12. I was almost 15 when I'd saved up enough money. Then she told me to look under the bed one morning, and there it was. I was so in tune to music that I picked it up as soon as I assembled it and played the same as I'm playing today—only I didn't know music. I was just hearing music. Which made me believe that every human being has some of that quality to do that: for one person it might be music, for another it might be writing, for another it might be analyzing acid or putting a laser beam together. There's a natural instinct that tells people how to do things even before they learn the skills of how to apply those things."

His father, Randolph Sr., left his mother Rosa, two sisters, a brother, and himself when Ornette was seven, and he grew up on the wrong side of the tracks. His father sang in church, and his mother was related to blues guitar great T-Bone Walker, so the Coleman kids heard lots of music. Texas is a fertile musical zone, and Coleman got input from childhood pals like King Curtis, Bobby Bradford, John Carter, and Dewey Redman. They were mutually supportive: when Coleman arrived in New York in 1959, broke but suddenly famous, Curtis, who led the studio band for Atlantic Records on hit after hit, met him in his Rolls Royce.

His family's acute poverty made Coleman put his horn to work right away. He'd taught himself to play hits from the radio and studied music. But when he joined a church band, he discovered a basic misunderstanding: he thought the concert scale began, like the alphabet, with the letter A instead of C. After being humiliated by the bandleader, he studied more, but also never lost sight of how creative mistakes can be, how they can release locked-up ideas.

By his late teens, Coleman was thrown out of his high school band (for improvising) and worked in pickup groups all over town. He played mostly r&b, although typically for the time, there were spicings of swing and jump blues and even bebop. Working at dives (his strict mother had his older sister chaperone), Coleman at 18 joined the young circle around Texas saxman Red Connors. Connors introduced them to the new jazz from New York, bebop. "All the other guys were talking about bridges and things," Coleman recalls, "and I didn't know what they meant, since the blues didn't have any of that." Coleman soon learned to navigate bop; historian Martin Williams used to tell how he heard Coleman warm up by playing Bird solos.

Still, the paying jobs in the South and Southwest were in pop music. When he was 17, after a football accident broke his collarbone, Coleman for three years switched from alto to tenor sax—the screaming, honking Texas tenor that yielded hits like "Flying Home" for Illinois Jacquet. And so during the late 1940s, Coleman, working with outfits like the Silas Green minstrel show throughout the South, tried to reconcile what his bosses and listeners wanted with his own leanings. He was ridiculed by audiences and bandmates, whom he tried to convert to bop, and fired by bandleaders. He had his horn smashed, got beaten up by whites and blacks alike for his music and his appearance (he had wild long hair and a beard), and a few times was lucky to escape with his life.

In 1950, Coleman joined guitarist Pee Wee Crayton's blues band, and ended up in L.A. There he spent the next few years at odd jobs while teaching himself music theory. His hair and beard and homemade clothes were flamboyant, but he was an unassuming soul who found the doors to a life in music slamming in his face. At first he lived in a musician's hotel with New Orleans drummer Ed Blackwell. Blackwell, a master of the Big Easy's parade-funk rhythms, would become a key collaborator. The pair found a house in Watts, and began practicing incessantly. Rejected by most L.A. musicians, Coleman, after a shave and a haircut, worked as a stock man and elevator operator at Bullock's department store. Cops routinely hassled him as he hitch-hiked to the downtown L.A. jazz clubs to try, usually fruitlessly, to sit in. But despite it all, his focus stayed fixed: he was developing the ideas that would shape his music—and the postwar jazz avant-garde.

Gradually, Coleman gathered sympathetic spirits. He married poet Jayne Cortez in 1954; their son Denardo was born two years later. By 1957, Coleman's regular cast, besides Blackwell, included trumpeter Don Cherry, a friend of Cortez's; Cherry's puckered tone and snaky lines became a magnificent counterpart to Coleman's extroverted alto. Cherry brought in drummer Billy Higgins. A bit later bassist Charlie Haden, whose deep, rounded tone and lyrical sense would be crucial to Coleman's development, met him at a jam session. They and others studied Coleman's theories of pantonality, as they rotated through his rehearsal bands. There wasn't any real work to be had by such a radical group, in L.A.'s cool-jazz environment. But, little by little, Coleman's evolving sound, pivoting on his alto's vocalizing, human cries, garnered him some ears.

Like bassist Red Mitchell, who heard him at a jam session and got hooked on his compositions—though not his playing. He introduced the altoist to Lester Koenig, head of Contemporary Records, who signed him in 1958: he liked the way Coleman and Cherry played Coleman's pieces at his audition. So Coleman unpacked his white plastic alto, like the one Charlie Parker used, and cut *Something Else!* Because Koenig wanted a piano-led rhythm section, this first disc kept Coleman within a recognizable harmonic context. Nevertheless, his edgy tone, slippery pitches, and sly rhythmic sense shine through the bars.

His marriage collapsed from the financial and personal pressures his vision created, but Coleman pursued it—and his next records let him out of the cage. Composer-pianist John Lewis of the Modern Jazz Quartet had been turned on to Coleman by fellow MJQers Percy Heath and Connie Kay. In turn, Lewis infected Atlantic Records jazz head Nesuhi Ertegun, who had worked with Koenig and arranged an amiable label switch. Ertegun set up a paid trip East and a scholarship at the Lenox School of Jazz for Coleman in August 1959—a sly way of introducing him to East Coast jazz honchos. Adored by some and rejected by others, Coleman edited the tapes for *Tomorrow Is the Ques-*

tion, his first pianoless disc. Without the piano's insistent well-tempered, key-centered attack, the album more accurately represented Coleman's new sound.

Following performances at Lenox and the Monterey Jazz Festival (where Lewis was music director), Coleman's quartet (Cherry, Higgins, and Haden) cut *The Shape of Jazz To Come* for Atlantic. This disc took the next step, and included one of his most haunting, oft-recorded compositions, "Lonely Woman." Here it is clear: his music pivots on the primacy of melody; as he points out, "You can use a lot of different chords to harmonize the same melody." Extending bop's insights— Charlie Parker playing the "higher intervals of chords" over standard harmonic sequences and achieving loose rhythmic interplay with drummer Max Roach—Coleman wanted not a spotlighted soloist but a bandful, all finding fortuitous harmonizing during open-ended modulations.

Soon after *Shape*, the quartet was booked at New York's Five Spot. There controversy flared—which prompted owner Joe Termini to stretch their gig from two weeks to two and a half months. Coleman became the darling of the New York intelligentsia. Through 1960, the group performed constantly and recorded *Change of the Century* and *This Is Our Music*, which document their growing subtleties. In fact, their version of Gershwin's "Embraceable You" (on *This*) shows how Coleman's alchemy works, much like Monk's readings of Ellington illuminate his brilliant eccentricity.

The 1960s kicked off an ironic pattern: this man who once couldn't find places to play began withdrawing from the scene for longer and longer periods. Coleman left Atlantic in 1961, broke up his quartet (too many of the rotating members had become unreliable drug addicts), and recorded fitfully. John Coltrane shared a bill with him at New York's Village Theater on December 26, 1966; six months later, Coleman, along with avantjazz tenor great Albert Ayler, played at Trane's funeral. Seeing the financial success of Trane, Miles Davis, and Dave Brubeck, Coleman began to demand larger sums for appearances and recordings—and succeeded at drying up gigs, since jazz audiences, traditionally drawn from collegiate and post-types, dwindled once the British Invasion and blues revivals claimed teenaged listeners. So Coleman began renting spaces, like New York's Town Hall, to showcase his music in ways he felt did it justice—and maximized his risks and profits. Despite all the tumult, in 1965 he recorded *The Ornette Coleman Trio at the Golden Circle Stockholm*. The heightened interaction between Coleman, bassist David Izenson, and drummer Charles Moffett make this one of his most accessible and rewarding efforts.

Coleman concentrated increasingly on composition, which led him to pick up trumpet and violin. While Coleman learned to play trumpet in a—for him—conventional manner, he sawed at the violin to produce unsettling textures. In 1972, he completed *Skies of America*, his most ambitious "classical" recording. Consisting of 21 movements, this series of tone poems matches Coleman's early 1970s quartet (Redman, Haden, and Blackwell) with the London Symphony Orchestra.

Tired of New York apartment hopping, he bought himself a loft on Prince Street in the late 1960s, then the storefront below it. He called it Artists House, and staged recordings and performances there—kicking off the New York loft jazz scene. But his neighbors threatened him with eviction, upset by music at all hours and frequently raunchy visitors. By the mid-1970s, Coleman sold Artists House—and pivoted once again musically.

In 1972, writer Robert Palmer played Coleman a tape of a mystical group in Morocco he'd heard about from Rolling Stone Brian Jones—the Master Musicians of Joujouka. Drawn by their unearthly beauties and powers, Coleman flew over with Palmer and played with the tranced-out musicians. Their effect on thousands of rapt followers reminded him of the visceral connections between blues and its audiences. "I started thinking about the electric guitar," he says, "and hearing how it had wide overtones, could sound like the whole string section of an orchestra. So I thought it would be good to get a sound like that for my music." The pieces were coalescing for his next move.

Which was Prime Time's first incarnation and first release, *Dancing in Your Head*. Coleman's first record in five years, it includes one track featuring him and Palmer, on clarinet, playing with the Master Musicians. Coleman observes, "We in the Western World suffer from too many categories and classes. We've forgotten we all have diapers on. We've separated music from life. These guys play to cure people of evil, which is what I've always thought I was doing—playing to remind people of something good." *Dancing* split Coleman's camp followers; many saw it as a fusion sellout. But thanks to it and later Prime Time discs, Coleman's influence and audience expanded. Take 1986's *Song*

X, where he joined guitarist Pat Metheny, who'd played Coleman compositions on disc and in concert for years. "Pat was the first person who hasn't played in my band who could play in my band," Coleman remarks.

In 1987 came *In All Languages*, from a small Fort Worth label called Caravan of Dreams, an oil-money project that funded other Coleman forays. (Coleman has long been adept at finding patrons.) The album was half with the "original" quartet (Cherry, Haden, and Higgins), and half with Prime Time—with the bands overlapping material. That year, at New York's Town Hall, Coleman, skewering expectations, put Prime Time on first, causing groans and walkouts by older fans and critics. In 1988 *Virgin Beauty* boasted three tracks with Jerry Garcia. Then silence again, until *Tone Dialing*.

For a lowkey, generous man, Coleman has had a tumultuous life. The IRS audited him for years. He was beaten and robbed in the lower East Side school building he'd bought at auction and turned into headquarters for Prime Time. But he never gets bitter or gives up. One of the most touching aspects of this permanent cultural revolutionary, this wildly dressed but near-ascetic man, is his desire to reach as many people as possible.

He says, "I think music should have meaning for people first of all, and secondly it should have a quality of you that people can appreciate. Language is what we use to identify whatever we're thinking about in order to express it to another, but the naturalness of music, of sounds, is basic to human expression. For example: most of pop music is songs, songs that have words that you can understand. Well, that particular format to me is a sound; to the music industry, it's a word. So I have always tried to match my sound on my horn to the word, since I'm not a singer. I've always felt that I would like to have the sounds I'm making be as pleasing and moving to people as words. Some words make people kill each other, some words make people racists, some words make people fall in love. I'd like to have a sound that makes the individual appreciate who he is and appreciate others, regardless of their color, race, or religion. That's what I've tried to pursue." [1996]

The Turtle
Abbey Lincoln

"I found that song in the *I Ching* in 1979," says Abbey Lincoln, on-stage at New York's Blue Note in early June. She means "Throw It Away," the leadoff cut from her new album, *A Turtle's Dream*. The song's melody at first ricochets in a downward spiral, then resolves in a stepwise, upward movement that signals optimism, even triumph. The music fits the lyric's point: "You can never lose a thing if it belongs to you." That mature sense of self-possession, hard won through experience, is at the core of Lincoln's art. Both songwriter and singer, she's delivering a personal, often mythic view of history—what some Asian cultures call "talking story."

One of the best stories I ever heard Lincoln tell deals with her film debut in *The Girl Can't Help It*. Ex-cartoonist Frank Tashlin's high-energy, absurdist 1956 romp through rock and roll and its rapidly evolving subculture starred the unlikely duo Tom Ewell and Jayne Mansfield (in a takeoff on Ewell's 1955's success in *The Seven Year Itch* with Marilyn Monroe), rock and roll founders (Little Richard, Chuck Berry), and a small host of what-ever-happened-tos. For her role as a singing femme fatale, she was given one of Monroe's dresses to wear, although their measurements were quite different. "It was stuffed when I got it," she says, with the same wryly ironic timing that her phrasing and her best songs display—and also like them, freighted with symbolism beyond the biographical. "I had the choice to wear it or not, but I wanted to—I was flattered by it. But it also gave me a reputation for being sexy and glamorous that I had to overcome to be taken seriously."

Born in Chicago in 1930, Anna Marie Wooldridge was the tenth of twelve children who, after some piano training and singing at school and church, won an amateur singing contest at 19. She soon was chasing a professional career under a variety of names—Anna Marie, Gaby Lee, Gaby Wooldridge, and finally, by 1955, Abbey Lincoln, when she recorded her debut of Sinatra-style standards arranged by studio top-notchers like Benny Carter and Marty Paich. The album was called *Affair . . . A Story of a Girl in Love.* "That cover had me upside down with my boobs hanging out again," she recalls dryly. So from that perspective, you could say that Abbey Lincoln has spent her 40-year-long career since struggling to discover what she is rather than settling into what she appears to be. Tall, still stunning looking, possessed of fierce dark eyes that seem to fill you with a penetrating sense of her often painful history, Lincoln can now fill prestigious, pricey rooms like the Blue Note. Performing there with her complementary young trio, she was in total control of her material and her audience in ways that reflected her long-time-coming ascension to the jazz pantheon. Not a note was out of place—not even the notes that, in fact, probably would have been, if they had been uttered by anyone else.

For like her fellow diva Betty Carter (also recently rediscovered by a mass audience), like her major influence Billie Holiday (to whom she's regularly been compared), Lincoln doesn't own a voice that's great in any strictly technical sense. Ella Fitzgerald and Sarah Vaughan she ain't. But she's got an evocative, idiosyncratic sound, a craggy, parched tone that can feel like a dry wind forcing its way through constricted canyons to couple magically with an elastically emotive attack. And she's learned to use her contralto to scale deceptive melodies with a seductive, shifting mix of vulnerability and control, as she lets declamatory sections trail off into outbursts of vibrato. The resulting tensions shape her extraordinary phrasing, creating psychological hooks that snag listeners before they know what's happening.

Lincoln's craft is, like the turtle's clear-eyed yet romantic self-knowledge on her new disc's title cut, the product of her checkered past. Her career and her life have shuttled between peaks and valleys. After years of living on the edge with Max Roach in New York ("We were carrying the stick—couldn't get arrested," she declares), she got a call out of the blue for the 1965 civil-rights-inspired flick *Nothing But a Man* and then, three years later, the lead opposite Sidney Poitier in *For Love of Ivy*. ("Nobody expected me to get those parts," she demurs, "because I had a big mouth—I didn't just do what I was told. I wasn't waiting around for a film career. I knew Dorothy Dandridge had died doing that.") Her films dovetailed with the direction her music began to take, once she'd hooked up with Roach at a California

club in 1954. (The two were married from 1962 to 1970.) Roach deepened her knowledge of Billie Holiday, and, along with friends like
Thelonious Monk, Charles Mingus, and John Coltrane, encouraged her
to move in a more modern and socially oriented musical direction. "I
learned from Roach about bebop and later kinds of jazz," she says.
"And through him I learned to adopt a more serious approach to my
career and work." Roach helped her get a contract that yielded 1957's
That's Him and 1959's *Abbey Is Blue*. With those discs began the long-
running and apt comparisons to Holiday that describe Lincoln's be-
hind-the-beat attack and stark tonal qualities.

During this period, Lincoln wasn't yet writing her own material. So
for her part of the collaboration with Roach and Oscar Brown, Jr., on
1960's *We Insist! Freedom Now Suite*, the classic jazz civil-rights cri
de coeur, she was, as she puts it, "the voice of the work. I would never
have thought of screaming like that. But I'd learned from Billie and
Bessie Smith that you could be social and credible." Based around
open-ended structures rather than song forms, weaving racial rage into
exploratory musical ideas, the album was a jazz watershed, presaging
the explosion of avant-garde, racially thematic recordings that filled
the decade into the 1970s.

By then, Lincoln had slid off the top of the mountain. Her relationship with Roach ended tempestuously. "I gave up my marriage," she
deadpans, "but I didn't know I was also giving up my career." For a
decade plus, she was, as she puts it, "out of style." She moved to
California and lived with her mother, where she read voraciously,
things like the *Encyclopaedia Britannica*. "I'm interested in all the
worlds that came before me," she explains. And she painted and began
to write poetry and music. "I finally graduated to lyricist and composer," she says. "It's made me a lot freer musically." Not that, at the
time, anyone was paying attention. Her recording career was virtually
nonexistent. Her starring days in Hollywood were a memory. In the
jazz world, rumors flew among the people who remembered her.

All of this points to why, like Billie Holiday's or even Judy Gar-
land's, Lincoln's life inevitably shadows her material, especially in the
small, often fractious jazz community. Still, like countless artists before
her, this show-biz pro has learned to deploy that confusion between
life and art as more material, to distill audience empathy into the mood
she seeks and work it to the max for aesthetic effect. At the Blue Note,

for instance, she poured her personality's daunting force into making meaningful eye contact with everyone in the nearly full house—an astonishing feat of communication. That skill helps her negotiate a delightful paradox: after unleashing often turbulent emotions in her listeners, she soothes them via the music that set the emotions off in the first place.

In 1982, a young altoist named Steve Coleman, who'd come to New York from his native Chicago, was playing on the street and living at the YMCA, working his way into the jazz scene. One night, he checked out an Abbey Lincoln gig at Sweet Basil. "He looked like a road worker," she recalls. "But he came up and talked to me, and I asked him if he was a musician, and invited him to come back and sit in. He did, and that Saturday night the audience went off. So I asked him if there were any more young players like him." Coleman put together the band that, in 1983, recorded what would become her comeback record, the stylistically ambitious *Talking to the Sun*.

"She told me she'd just moved back to New York, that she wanted to get back into the music," Coleman says. "I really liked her timing. The way she laid back on the beat and redefined it reminded me of Louis Armstrong, Billie Holiday, Lester Young, and James Brown." Like many jazzers, Coleman doesn't generally hold vocalists in high regard as musicians, but he makes a pointed exception for Lincoln: "She was part of the band. Her tonal sense was something: she really improvised, not like most singers, who have set arrangements and moves to fall back on. I remember that when I met Cassandra Wilson around that time, I turned her on to Abbey—and that's where a lot of what Cassandra does comes from." Thus Lincoln's influence—at that point almost subterranean in jazz circles—rippled into the cooperative group of young jazzers called M-BASE, whose graduates include Coleman, Wilson, and Geri Allen. They were out to blend funk and African rhythms with jazz, building on earlier outings by the likes of Roach, Mingus, and Miles Davis. Now, the fortysomething Wilson's own smokey voice and slyly supple attack has made her a crossover diva, thanks to 1994's chart-topping *Blue Light Til Dawn*.

In 1989, Jean-Phillipe Allard, the head of Polygram France, called Lincoln and asked her what she would like to do. It was part of a larger strategy to rehabilitate key jazzers like Betty Carter and Joe Henderson, who, for one reason or another, had had important careers derailed in the 1970s. Hence the flow of solid discs (*You Gotta Pay the Band, Devil's Got Your Tongue, When There Is Love*), with stellar accompanists like Stan Getz, Hank Jones, and Charlie Haden that have come from Lincoln ever since. "It's the first time I've ever been produced," she explains. "You need to have the chance to repeat yourself so you can grow. Now I've got that, and I'm grateful. Good thing too: if it came any later, it'd be too late." Nobody talks story better than Abbey. [1995]

Portrait in Three Colors
Charles Mingus

As famous for brawling and brooding and womanizing as for musical genius, Charles Mingus is one of the most fascinating, contradictory, turbulent, and important figures of jazz's first century. (In 1994, Mingus became the first jazzer to have the Library of Congress acquire his archives.) And he knew it. He was a gargantuan figure with a huge ego, a deeply spiritual streak, bruising insecurities, and insatiable appetites: his love for art, from music to writing to film, was like his love for women: all-embracing and all-consuming, a Whitmanlike gathering of possibilities.

Mingus was one of the premier bassists of American music. He followed in the footsteps of Jimmy Blanton, an Ellington band member until his early death and a contemporary of Charlie Christian's. Like the guitarist, Blanton revolutionized the attack on his instrument, striving for the vocalizing nuance of a jazz horn. Mingus expanded on that, and his virtuoso lines spilled over from jazz into pop and rock. The propulsive bass patterns of classic 1960s soul music, for instance, are his children.

As a composer, Mingus rewrote the rules in typical American fashion. He dismissed limits, crashing the frontiers to gather and synthesize. His music was an extension of his personality, like any good jazz musician's; but from his small-combo tunes to his extended orchestral works, Mingus's jolting but effective use of rhythmic and thematic jumpcuts (instead of linear development), and his method for composing and arranging (an interactive approach demanding considerable input from his musicians), made his voice representative of American culture's postwar directions. For instance, he used jazz to make social statements, writing pieces with titles like the wry "Fables of Faubus," after the Arkansas segregationist governor of the time, and "Please Don't Let Them Drop That Atomic Bomb on Me."

Mingus the man had many sides: the outspoken antiracist and antiwar activist; the Beat-era intelligentsia darling who wrote Kerouac-style autobiographical fiction; the Horatio Alger who went from Watts to Park Avenue; the public person who ranted on the bandstand about social issues, who stopped the band midtune to berate the audience or a bandmember; the private person who almost never hung out with musicians, could sit without saying a word for hours, and published a training method on how to get cats to use the toilet; the insomniac who checked himself into Bellevue for a rest; the meditator who had out-of-body experiences; the conspiracy theorist who first read Freud in high school; the disappointed romantic who talked about becoming a pimp and fell deeply in love with a parade of women; the tireless letter writer to jazz magazines who cc'd heads of state like Charles DeGaulle. Such was Mingus's prismatic temperament, and he almost never self-edited. "If he thought it, he said it," recall friends and acquaintances alike.

Born on April 22, 1922, in Nogales, Arizona, a U.S.-Mexico border town where his father, then in the army, was stationed, Charles Mingus, Jr., was raised in Watts—the part of L.A. famous, like South Central L.A., for riots. But when Mingus was growing up, Watts was home to a cosmopolitan working-class mix. Latinos and Asians, blacks and whites walked its streets. Mingus himself had white, black, and Asian blood. That made him an outsider in a color-charged society. A large, pigeontoed boy, he was a target for bullies until Asian friends taught him judo. But music ultimately defined his ethnic niche. As childhood pal Buddy Collette recalls, Mingus started hanging around with blacks once he began playing bass with Buddy's teenaged band.

As Mingus tells it in his powerfully fictionalized, Kerouac-style autobiography, *Beneath the Underdog*, the first music he heard was in the Holiness Gospel Church, which his mother attended. (His father, who could "pass" for white, preferred less "black" surroundings. Mingus was razzed about his light "high-yellow" complexion, especially once he took public stands on racial issues.) Gospel was a crucial sound for the rest of his life, echoing through popular pieces like "Better Get Hit in Your Soul." The intensity and fervor, the way a group of inspired people join to improvise around a joyful noise—the creation of a community—were at the heart of its appeal to this loner.

As a kid, he tried to learn trombone, then cello. But he had crummy teachers, the door-to-door kind who sold home lessons in poor neighborhoods back before radio and TV killed amateur musicmaking in the U.S. He took up the bass in junior high, when his sax-playing pal Collette suggested it. The two of them joined rehearsals led by teacher Lloyd Reese, who schooled a number of L.A. jazz-greats-to-be in notation and ear training. Mingus studied the bass with jazzer Red Callender, then former New York Philharmonic bassist Herman Rheinschagen. He was determined not to be hemmed in by idioms as he became the best at his instrument.

From early on, Mingus saw himself as a rebel, but he also had to earn his keep in the mainstream jazz world. He found work, but not much or for long. (At a couple of despairing points, he took post office jobs, as his father had suggested after high school.) His bass virtuosity, his composing and arranging, and his personality produced a volatile mix most bandleaders couldn't handle. So he toured briefly with Louis Armstrong in 1943 and Lionel Hampton in 1947–48. For Hampton's band Mingus produced his first recorded chart, "Mingus Fingers," a bebop-flavored big-band piece that became a minor hit. (One version is on *Mingus Revisited*.) As a leader, he rechristened himself "Baron" Mingus, to mark his place among jazz royalty like King Oliver and Duke Ellington and Count Basie. For Mingus, Ellington's impact equalled gospel music's. He heard Duke's "East St. Louis Toodle-oo" come over his father's lo-fi crystal radio set in the late 1920s. The low timbres and rich harmonies filtering over staticky airwaves predicted some main lines of Mingus's future.

Mingus came to national attention in the Red Norvo trio of 1950–51. This West Coast group—bass, vibes, and guitar—was, like the Modern Jazz Quartet, part of the cool-jazz reaction to bebop. Their take on a standard like "I Get a Kick Out of You," with its tightly interwoven voices and episodic nature, its refusal to repeat any element during its three minutes, forecasts Mingus's development as a composer and bandleader. (Find *The Red Norvo Trio*, unfortunately out-of-print.) With one crucial difference. From the mid-1950s on, Mingus—who had been the only black in Norvo's trio and confronted American apartheid on the road—would multiply the voices in his compositions. But he would also factor in more emotional raggedness, derived from gospel and blues—what he called, in one title, "slop." What he meant was the music's human aspects, the divergences from a strict norm that make sound breathe.

Mingus loved experimenting with form. As he extended his pieces, he used smaller mosaic-like units to build from, instead of linear development. Juxtaposition and jumpcutting became key tools. With American composers like Charles Ives and John Cage, Mingus wanted a new way to organize form that would allow for maximum individual freedom within meaningful structure—a problem central to American culture. And improvisation—instant composition, he called it—was key.

His early recognition with the Norvo trio brought problems. In 1951, the trio was offered a TV shot with Mel Tormé, but the union wouldn't let Mingus do it—he had no New York card. Characteristically, he saw this as racism. Norvo replaced him for the shoot, hoping he'd remain in the trio, but Mingus, insulted, decided to remain in New York. He got a brief gig with Duke Ellington, but was bounced after trombonist Juan Tizol drew him into a knife fight. He worked with Charlie Parker, Billy Taylor, Stan Getz, Art Tatum, and Bud Powell. Meantime, his second wife, the first of his three white spouses, left him. Celia Mingus would later marry Saul Zaentz, the up-and-coming head of what would become Fantasy Records, a major label. The pair would help keep Mingus financially afloat, backing his entrepreneurial dreams of distribution mechanisms for his music.

In 1951 Mingus, with Celia and drum great Max Roach, founded the first of those—Debut Records. He felt the existing record-company and promotional and concert-booking structures did the job badly, that the compromises between commerce and art were almost always on the artists' side. An independent record company was a rare bird at that time, becoming more common from the mid-1960s on. The hurdles were daunting. A handful of major labels—RCA, Columbia, Decca, Capitol, Mercury, Verve—had the recording studios and national distribution of recordings sewed up. Distribution is one of the most costly parts of any entertainment business: warehousing, shipping, sales forces are fixed, and high-priced, overhead. Mingus couldn't afford those luxuries. And so you could buy Debut records by mail or in a handful of major cities that could order them from him—New York, Chicago, L.A., maybe Detroit and Philadelphia. And that was it. Debut lost money from the outset, while Mingus stretched out musically with it, recording then-rare excursions with French horn as the lead voice. (*The Complete Debut Recordings* delivers just what it says— minus Mingus's own groups.) He also taped early Jazz Workshop dates at its Brooklyn club base.

Mingus the entrepreneur had hit a high point: the famed Massey Hall Concert of May 15, 1953. Toronto's New Jazz Society asked him to put on a concert with what they called "The Creators of the New Music." So Mingus and Max Roach and Bird and Dizzy Gillespie and Bud Powell joined forces. Because Mingus's bass was badly recorded onstage, before he issued the album, *Jazz at Massey Hall*, on Debut several months later he rerecorded it. Editing and overdubbing were extremely rare then, and for a long time afterwards most jazzers still thought of it as cheating. Mingus, however, felt the need to properly capture for repeated listening what had been created in the moment. One of Mingus's Workshop cohorts, Teo Macero, would later expand this technique as Miles Davis's producer.

Back in Brooklyn, the Jazz Composers Workshop ran from 1953 to 1955. Among the participants: Macero, Lennie Tristano, and Teddy Charles. (Some of their work is on *Jazz Composers Workshop*.) Mingus reworked the stylistic tactics of the Norvo trio, like counterpoint and episodic development. And while he was still densely notating his cool bop-inflected music, both procedure and style would shift once Mingus began his own Workshops in 1955. By then, Mingus had begun to feel that musical notation couldn't capture the nuances he wanted. In his Jazz Workshop, which had a revolving cast, he wanted the vocal tinges that elude notation. For Mingus, it became the only model to convey the depths of feeling, the subtleties of rhythm and tone he demanded. His key cohorts: Jimmy Knepper, Dannie Richmond, Jackie McLean, Mal Waldron, Booker Ervin, Charles McPherson, John Handy, Eric Dolphy, Roland Kirk, and Jaki Byard. In 1956, Mingus recorded *Pith-*

ecanthropus Erectus. The title track previewed his ambitious new directions: its name is ironically underscored by a nearly 11-minute-long excursion through human evolution via often onomatopoeic effects. The following year, he cut *The Clown*, which kicked off with "Haitian Fight Song," his roistering tribute to rebellious Haitian slaves, and finished with the title cut's collaboration with improvising writer Jean Shepherd. Then came *New Tijuana Moods*, a provocative Spanish-tinged experiment in extended forms that wasn't released until five years later.

In nightclubs Mingus directed his Workshops, often ostentatiously, from the bass. By 1961, his focus shifted so heavily from playing to leading that he used other bassists and conducted or played piano. Now he attracted notice for his eccentric bandstand behavior. He'd stop mid-tune if a musician made a mistake, or if he didn't like the way the performance was going, or if he got a new idea. Besides, Mingus—like Ellington, the MJQ, and others—grew to hate the club ambience. He felt it limited appreciation of his music. So the ringing phones and jangling cash registers and noisy help or crowd could become the subject of a stage harangue or the cause of a walkout. This didn't exactly endear him to clubowners or some musicians. But audiences loved it, and he usually packed houses for long engagements.

For Mingus's focus was on his music. The public, he thought, should follow the artist-visionary where he led. In fact, many did, and Mingus became a success by the late 1950s; for a time he lived on Park Avenue. His albums came in a remarkable cluster, with a consistently high standard of exploration. *Blues & Roots* kicks off with "Wednesday Night Prayer Meeting," one of Mingus's wonderfully rousing gospel-based outings. *Mingus Ah Um*, produced by Macero in 1959, was a rich melange of gospel, blues, and postbop spiced with wit and passion. The next year, *Mingus at Antibes* featured Bud Powell on one cut. That summer, Mingus arranged the "rump" Newport Jazz Festival, to protest the lack of diversity on the actual Festival's program. That led to the Jazz Artists Guild, which tried independent jazz promotions but failed.

This period came to a disastrous head with Mingus's concert at New York's Town Hall in 1962. Mingus had arranged to have United Artists record a 32-piece orchestra that he was composing for, live at Town Hall. But the company forced him to push the concert up by six weeks. The pressure cooked Mingus. He had musicians frantically writing, arranging, and copying music right up to the concert itself. The night before the concert, things came to an ugly head. Knepper pointed out some errors in a piece. Mingus told Knepper to finish it. The trombonist, frazzled and sleepless from furious scoring and running back and forth to the music copyist, snapped back, "Do it yourself." Mingus balled up his big fists and swung on Knepper, knocking out his four front teeth and cutting his range on his horn by an octave plus. The Town Hall concert was a disaster and its edited recording confused fragments—far from Mingus's overarching plan. (This music was the basis for Gunther Schuller's highly rearranged version, premiered at Lincoln Center in 1989, called *Epitaph*.} The original album has been restored and reissued as *The Complete Town Hall Concert*.

Mingus knew he was having a kind of nervous breakdown, some of it thanks to his own restless nature, some to the drugs he was trying to use to control himself. So after finishing already-contracted gigs, he throttled down into near-inactivity, holing up at a Harlem gospel church run by Red Callendar's cousin. His widow Sue describes what came next as "a classic Mingus": he checked himself into Bellevue. Apparently he wanted to get some rest, and he'd heard that the psycho wards at Bellevue were real quiet and organized, so he thought it was like a resort hotel. But he hadn't thought about the fact that they were wards, that they wouldn't let him leave unless a shrink certified him as okay, and the staff shrinks wouldn't, because the frustrated Mingus started to get abusive and threaten them. Finally, critic Nat Hentoff (who'd been getting constant calls from Mingus at the ward's pay phone) hooked Mingus up with Dr. Edmund Pollack. Pollack, after speaking with Mingus, signed the necessary release papers and got him out.

By 1963, Mingus had left his third wife, Judy Starkey, and two kids, and was back on the road, touring Europe and the U.S. But disasters began to mount up. His second small label, called Charles Mingus, only put out a handful of titles for mail order in 1964–65. Publishers rejected the mammoth manuscript for *Beneath the Underdog*. Nevertheless, Mingus's muse still dwelled at Olympian heights. Take *The*

Black Saint and the Sinner Lady, an album devoted, à la Ellington, to extended "portraits." Mingus ransacked a stunning range of musical idioms its raw materials but integrated them into something new. His use of techniques like overdubbing had evolved, and he now routinely joined many puzzle pieces to make a final cut—like a movie director in the editing room.

Between 1966 and 1969, Mingus essentially withdrew from public life. Tom Reichman's film *Mingus* documents his eviction from his downtown loft, where he'd wanted to start a school. Mingus had reached financial and emotional collapse. Eric Dolphy, one of his closest collaborators, had died in 1964 at 36; John Coltrane, who'd learned from Dolphy and whom Mingus respected enormously, died a couple of years later. Many of Mingus's longtime cohorts were drifting away or gone. So it's not surprising that, given his volatile personality, he lapsed into a long-term depression; he told Nat Hentoff he was unable to get out of bed for days at a time, even though he couldn't sleep. He was using diet pills to try to control his weight fluctuations, and downers to counter the diet pills. The situation snowballed. Finally, Mingus was incarcerated at Bellevue again, after a sad incident at his daughter Carolyn's birthday party in Central Park, where he pulled his clothes off and began leaping around. They put him on Thorazine, among other things, which at times left him catatonic, at times in a rage. He could barely function, never mind play.

Mingus started performing again in 1969. In 1971 he got a Guggenheim and published *Underdog*. He continued to write big-band music and extended pieces, started doing film scores, and continued recording and performing with a fine quintet, as *Charges One* and *Two* document. He led tours until 1977, when his health ebbed rapidly— he was gripped by Lou Gehrig's disease. Ignoring the growing symptoms, he toured until sidemen had to lift him in and out of the car and carry him onstage—a ghastly experience for a man so proud and private. Even then, nearly unable to speak, he collaborated with Joni Mitchell on *Mingus*, an album of his work. He supervised his last recording session in January 1978 from a wheelchair. In June, he was honored at the White House, with other jazz musicians. Hence the famed photograph of Mingus with tears in his eyes, as he slumps in his wheelchair while Sue and President Jimmy Carter try to comfort him.

On January 5, 1979, he died in Cuernavaca, Mexico, where Gerry

Mulligan had advised him and Sue to find a Mexican healer. Buddy Collette, who was there, announced to the press that a heart attack had finally released Mingus's tempestuous spirit. Sue scattered his ashes over the Ganges. [1996]

The Bulldog
Ray Drummond

B assists, lugging their oversized fiddles from gig to gig, are jazz's invisible workhorses. Invisible, that is, to the record industry, which generally ignores their potential as bandleaders or composers because they're part of jazz's traditional "back line"—the rhythm section—not the "front line"—the horn or piano players who take the solos that bring applause. And invisible to most listeners, except for hardcore jazz fans, because of the very nature of their musical function.

When a bassist is doing his job, his contribution to group improvisation can virtually disappear. The bass anchors the beat, along with the drums. It also helps set the shifting harmonic framework that jazzers superimpose on often hackneyed Tin Pan Alley material—what mainstream jazz has used as launchpads for improvisational flights since Louis Armstrong first annexed pop tunes to jazz's terrain in the 1920s. Think of the bassist as an improvising quiltmaker, who listens carefully to his cohorts' pieces of the musical puzzle, plots more or less instantaneously how they dovetail, then sutures them with a bass line.

As bassist Ray Drummond puts it: "The magical moments are when I'm sitting in the audience listening to what I'm playing, where it's really transparent, when the river of artistic inspiration goes through unimpeded. That, to me, is what this is all about—the connection between the artist and the audience, even when neither is quite sure what exactly is going on."

At age 48, Drummond is one of the finest bass players there is. His bulk should prevent him from being invisible: like Charles Mingus, one of the few bassmen who escaped the backline ghetto to become an influential bandleader and composer, Drummond makes his instrument look almost cuddly. So should his skill, which extends how Mingus and others pushed the recalcitrant bass closer to the fluency of the frontline horns. So should his reputation among his peers: over the last dozen years, Drummond has graced some 150 albums as a sideman because he can speak many of jazz's tongues, which have proliferated since the music's birth a century ago.

Though Drummond works in many contexts, one of the most revealing gigs he regularly tackles is with pianist Chris Anderson at Bradley's, the 25-year-old piano bar up the street from New York University. Bradley's functions as the mainstream jazz world's late-night hangout, where record label execs, agents, writers, DJs, and musicians gossip at the bar or back tables, checking out the duo or trio playing standards in the corner beneath the late Bradley Cunningham's ironic self-portrait.

Anderson is that all-too-common jazz phenomenon, a musician's musician, unknown even to most jazz fanatics. A bone disease has left him a dwarf; he's also nearly blind. But as onetime student Herbie Hancock has attested, his sense of harmony and melody is huge and unique. As is his sense of rhythm, in a rather different way. Anderson, who lives at the Lighthouse for the Blind in New York, rarely plays with anyone. (It was Drummond, operating, as he often does in the jazz world, as a behind-the-scenes catalyst, who brought him into Bradley's. It's still almost the only club Anderson appears at.) Anderson spends his time on the Lighthouse's piano conjuring improvisational fantasias—the dreamy, baggy form his musings on tunes tends to take. Most bop-based players run through the cyclical chord changes of pop tunes and thicken them while subtly shifting beats. By contrast, Anderson's rhythms are self-referring, gnarled, irregular—in a word, crotchety, like the man himself.

At Bradley's last fall, Drummond and Anderson probe a set pulsing with ideas. Anderson is exploding song forms, while Drummond is dancing on his bass, smoothing the pianist's rhythmic jolts into an arc, representing Anderson's harmonic choices as sequential rather than brilliantly abrupt. That way, the experience was clarified for the audience. It worked brilliantly—but it's clearly work. "He sure doesn't want to stick with any grooves or harmonic patterns tonight," Drummond said when the set was over, "so he's got me scrambling all over the place to make it seem like everything's going down in 4/4. But boy, do I have to fight with him about it!"

•   •   •

It's the lunchtime break between workshops and panels at the Jazz-
Times convention, the industry's annual gathering of record company
execs and small fry, promoters and managers and booking agents, and,
of course, musicians. You can usually tell, even if you don't know, who
the musicians are at a glance. They look the edgiest, crack the biggest
smiles, laugh just a little too loud and fast for the punchline. Why?
They're at the bottom of the pile here and they know it.

In the middle is Drummond, whose girth makes him look like a
boulder in the midst of a human rapids. The Bulldog has taken one of
his few stretches of time off—he's typically working 200-plus days
annually—to hit the convention. "I just want to hang, to mingle," he
explains. "I'm not chasing after anybody for a deal. I'm really interested
in just seeing folks that maybe I wouldn't otherwise get a chance to
see, what with my crazy schedule. If it's part of a strategy on my part,
it's my grass-roots thing, the same thing I've been working on ever
since I first came to New York: let people know who you are, let them
see what you can do, and let word of mouth take over."

Drummond doesn't seek out publicity, but here he is, one of the
few musicians who's a center of attention, awash with people who want
to say hi (usually musicians), or to check on his schedule (musicians
and managers), or to give him CDs (musicians, managers, and record-
label types). The afternoon is full of impromptu conferences. Drummond plants himself at the lobby's bar and downs a few double Ab-
soluts with lime to no effect except that his eyes narrow more
frequently, while people drift by to talk.

Around 9 P.M., we clamber into his Peugeot station wagon to check
out a few gigs around town. First is the Vanguard and young pianist
Geri Allen, an emerging star who Drummond has, inevitably, worked
with: they overlapped in a mid-1980s Mingus Dynasty lineup. "I remember she seemed overwhelmed by the music," he recalls, then adds
immediately, with his usual generosity and insight, "but then again, we
all were. I remember playing with that band and feeling like I had no
control over the bass, that someone else—Charles—was playing, not
me. When that music's done right, there's a powerful presence of his
that comes onto the bandstand."

Tonight, Allen is doing her music, fronting a trio with bass veteran
Ron Carter. Drawing big smiles from the waitresses, Drummond heads

to the last bar stool at the back of the club, and hunkers down. The set is already in progress. For the first few minutes, he mutters about the disturbing aspects of Carter's playing—that he rarely puts his heart into it anymore, that his sound is sloppy, that his ego has run away with his taste. But playing with Allen has clearly energized Carter this evening, and Drummond soon warms to Carter's unusual urgency. "That," he squawks suddenly, eyes bugging, "was some real Wilber Ware shit. Imagine, Wilber Ware!" (Bassist Ware, who played with Rollins and Thelonious Monk, is most remembered for his thick tone and rhythmic inventiveness.) "All right, Ron!" And he puts his big mitts together, leading applause that crescendos across the club. Afterward, in the unused kitchen that is the dressing room, the two trade quips and equipment info and travel tips.

Drummond has been in motion virtually since he was born on November 23, 1946. His father Charles, a World War II vet, started as an enlisted man playing saxophone and clarinet in an army band—a key outlet for innumerable black musicians since the turn of the century. But in 1943, he went to Tuskegee Institute for flight training, where he married. After the war, he stayed in the reserves and kept flying—and getting checks. Meanwhile, settling his family in Brookline, Massachusetts, he tried his hand at music ("I'm told, because I don't remember it, that when I was small I went to the musician's hall with him," says his son), cabdriving, law school. But nothing panned out. So when the Korean War came along and the army offered to remobilize him, he packed his fledgling family off to his in-laws in Pittsburgh—a trip they'd make again in succeeding decades.

So Raymond, as his family still calls him, learned early about the mechanics of being on the go. "We left Boston in 1951 and went to Germany, Nuremburg," Drummond continues, as we sit, just before Christmas, in the recently refurnished living room of his prewar bungalow in Englewood, New Jersey, a twenty-minute ride from New York over the George Washington Bridge and home base for many black jazzers. "I have the dubious distinction of graduating from the very same school that I started in—a rare thing for an army brat. I started elementary school in Nuremburg, and graduated from Nuremburg American High School in 1964. But in between I went to fourteen schools in twelve years. We left Germany in 1954 and went to Colorado, Kansas—twice, once in the 1950s, once in the 1960s—and so on.

"It wasn't as tough as you'd think. I have five brothers and sisters. The two youngest were born in the 1960s, so they're effectively from the Monterey Peninsula, where my folks had settled by then. But the older four—I'm the oldest—were used to Pop coming in and going, 'Okay, in ten days the movers are coming and we've gotta pack up everything.' So we'd dutifully get to work. We'd say good-bye to the friends we met, jump in the car, and that was that. It wasn't dramatic. It was just what we did. We knew there'd be another PX, another post theater, new friends.

"You'd get a glimpse of people who grew up in one spot, like the kids in Junction City high school in Kansas, where I also went. Or my wife, Susan, who grew up in one place in Boston. Or my daughter, Maya, who's grown up here with all the same kids, who are now sophomores in high school. That was unheard-of for us. For us, moving was a way of life; it was never a trauma. I didn't really think about it until college, when I was finally in one place for four years."

College for Drummond was in California. Claremont—Claremont Men's College, as it still was called in 1964, when the Bulldog landed there from Nuremburg. He'd never seen the place, just the brochures. "They somehow got lists of prospective minority candidates, which included kids at overseas military school," he explains.

Starting as a chemistry major, he switched to political science and wrote his senior thesis on "Black Power and the Rise of Cultural Imperialism." These were the war years, and Drummond, as a member of ROTC and the ROTC band commander, came under scrutiny for his antiwar beliefs, which led him to stop attending classes and ROTC functions. Even a visit from his father, the colonel, didn't temper him.

The one thread running through the young Ray Drummond's life was a hobby: music. "Initially, being at Claremont was a depressing time for me," he explains. "That's when I taught myself to play piano—a lot of days and nights in practice rooms. And of course I was listening to music and collecting records. I bought my first Bill Evans record in Germany—for $2.35! Same thing with the early Ornette. I was reading *Downbeat* and *Metronome*. I'd get books out of the library. And I'd take myself to local clubs and hang out to listen. So I was the teacher and student at the same time, which is how I've become the bassist that I am."

Seated at a piano in a yearbook photo, the 20-year-old future bass stalwart looks like a young McCoy Tyner. He'd started his musical odyssey at age eight, when the family was living in Kansas. His mother bought him a mail-order Sears Silvertone trumpet and got him formal lessons. From then on, he played trumpet or French horn in school bands wherever the family landed. He took up the bass at 15, in California: "One of my teachers had a summer school, where he had more than enough French horns, but he needed another bass player." Mingus had a similar experience: he switched from cello to bass when a pal, reedman Buddy Collette, explained that, as a black musician, he wasn't going to get classical work, so he should learn a related jazz instrument. "So the music was always there. It was just never at a level where I wanted to make it into a career. When I taught myself piano, I could read music already. I already had a knowledge of melody and harmony. The piano was just like having the music notated on the keyboard in front of you. I could hear the notes, and so by trial-and-error and serious mathematical induction, or deduction, or conduction, I got there."

Drummond dutifully applied for nine-to-five jobs as he got ready to graduate in 1968. After his last summer teaching math in the Upward Bound program, he started work at Allstate—a plum job in Menlo Park, a small Bay Area town near Stanford. So it was that Allstate inadvertently led him to San Francisco, which happened to have a thriving jazz scene in the 1960s and 1970s—a scene that soon seduced him.

"I was responsible for hiring minority folks for sales or administrative jobs in both regions out of the Menlo Park and Sacramento offices," he recalls. "The company went to bat for me with the draft board, and got me deferred as indispensable. I know they were very happy with me, because they had me on the fast track to become a regional manager, rotating me around the company to learn all its different operations, and they gave me a leave of absence when I went to Stanford's MBA program in 1970." To the newly married Drummond, it seemed like the second rung on the ladder to corporate success.

Drummond recalls: "They gave me a full fellowship—a food stipend, they were paying the rent, tuition, books. It was unbelievable." After a year, however, he bailed out. "Two things put me over the edge. The work load meant I wasn't able to play as much music as I had been. Even at Allstate I'd been playing weddings and bar mitzvahs and little gigs around town. I had a little jazz group that got together every Saturday morning. I met this guy who was a clerk for Western Airlines when I had the bass sent up to Palo Alto, and he played drums in a group in Berkeley. The piano player was an engineer at Ampex, the sax player was a resident intern at Stanford Medical Center. And they said, 'We've got this really great trumpet player.' This is 1968, right? One Saturday morning, in comes this guy" (Drummond hunches his bulk into a question mark and shuffles slowly across his living-room floor). "I said, 'Oh shit, what's this?' So we start playing a Horace Silver tune, and he goes, 'Bleeedleleelele.' Whoa—he's Tom Harrell." Harrell, a functioning paranoid schizophrenic, is one of jazz's finest trumpeters, and an outstanding composer-arranger. He and Drummond still work together whenever they can.

"The other thing," he continues, "was just looking around at my classmates and realizing I had nothing in common with these guys. I could just see it was gonna be a rough 35 years, talking about their kids and what was on TV last night. My wife and I were just totally bored with that. So I figured, 'We don't own anything, we don't have any kids—now's the time for me to take my shot and see what happens. If I don't do it now, I won't do it.' " So he took his last stipend check, and moved to San Francisco to try to break into the jazz scene—which he did quickly, recording "Spirit Dance" with violinist Michael White's band within a couple of months.

In jazz, your first gig can be the outer strands of a web: one thing, for the committed and talented, leads to another. By 1973, Drummond was playing with hard-bop elder Bobby Hutcherson, recording *Live at Montreux* and *Sirius*. But as he got steady gigs with local heroes, Drummond got the word: "A week after I got to San Francisco in 1971, people started asking me how come I wasn't in New York.

"But I was doing fine. I mean, I wound up getting divorced. But I needed to live my bachelor life in my little studio to get the music together. It was the time of my greatest musical concentration, most of my serious woodshedding to get together the technical and mechanical aspects of performing. A lot of my earlier compositions came from there. I was playing 6, 7, 8 hours a day. It was a great time for me—no responsibilities. So I could be creative. I was working in the Keyhole, a black club near Candlestick and the Cow Palace, with a band led by Jules Brissard that played everything from top 40 to bebop. No admission charge, no singers, no dancing—but the place was always packed. We had to learn new shit every week, and it was always a challenge, and always fun. It gave me a glimpse of what earlier eras must have been like. The cops never got called, and trouble was almost nonexistent. I lasted in that until Hutcherson picked me up."

That was also when Drummond met his second wife, Susan Paone—at a Cecil Taylor gig. "I was talking to a DJ from KJAZ when Susan walked in, and it was like, I gotta go talk to her. The rest is history—21 years now. She's my heartbeat, a fellow Bostonian. She's been a nurse in the army, and the nurse for the Monterey Pop Festival, for Hendrix and all them in 1967. First time I brought Susan home, my mother snatched her away from me and said, 'She's my daughter'—even though she has two of her own."

Drummond's family ties combined with his business training to yank him out of music in early 1974, just as he seemed to be hitting his stride. In 1970, his father retired from the army, and opened a business, Harris Management Company, to provide services, like food preparation and janitorial work, for the army and air force as well as private firms like Bank of America and Pacific Bell. The contracts kept coming in, thanks to the ex-colonel's contacts.

"He asked me to join him. At first I resisted, but I finally gave in after about two years. Since his business was labor-intensive, and my background was in labor laws and relations, I was the perfect choice for personnel director. Later I become executive vice president, and designed management systems to set up and track the very complicated crew schedules we had to follow."

Drummond turned the company around, but the wheel came around for him, too: "After three and a half years working there, I realized, I miss music. I mean, I'm good at this stuff—but it's BORING. There's nothing in it for me. I was still playing, working a couple of nights a week in Berkeley. I talked with Susan, and we agreed it was time to go to New York." It was November 1977.

In New York City, Drummond blossomed. Thanks to luck and skill, he moved quickly through the concentric rings of possibility that greet a neophyte on the scene. He and Susan rented a house in Englewood, down the block from California-born bassist Sam Jones. According to Drummond, "Sam took me under his wing after he heard me in January with the Thad Jones–Mel Lewis orchestra at the Vanguard—the first gig I had here, which [bassist] Rufus [Reid] recommended me for. In February Sam asked me to work for him at Bradley's with [pianist] Jimmy Rowles, which is how I started working there. I was excited. As a new young guy, I was hanging in there all the time, trying to break in."

For all the talk in recent years about the "jazz tradition," there's often been a flagrant disregard of the tradition's older standard-bearers and of the fact that jazz is still overwhelmingly an oral tradition, a series of insights and gestures passed from one generation to the next on the bandstand. Witness, in 1993, the firing from the Lincoln Center Jazz Orchestra—whose artistic director, Wynton Marsalis, is one of the loudest advocates of "the tradition"—of nearly everyone over the age of 50. How exactly, Drummond and his middle-aged peers ask, can that tradition be sustained when few of the Marsalis-led Young Lions join their elders on bandstands for rigorous testing, when most come out of sleek supermarket-style music schools like Boston's Berklee expecting to be instant bandleaders with groups of their ex-dormmates, and so don't get introduced in any but superficial ways to the very tradition they spend so much time talking about?

"The gig I had with Rowles that night at Bradley's was the kind of thing we used to do, that we were prepared to do," says Drummond, visibly agitated—a rarity for him. Here, his voice ascends registers in leaps, underlining his anger and bewilderment. "We'd already sat down and listened to hundreds of tunes, learned and practiced them, developed our ears. Because when I'm following some of the older guys especially, it's not necessarily that I've played the tune before, it's just that I've heard it, so I can figure out how it goes—I know the architecture. And you've got to know who you're playing with, and be able to figure how they'll approach it.

"That's the kind of discipline you're supposed to bring to this job. You're supposed to develop a personal sound, you're supposed to give something back to the jazz community that helped make you, and you're supposed to make the other people onstage with you look great. It's a team. Few of the younger guys realize that. I mean, I remember Wynton saying when I was playing in his band in the mid-1980s, 'Playing in a quintet is like playing on a basketball team.' But on a basketball team guys are feeding each other the ball. Not in Wynton Marsalis's band. There's only one guy with the ball, therefore you have to play the game according to his rules.

"A lot of those younger guys have no idea that an artist is supposed to have a vision. One reason I stopped teaching (teaching music is a standard jazz musician's income supplement) is that I'd be pitching that line but I could see that these kids couldn't withstand commercial intrusions to do justice to their vision and develop it. Unless they're seriously motivated to go through the process of growth and pushing themselves, they're not gonna be able to stand up to the temptations. You can see it: Wynton's there already, the first one of the onslaught of manufactured jazz stars, where other factors are so important in the creation of the product, more important than the music, the artist's vision.

"I was telling a seminar in Pittsburgh a couple of months ago: "Isn't it curious how all these young bass players talk about how they eschew any kind of electronics, but when you hear them in performance or recording, you can't tell who they are?" I can tell Christian McBride and Peter Washington—my youngest and oldest sons, as I call them. But the other guys? I'm a bass player, and I can't tell them apart. They have a generic sound, packaged in a white box, that they pour out. On the other hand, Ron Carter, Buster Williams, Cecil McBee, Rufus Reid, George Mraz, me—two notes are enough to ID us. Isn't that curious? What do you think that might say?

"The answer is that developing a personal sound, a personal vision of who you are as an artist, is not an issue they address. It's not important to them. Neither their peers nor their elders are making them address it. And it's a serious issue that cuts to the heart of the credibility of the artistic process: the integrity of that process is only as good as the issues the artists themselves recognize. That's what makes us different from computers, what makes the masters different from the students. But the support structure isn't demanding that these musicians create a personal vision. In fact, just the opposite—which is why so many younger players on all instruments sound the same."

For Drummond in 1978 and after, things happened with what, in hindsight, looks like inevitability. The Jones-Lewis Big Band and the Bradley's gig led to a stint with the vocalist who runs jazz's finest on-stage finishing school, Betty Carter. Carter's bands—another of mainstream jazz's key entry points, like a regular gig at Bradley's and the

Vanguard—have graduated the likes of pianists John Hicks, Mulgrew Miller, Cyrus Chestnut, and Jacky Terrasson into jazz-virtuoso star status. As a bassist, Drummond doesn't have access to that status— after all, he doesn't even rate an entry in the *New Grove Encyclopedia of Jazz*. But he could, and did, trade on the respect other musicians paid his craft, becoming one of the busiest sidemen in New York. Soon he was touring with saxman Johnny Griffin, pianists Kenny Barron and Hank Jones, whirlwinding his way across Europe, hopping the international date line to Japan, becoming de facto house bassist at Bradley's, beginning the feverish pace of recording that's resulted in a stack of album credits—in short, leading the fractured life of the successful jazz journeyman.

"I have a lot of trouble leaving this house," he says wistfully. "I spend a lot of time puttering around before I actually get on a plane. I'm really attached to this little starter house we've expanded into something else. We had new siding put on a year ago. The bathroom's just been redone. This is home. The basement is a mess—my office, the records and CDs and old reel-to-reel tapes, my music. But it's my mess, and I really miss it when I'm gone."

During the last two years, different elements have gotten Drummond to slacken his frantic pace—his consistent ability to make a living, his daughter, whose photos pop up everywhere around the house, having a rocky adolescence, his desire to focus on his own music rather than working as a sideman, however lucrative. "No more getting off the plane from Japan, hitting a weeklong gig at Bradley's that night, and doing a record date or two in between," he says, shaking his head with conviction. "I don't need to do it anymore. And I need time to focus on my own creativity as a composer and leader. I wrote my first grant proposal this year to the New Jersey State Council for the Arts. It was weird, because I basically had to say, 'I need this grant so I can stop working so much and have time to think and write.' "

Over the last decade, Drummond's own albums have shown his growth as a leader and composer, as he's abandoned the neobop approach favored by Wynton Marsalis and his followers for an amalgam of African roots and post-Coltrane open structures. *Excursion*, one of his latest CDs, paints a promising musical landscape. "I come from the Miles Davis school of bandleading," he says. "You get the right guys for the gig together, feed them good material, and just help the chemistry along. If you've made the right choices, the music should happen organically."

Maybe Drummond can move into the public's field of vision. Take his stint at the Village Vanguard, jazz's most famous basement, this wintry post-New Year's week. Drummond is leading his fierce individualists—tenor saxists Craig Handy and David Sanchez, pianist Danilo Perez, drummer Marvin "Smitty" Smith, percussionist Mor Thiam—to a full house. The powerful 90-minute set has the crowd applauding wildly: the solos are topnotch, the ensemble work is sharp, and the show flows brilliantly. Beginning with a witty second-line-strut on Dizzy Gillespie's classic "A Night in Tunisia," Drummond pilots his crew through open-ended segues, from blues eddies to free-jazz white water, a roaring piece by McCoy Tyner, and a lilting, African-inspired original foaming gently with crossrhythms.

"I was hoping," he says with a mix of resigned good humor and annoyance during the break, "to record this band, to document it on tape this weekend. But Columbia won't give me a release for David (who's currently under contract to that major label). They say he's been exposed too much, that they want to pull his career back under control. So I guess it's not gonna happen." Partly, this is because Ray Drummond isn't, say, a pianist like Perez—one of the many leaders outside the Columbia stable who've gotten the nod to record with Sanchez over the last year. Partly, it's because Drummond isn't signed to a major label: not a pianist or hornman, he's too old to be a Young Lion and too young to be an Old Master—the major jazz labels' main categories of preoccupation in the post-Wynton years. That means there are no significant trading points for Columbia in okaying Sanchez's participation in his recording. And so they don't. Which means that the larger audience who might hear about this stirring gig from the hundreds who'll pass down the Vanguard's narrow staircase this week, and who might want to find a document of it, won't.

The late afternoon has yielded to evening while we've been talking in Drummond's home. The Bulldog pauses, and wanders back to the coffee machine in his cozy, well-stocked kitchen, where the table is covered with music magazines like *Downbeat* and the jazz supplement to the *Village Voice*. "The last two years the whole circle of my life has been coming to a focus," he says quietly. "People I haven't seen in years—all of a sudden, boom, there they are. All over the world. Some of them I haven't seen in 10 or 20 years. It's obvious that things are about to happen, that things are on me. I'm ready." [1995]

The Two of Us
Tom Harrell

At age 48, Tom Harrell has become one of jazz's outstanding figures. He wields trumpet and flugelhorn with unnerving agility, and can go through an entire set without repeating a phrase—no mean feat. As a sideman, he's a veteran of the Stan Kenton Orchestra, Woody Herman's Thundering Herd, Horace Silver's Quintet, Phil Woods's Quintet, and Charlie Haden's Liberation Orchestra. He's co-led avant-tinged groups with saxist Joe Lovano, and for the last few years has fronted various topnotch, mainstream bands of his own. And he's widely recognized as one of the music's premier composers and arrangers.

What makes his list of credits even more formidable is that Harrell is a clinically diagnosed paranoid schizophrenic.

"I had feelings of unreality and obsessive thoughts when I was a teenager," he explained to me one recent afternoon at the small Upper West Side apartment he shares with his wife Angela. The main room is crammed with electronic keyboards and file cabinets stuffed with his music and open traveling trunks full of clothes. A small table and a couple of folding chairs are in the room's center; a bed takes up one corner. "I started drinking in high school, then I stopped. I started therapy in the 60s, and that's when I started taking medicine for paranoia. Then I was diagnosed as a borderline schizophrenic in the late 60s, after I made a halfway suicide attempt, and started treatment after that. It helped me adjust to social situations. It also helped me get started writing again—until I got medicine, I stopped being able to write."

Harrell's medication—the only thing that keeps him from being institutionalized—helps depress his illness's symptoms. (He also follows a fairly strict physical regimen: "I try to exercise by walking three times a week, a long walk. And I eat protein: I like steak and spinach every two days. And I take multivitamins.") It also, inevitably, depresses his outward affect. He talks in a low near-monotone, and rarely faces you, although he turns his face toward you regularly, and fixes you with his bright, glistening eyes—windows so suggestively open you can scan both his intelligence and his vulnerability at a glance. He pauses often to grope for a phrase—although once he's on a thought-train, he rolls. As his longtime friend and musical associate, bassist Ray Drummond, puts it, "The guy is so garrulous it's ridiculous." When he walks onstage, he looks like a human question mark: his head, with its slicked-back hair, bent almost perpendicular to his body, eyes on the floor, arms stiff at his sides. Then suddenly, when it's time for him to blow, he straightens to his full thin six-foot-two height, puts the horn to his mouth, and proceeds to carve the splendid sounds that have made him such a reputation among his fellow musicians and critics and fans.

"The playing of a wind instrument is also a sort of yoga exercise," he explains. "The breathing involved can make you very centered. Even before I realized I had mental problems, like when I was in high school, I noticed that when I first found out about the concept of breathing from the diaphragm, I saw that it gave a feeling of relaxation and peacefulness. It would calm me." He pauses. "Music gives me positive energy. It gives me passion. It gives me a reason to live. I'm really lucky, because I've heard people say, 'My life is meaningless.' I've said it myself. But then I remind myself that my life has meaning, that I can make people happy by what I do, and make myself happy while I'm sharing it." Pause. "Playing with bands at a really high level of creativity, and having the audience involved in what you're doing . . . when there's that interplay, when the music takes off, it gives you the experience I have, maybe once or twice a year, that the music is playing me. You lose your sense of self in the music. It gives you the feeling that there's something bigger than yourself, that there's a higher power. That helps me deal with illness, having that personal experience—although I guess you could say it's beyond personal, because it's creating a community. Playing with Joe [Lovano] last year at the [Village] Vanguard, I remember that the music reached such a peak that there was one point where I played one note and someone in the audience screamed—and that was the way I felt too, and the whole group felt that level of intensity, of joy, of really positive energy."

Garrulous, indeed. Talking with Harrell, the trick is to learn to distinguish when his lapses into silence mean he's formulating the next leg of the verbal journey—which can then pour out—and when he's finished what he had to say and is simply waiting for your next input into the conversation. It's the verbal equivalent of playing in a jazz band with him.

Thomas Strong Harrell was born on June 16, 1946, in Urbana, Illinois. His father was an industrial psychologist, and soon relocated the family to California's Bay Area, when he became a faculty member at Stanford University. Harrell's parents were fond of music, and introduced the youngster to their favorite sounds. "I was very lucky," he says. "My parents played a lot of music when I was a kid. The Louis Armstrong recordings with the Hot Five and Hot Seven were what made me want to play the trumpet. I started when I was 8, and I started improvising right away. It was fun, because there didn't seem to be any rules—which really appeals to a kid." Soon he was also studying piano—an instrument he still loves to play and uses to compose with. Among his teachers were such jazz stalwarts as saxists Lee Konitz and John Handy. So it's not surprising that, by age 13, the precocious musician was gigging around San Francisco Bay on both instruments. It was while he was enrolled as a music major at Stanford that he attempted suicide; after his diagnosis and treatment, he finished with a BA in music composition, in 1969.

Which is where Drummond—himself such a fixture around the mainstream-jazz scene that he's appeared on more than 150 albums in the last decade or so, and works 200-plus days a year—first met him: "And could he write then? Let me tell you, the Big Band that's been playing every Monday night at the Vanguard for nearly 30 years has a chart in its book that we first played out in Berkeley with that little band. And it still sounds totally fresh." Harrell nods when I tell him that story, and adds: "That Vanguard chart is one of the first pieces I wrote after I started taking medicine. I started it before I started my medicine, but I couldn't finish the big band arrangement until I started taking medicine. I did a three-horn arrangement in the mid-1960s, but I had to start medicine to finish the big-band chart."

Harrell's music, both composed and improvised, is complex post-bebop; among his idols are composer Tadd Dameron, who penned a number of melodically serpentine, densely harmonically textured bop-era classics, like "Hot House." His solos and his charts are subtle and rich, fertile with (to nonmusicians) barely noticeable feats of harmonic modulation and dynamic tension and, for the big bands, powerful section writing as well as undeniable, in-your-face outpourings of virtuosity and swagger—like when he'll string several choruses of sixteenth notes across a jagged, shifting harmonic plain.

Harrell—who, like most jazzers, views improvisation as instant composition, seeing the two as a continuity—nevertheless often feels torn between his composing and performing sides. "I practice all the time," he says. "The demands of a brass instrument are such that I have to restrain myself from writing or playing the piano, because once I get started writing, sometimes it's hard for me to tear myself away. So I try to force myself to practice trumpet as much as possible. I've been playing more flugelhorn over the last year. I love the sound of it. Trumpet and flugelhorn are like two different personalities. But you can approach them both with the same melodic concept. You can take a lot more melodic chances with flugelhorn than many people might think. I like to play both of them. In a concert situation, they complement my physical makeup: when I get tired of one and play the other, it rejuvenates my chops. Shifting also rejuvenates me musically, because it inspires me to try new things. It's hard to be creative, period," he says with a laugh, "but it's difficult playing the same instrument all night—it places a great demand on the improviser to be interesting." He pauses, then unleashes an ambitious bombshell: "My next target is playing multiphonics on brass instruments—more than one note at a time." Something saxists have done more or less routinely for decades, but a relatively uncharted territory on the more rigid trumpet.

"For me," Harrell continues, "composition happens different ways, although sometimes it can turn into a ritual. Whenever I practice, I might hear a fragment in my mind, or it might come out in my playing, so I write it down or record it. Then ideally I extend the fragment as soon as I write it down. It's nice to have three or four weeks off from performing so I can develop the fragments—that's when I compose every day. It's easy for me to have melodic ideas, and chordal ideas, and rhythmic ideas—but they're isolated ideas. To be able to conceptualize an entity, though, I have to be in a certain frame of mind. When I'm doing it every day, it comes much easier. It's almost like a door opening every night—a melody would emerge in my head."

Harrell's current quintet—saxist Don Braden, pianist Kenny Werner, bassist Larry Grenadier, drummer Billy Hart—has him writing in a more open-ended, free-jazz vein for some tunes than he has before. And he is quick to credit their abilities with his expanded music ambitions. Watching him onstage, it's possible to see, more starkly than in most other musicians, just how much Harrell is listening to his cohorts: when, for instance, another player's solo is winding down, he hears it before almost anybody, and suddenly punctuates the musical movement by straightening up and putting the horn to his mouth, ready to blow.

Harrell is as quick to poke fun at himself and his condition as he is to praise others. During his high school days, he harbored ambitions to become a cartoonist—and still has his strips. As Drummond puts it, "He's a real comedian, once he gets to know you." So I tell Harrell a story I've heard to confirm its truth, and he laughs so hard he nearly falls off his chair. The story: he's on tour, and checks into a hotel, where he's given a two-room suite. He puts his bags down, and slowly looks around, then cracks, "One for each of my personalities, huh?"
[1995]

Across the Great Divide
Don Pullen and Joe Lovano

At age 53, after two years of cancer treatments and hospital bouts interrupted by recording and tours, pianist-composer Don Pullen died on April 27. His death wasn't a surprise; he'd made financial arrangements for his kids with his record label, and then left Sloan-Kettering for his brother's Orange, New Jersey, home the weekend before. But it was still stunning. That's partly because it followed so closely on saxist-composer Julius Hemphill's lingering illness and death. (Hemphill was 57 when he died of multiple causes on April 2.) But it's also partly due to the arc of Pullen's career, which ironically (also like Hemphill's) garnered increasing accolades and audiences before he left the life he (like Hemphill again) loved so dearly, if not always so wisely or so well.

Pullen's music, most brilliantly crystallized in his last band, the African-Brazilian Connection, ignored stylistic divides with the casual aplomb that comes of vision, time, and training. Born in Roanoke, Virginia, on Christmas Day, 1941, as a youngster he began to accompany vocalists in the gospel church, and soon did the same for r&b singers. At college he discovered Art Tatum—"God" to all jazzers for the sheer force and power of his technique. But Pullen's questing musical intelligence soon led him to the revolutionary sounds of Ornette Coleman and Eric Dolphy—people who were (and are) often accused of lacking technique completely. In Chicago in 1964, he played with the Experimental Band of Muhal Richard Abrams—precursor of the AACM, that wellspring of post-Ornette probing into jazz's edges.

Moving to New York, Pullen once again found rent-paying work backing singers like Big Maybelle, Ruth Brown, and Arthur Prysock while gigging with soul-jazz organ trios in New Jersey nightclubs. By 1966 he'd joined drummer Milford Graves and the great saxist Albert Ayler, whose frenzied, possessed "energy music," pushing at the rhythmic and harmonic bounds of jazz, often radically deconstructed churchy roots. After a shot as Nina Simone's music director, Pullen signed on with Charles Mingus's 1972–75 group, a comeback powerhouse for the bassist-composer that included trumpeter Jack Walrath, drummer Dannie Richmond, and tenorman George Adams. (The group is documented on *Changes One and Two*.) By this point, Pullen was regularly deploying his patented "crushed" runs. This rapid fingering extended Cecil Taylor's breakthroughs and built on Pullen's experience as an organist. Translating organ glisses to the more recalcitrant piano via wrist acrobatics, Pullen's solos whimpered and imploded. Not surprisingly, Mingus's polystylistic ideas inspired Pullen, though the two had the usual Mingus-sideman fights, and gave him room to synthesize his diversity into a voice.

Making his solo debut in 1975 for overseas labels (a common jazz story), Pullen a year later came home with the aptly named (and out-of-print) *Tomorrow's Promises*. In 1978, he, Adams, Richmond, and other Mingus vets became the first Mingus Dynasty. Soon afterward, he and Adams led Richmond and bassist Cameron Brown in a quartet featuring dynamic interplay between Adams, with his careening from-a-bass-blast-to-a-scream horn, and Pullen, with his tone-clustered, rhythmically scintillating runs. His trio recordings (*New Beginnings* and *Random Thoughts*) finessed Pullen's coming into his own voice. Then, in 1990, he organized the African-Brazilian Connection.

Born while Pullen was artist-in-residence at Pennsylvania's Yellow Springs Institute, the Connection proved to be the perfect vehicle for Pullen's multifaceted tastes. Carlos Ward's now lyrically crying, now post-Trane lunging alto sax and his bracing flute served as Pullen's melodic alter ego and soloing foil, and the syncretic beats pulsing through the deftly relentless rhythm section—Nelson Matta—under-pinned the catchy heads. Their rich recorded legacy: *Kele Mou Bana, Ode to Life* (with its haunting 13-minute elegy for Adams, "Ah, George, We Hardly Knew Ya"), and *Live . . . Again*, recorded at the Montreux Jazz Festival in 1993.

Last July, after he'd come out of chemotherapy and done a five-week tour of Brazil and then Europe, Pullen brought the Connection to New York's Sweet Basil. They ate the place alive. They'd been clev-erly conceived as a vehicle to mix avant and mainstream elements in an accessible way. But faced with death, the band further heightened the *Ode to Life* material with a ferocious vengeance, winding seamlessly in and out of free-jazz blasts and classical fantasias and roots of all sorts. It was a stirring affirmation of jazz's essential impurity, of the vanguard's potential ability to reach an audience—and, in the process, undercut neo-pundits who, ignoring Mark Twain, have been proclaim-ing the death of the avant-garde set and its following. The shows I saw were packed and breathtaking, the full houses scorched by the voice of a man who's on fire with nothing to lose. And now it's over.

Except, of course, for the voices from beyond the grave that art Orphically preserves. The Connection's last album, *Sacred Common Ground*, was recorded in early March 1995, while Pullen was in re-mission, and has just been released. It had been conceived as a vehicle for choreographer Garth Fagan when Pullen was performing at the Helena, Montana site for the Lila Wallace Jazz Network—the single best argument in favor of that Network I know of so far. *Ground* is a provocative attempt to annex to jazz, that roving omnivore, yet more territory—Native-American chants. (Yes, others have tried it, usually with mixed success.) Opening with Native-American singers and drummers, it gradually weaves the Connection in, layering and interweaving rhythms and sounds in ways you could never predict from the raw ingredients—ways that underline what Sonny Rollins once told me, "Jazz isn't a thing; it's what you do with things." What Pullen did, with his cohorts, produced a beautifully moving last testament that befits his large and restless musical spirit. The week before he died, the troupe chanted and drummed in his hospital room as he prepared, soothed and ready, for the inevitable.

Like his late labelmate, Joe Lovano walks the fault lines in jazz between the mainstream and the outside—and does it with conviction and results. That's at least partly because the 43-year-old multi-instrumentalist came up through the ranks and paid his dues while playing around jazz's many and multiplying interstices. Born in Cleveland in 1952, to a jazz-loving, sax-playing barber-father, Lovano picked up his horn and the music early. Growing up in a family where Sonny Rollins and John Coltrane records were normal listening fare, practicing his horn alongside his semipro dad in improvising dialogues, he learned standards and the value of listening—jazz's motive power, the art of musical conversation.

Lovano first broke into the touring circuit the way many younger jazzers traditionally did—playing around. A mid-1970s stint at the Berklee College of Music introduced him to guitarists John Scofield and Bill Frisell, and pianists Kenny Werner and Mulgrew Miller—all of whom he's recurrently worked with ever since. He paid the usual clubland and roadwork dues, playing in organ trios, like Jack McDuff's and Lonnie Liston Smith's, and in big bands, like Woody Herman's umpteenth Herds and Mel Lewis's long-running Vanguard outfit. That last outfit was where he met Tom Harrell, who became an ongoing collaborator, in the early 1980s. Soon he was branching out. He joined Charlie Haden's far-reaching Liberation Music Orchestra, and he entered the sometimes surreal space of one of my favorite groups, the Paul Motian Trio. There Motian, Frisell, and Lovano serve up an uncanny sound like nothing else, juxtaposing Motian's melodic drums, Frisell's dreamy-to-buzzsaw guitar, and Lovano's now-shrieking, now-crooning sax in atmosphere that continually shifts unpredictably, with sly charm and wit and a Cheshire-cat smile. Lovano, for instance, can become the rhythm instrument, while Frisell solos to Motian's obbligatos.

The result of all this journeyman traveling: Lovano understands the music's history, not as dogma but as living, evolving art that reconciles and even transcends definitions. That's become clear as he's slowly matured into his own voice over the last few years. Beginning with his 1985 recording *Tones, Shapes & Colors*, Lovano consistently sold in the high three to low four figures—all too typical jazz-journeyman numbers. Meanwhile Blue Note had signed him, believing in his possibilities; and to its old-fashioned credit, the label released four Lovano albums while it waited, usually patiently, for his audience to find him. His *Tenor Legacy* paired him with then-emerging younger saxman Joshua Redman, and the sparks between the two flew engagingly as they prompted themselves and the music to strenuous heights. Coming out just as Redman's star was rising high, it helped pull Lovano, already on an upward career trajectory of his own, farther along. *Rush Hour*, his interesting 1995 chamber-jazz collaboration with Gunther Schuller, verified his arc. Now, ushering him through the door of his big breakthrough, is his two-CD release, *Quarters Live at the Village Vanguard*, recorded live almost a year apart, over two weeks with two different quartets at New York's clubland jazz mecca.

The two CDs have distinct feels, but on both the music is consistently engaging and open, stretching, reaching. Along the way, the pair of recordings essentially outlines one player's history of postwar jazz, in a kind of musical bildungsroman, but in retrograde. The first CD, recorded in 1994, captures Lovano with horn wizard Tom Harrell, versatile bassist Anthony Cox, and drum stalwart Billy Hart. The material is mostly Lovano originals, which cover the spectrum from ballads to uptempo movers. Some tunes, like "Fort Worth," are homages—in this case, to Ornette Coleman, Dewey Redman, and the other postwar avantjazzers born in that Texas ex-cowtown. And certainly the other sounds that interweave through Lovano's own voice—Coltrane, Sonny Rollins, Miles Davis—filter through the extended improvisational interplay, which is fast and loose and consistently scintillating in its risk-taking and resolution.

What's interesting about the second CD, recorded in early 1995 with the *Tenor Legacy* rhythm section—pianist Mulgrew Miller, bassist Christian McBride, and drummer Lewis Nash—is that Lovano chose this more straightahead setting to unearth the roots of his own development, tunes written by or identified with Charlie Parker, Miles Davis, Sonny Rollins, and Charles Mingus. This is, as Lovano himself puts it, "the classic jazz language, moving from bebop to post-bop to modern modal. Classic jazz quartets are at the root of my playing." So the material is meant to have personal resonance. "This Is All I Ask" is a tune Lovano learned from a tape his father made for him, and "Little Willie Leaps" is something his dad taught him as a kid.

One of jazz's key aspects is supposed to be experiential: as Charlie Parker put it, "If you don't live it, it can't come out of your horn." As a jazzer, your goal is to synthesize your experience and coalesce it into your own distinctive voice and outlook, then reintegrate that individualism back into group dynamics for the overall good. It's a model that's been at the heart of jazz from its beginnings a century ago, and it surely reflects how post-Madisonian American civil society and culture is supposed to function. Lovano, as he crisscrosses stylistic lines with maximum attention to the demands of the music at hand, is evidence that jazz's ever-multiplying dialects can, in fact, nearly all be spoken by a dedicated, talented individual. By extension, then, it offers a hope that an increasingly fractured American culture may yet rediscover some common ground, if only, as the telephone company ad used to go, people would just listen.

Lovano has come a long way in terms of recognition over the last couple of years. After all, he's not even listed in the error-and-omission-riddled *New Grove Dictionary of Jazz*. And only two years ago, he was being used by certain Lincoln Center honchos as a target, a prime example they'd consistently cite of somebody who couldn't/didn't play real jazz. It's a measure of at least a few things around the ever-squabbling jazz world that this December, Lovano was a key participant in "We'll Take Manhattan," a night of commissioned compositions put on by Jazz at Lincoln Center at Alice Tully Hall. [1996]

Out of the Tradition
Julius Hemphill

When multireedman Marty Ehrlich, now one of the most accomplished composer-musicians of his generation, was a teenager in St. Louis, alto saxist Julius Hemphill came back through town. Ehrlich, who already knew him slightly, admired him as both a player and a composer. So he jumped at the chance to ferry Hemphill around town one day—a day that led to a deeper, lasting relationship.

"I was really nervous," Ehrlich recalled for me recently. "But Malinke Elliot, a writer-director who was a mutual friend of ours, told me, 'You can ask Julius anything. He's open, and he'd be glad to answer any questions.' So while we were on our way to the first stop of the day, I asked Julius what he thought the key ingredients for a good composition were. He nodded to let me know he'd heard the question, but didn't say anything." Nor did he say anything about the topic for the rest of the day, so as the duo wound their way around St. Louis the conversation also took various turns. Until, that is, that night, when Ehrlich was dropping Hemphill off at the place he was staying. "Contrast," is all the older man said.

Succinctness is one hallmark of the far-reaching body of work that Hemphill has amassed over the last twenty-odd years of recording and performing. Unlike many of his comrades who came up during the free-jazz heyday, he's never surrendered to the sheer energy of note cascades for their own virtuosic sake. Though he has a formidable conceptual musical mind, he's avoided the more abstract explorations some of his peers found so appealing. Instead, he uses his marvelous gift for lyricism to leaven even his earthiest or most avant-garde, noise-perforated outings. That thoughtful and balanced approach, that distinctive sense of control over texture and space, shows clearly in his composing as well as his approach to his horns.

Hemphill's oeuvre is even more astonishing when you consider that, like virtually all jazzers, he's had to rely largely on grants, like those from invaluable new-music-friendly organizations like Meet The Composer, to fund his often ambitious projects—large-scale groups and multimedia pieces like his critically acclaimed saxophone opera, *Long Tongues*, and the three-and-a-half hours of music (35 separate themes!) he wrote for Bill T. Jones's *Last Supper at Uncle Tom's Cabin: The Promised Land*. Yes, the World Saxophone Quartet, which he cofounded, finally made what is, for jazzers, a big splash and some big money. But that was after years of small-label dues. And inevitably, Hemphill, like so many artists, plowed much of what he made back into what he wanted to do.

As a composer, Hemphill is more than just a study in contrasts. His pallette suggests an unfettered but disciplined imagination, a willingness to go for the uncommon and untried that resounds with his sense of music history. He enjoys tackling offbeat instrumental lineups, whether the WSQ or his saxophone sextet. His earliest recorded band, on 1972's self-produced *Dogon A. D.*, features himself on alto and flute, Baikida E. J. Carroll on trumpet, Abdul Wadud on cello, and Philip Wilson on drums. He used overdubbing for 1977's fascinating and far-ranging *Blue Boyé*, a solo record stuffed with outrageous sonic effects, from growls and groans to screams and yelps, as well as enticing mainstream and melodic ideas. (That disc's associate producer was altoist Tim Berne, who is, along with Ehrlich, one of Hemphill's major disciples.) And his writing for large ensembles, as his *Julius Hemphill Big Band* demonstrates, is replete with incisive, seductive section charts. If they recall masters like Ellington and Gil Evans, their curving, at time implosive voicings are Hemphill's own. According to Ehrlich, who worked with Hemphill on that and other dates, "He actually hears the way these things will sound when he writes them—which is a lot rarer than you might think."

In his own alto work, Hemphill seamlessly meshes bebop and blues. Along with the gutbucket Texas traditions he grew up with, Charlie Parker's human-touch-of-blue horn echoes across the glowing, often jagged lines that scissor and weave throughout his work. ("Kansas City Line," on *Blue Boye*, is a Hemphill tip-of-the-hat to Bird, but with a characteristic twist—it's a 10-bar blues.) Never one to be confined to predetermined formats, Hemphill has admired Gerry Mulligan, especially his pianoless groups, and Lennie Tristano and Lee Konitz from his youth. And one of his stock tongue-in-cheek aphorisms for interviewers over the years has been, "I like making things. Noise is one of them."

It's easy to hear why Berne, whose interests in soul music and punk-style noise collide on his own efforts, would seek Hemphill out, why his composing, arranging, and playing are influenced down to the bone by the older man, why his most recent disc, which features fellow Hemphill admirer David Sanborn—yes, *that* David Sanborn—is called *Diminutive Mysteries (Mostly Hemphill)*. "The primary focus of what he taught me was about tone," Berne explained to me not long ago. "The rest of the time we'd hang out, and it'd be pretty free-form. He wasn't interested in trying to feed me systematized information in the typical teacher-student way. He'd question my questions. He provoked me into thinking for myself." Indirectly as well as directly, he's opened the same Socratic path for other younger players. Guitar hero (and ex-Berne sideman) Bill Frisell, for instance, has an evocative dirgelike piece on his *This Land* called simply "Julius Hemphill."

When Hemphill was born in Fort Worth, Texas, on January 24, 1938, what we call jazz was still very much what it had been from its birth: a fluid, open-ended collection of idioms. Most musicians kept it that way deliberately; they refused to define what they did for fear of limiting it. In fact, they generally resented anyone else's attempts at definition. Descriptive titles like bebop—and for that matter, jazz—were attacked or dismissed for their confining overtones. Many of Fort Worth's native sons—Ornette Coleman, John Carter, Dewey Redman, James Jordan, King Curtis, Cornell Dupree—felt the same way. What they heard growing up was a musical stew that included blues, r&b, and bebop, and they saw no reason not to draw on whatever ingredients they wanted for what they did. As Hemphill recalls, "The music people played live was an indiscriminate mix. They'd stick bebop into rhythm and blues routinely."

His career has been a reaffirmation of that dismissal of labels in pursuit of an elemental American sound—Robert Johnson and Bird are two of the biggest heroes in his pantheon. He studied some classical music at North Texas State and Lincoln University. "It was," he says dryly, "an academic pursuit, largely hypothetical, since there were so few African Americans in the classical world." He took jobs with r&b

bands, including guitarist Ike Turner's. And he played in an army band—a crucial vehicle for more than a few black musicians of his generation.

While he was in the army, he met and married a St. Louis woman, and moved there in 1965. St. Louis had earlier been a sonic incubator for Ike Turner's r&b and Chuck Berry's rock and roll and the trumpet sounds of Clark Terry and Miles Davis. By the time Hemphill arrived those scenes were played out. But the Black Artists Group (BAG), a community-organizing and multimedia-based cooperative modeled on Chicago's Association for the Advancement of Creative Musicians— one of the AACM's prime movers, trumpeter Lester Bowie, was a St. Louis product—drew him in. There he met fellow altoist Oliver Lake, who in 1976 would join him, baritone saxman Hamiet Bluiett, and tenor saxist David Murray in the celebrated World Saxophone Quartet. Under Hemphill's guidance—he put together most of the group's charts and original compositions—the WSQ melded such apparently disparate elements as gospel, blues, soaring lyrical flights, and raunchy flickerings of free improvisation.

BAG energized Hemphill, who began to finesse his own sound as both player and composer and to work in the multimedia formats he still favors. In 1972 he started his own label, Mbari Records. This was in accordance with key dicta of both the AACM and BAG—control your own music and its presentation as much as possible, and don't let the record companies get your copyrights. (One of his first Mbari releases, *The Collected Poem for Blind Lemon Jefferson*, showcased his proclivity for matching words and music: it paired his sax and flute with the voices of poets K. Curtis Lyle and Malinke Kenyatta.)

The Mbari records are stunning, not least because they present Hemphill's voice in its fully formed guise. There's the mix of bop and blues that runs through so much of his music on the title cut of his first release, *Dogon A. D.* Cellist Wadud seesaws back and forth on a minor third that essentially inverts and remeters Willie Dixon's "Spoonful," while Hemphill filigrees alto in and out of the spaces, flying against the time and often the grain. There are, of course, his patented thick textures, often contrapuntal, with their gyring lead lines and occasional outbreaks into ferocious overblowing. Parts of *'Coon Bid'ness*, recorded mostly in 1975 with folks like Bluiett and Arthur Blythe, are fairly bursting with that direction: pieces like "Skins 1" foreshadow much of the early World Sax Quartet. (Historical irony: Blythe took Hemphill's place in the WSQ when he was ousted from the group in September 1989.) But there's also the subtle and rich chamber-music introspection of an evocative piece like "Reflections." And there's his dry, sardonic humor: the sudden grungily sawed cello that signs off on the ironically titled "Lyric," or the brittle donkey honks that punctuate and end "Skins 1." (None of this stuff is in print. Some record company could do us all a favor by picking it up for CD reissue.)

The WSQ was initially Hemphill's band, in the sense that he gave it impetus and shape. But there was always a tug of war between his more arranged notions and those of some of the other players, who wanted to blow more freely over vamps. Over the years those tensions hardened, especially when, as Hemphill puts it, "I was getting too much credit. I always told interviewers we all contributed, but people had the perception that I was the leader because I wrote the bulk of the music. And that didn't sit well." When Elektra Nonesuch head Bob Hurwitz suggested the foursome cut an album of Ellington tunes, the group went along, and turned in a sterling job (*Plays Ellington*) that netted them mainstream media attention and sales bigger than any they'd had. But it also marked a key change of direction, and exacerbated the group's already almost insoluble inner divisions.

In 1988, Elektra Nonesuch offered Hemphill a shot at doing what he wanted as a leader, and he came up with his *Big Band* album. Even though it drew some critical raves, *Big Band* got what Hemphill characterizes as "an ambiguous response" from the label. It wasn't a high marketing or publicity priority. So it didn't exactly blow out the doors of record stores, and Hemphill found himself back recording for small indies like the indispensable Black Saint.

He'd been recording for that Italian label, actually, pretty much all along. (The early, grittily powerful WSQ discs were on Black Saint, for instance.) And now, thanks to CD reissues, some of Hemphill's non-WSQ work has resurfaced. With Wadud and drummer Don Moye he created powerful, slashing statements like 1978's *Raw Materials and Residuals*. He plays flute and, unusually, tenor sax on *Flat-out Jump Suite*. And until this last year, he's continued to record. *Julius Hemphill Trio: Live from the New Music Cafe* reunited him in late 1991 with Wadud and test-drove drummer Joe Bonadio as they hit Hemphill standards like "Dogon A. D." and "Bordertown" and the lustrous "Georgia Blue." His sextet, which includes Ehrlich, the fiery young James Carter, and veteran Coltrane scholar Andrew White, convened that same year to cut the fiercely but smoothly driving *Fat Man and the Hard Blues*. Kicking off with "Otis' Groove," a sinewy tribute to soulman Redding, it unwinds a stunning diversity of entwined lines through a dazzling variety of moods and settings—the titles include "Floppy," "Headlines," "Anchorman," and "The Hard Blues," a gutsy, wailing track he first recorded in 1972, and which clearly reflects his early Fort Worth days.

I cite the titles in deference to a revealingly dense but rich passage from Hemphill's own notes to *Blue Boye*, which Ehrlich pointed out to me, and which I've been chewing on ever since: "Since it is my understanding of the matter that instrumental music is not readily capable of delivering specific imagery and messages under our cloak of anonymity, it appears that one must be content to resort to titles and style to convey what might be termed 'probable intent.' With that line of thinking in view, I hope that some more immediate level of communication has been established. I think that music as we know it is autobiographical." [1994]

I Have a Dream
Marty Ehrlich

When Marty Ehrlich turned 40 last year, he and his wife had a second child just before he underwent surgery for a persistent larynx condition, after years of unsuccessful treatments. A cyst was removed, his diet and regimen were changed, and he endured three weeks of silence after the operation. The whole thing was scary. As a multireed jazzman, Ehrlich leans heavily on his pipes. It's hard to get much more than a monotone out of your horn without tugging at your throat. And yet Ehrlich reacted with the combination of understanding, resolve, and acceptance that courses through his richly developed, polystylistic music. When it was over, he healed and went back to the teaching, sideman gigs, and too-few shots at recording and performing his own stuff that pay his East Village rent.

Neither flashy nor flamboyant, a team player in the jazz spectrum polarized between neocon young Lions and selfconscious avant-shock troops, Ehrlich emerged a decade ago, with the likes of Tim Berne and Bill Frisell, from the so-called downtown New York scene around the Knitting Factory. Sharing that stage with fiery extroverts like John Zorn, Ehrlich seemed quiet, almost conservative. Turns out, he's one of his generation's original thinkers, as a player and a composer. He works primarily in flowing melody, tonal contrast, rhythmic displacement, and ensemble interaction; the mix can produce dreamlike results, where the inner logic's inexorable thrust is emotional as well as formal. But because he's subtle, working in substance rather than effect, because he's always got an ear on the structure of a performance instead of just blowing his own horn, Ehrlich is less visible (or audible) than players who go for the crowd's jugular with honks and screams, solos that arc like guided missiles to an inevitable fever-pitch close. "I try never to play a solo that has a predictable shape," he says. "I don't want them all to end with a big climax. Sometimes I like to let my solo just go back into the texture; sometimes I'll just bring it back around to where I began." It's characteristic of his self-effacing sense of the whole that his engaging new album, *New York Child*, has tenorman Stan Strickland, a longtime Ehrlich cohort, taking the opening cut's solo.

Since he moved to New York in 1978, Ehrlich has been trying to make his mark, and his living, in jazz's interstices. Few players can match his dexterity and content as he moves from clarinets to saxes to flutes; his early hero Eric Dolphy is one of the scarce role models in this shapeshifting zone. And like Dolphy, an underrated leader who was a brilliant sideman for explorers like Charles Mingus and John Coltrane as well as mainstreamers like Oliver Nelson, Ehrlich has a rare and wonderful talent, a now yearning, now biting attack with a stunningly voicelike expressiveness. In the paradoxical way of art, his fluidity reflects his discipline; the combination has gotten him on fifty albums. Ironically, his gift's superficially chameleonic nature can mask his unique voice.

Ehrlich's chops have made him a valuable sideman for varistriped leaders. For the last decade, Muhal Richard Abrams, co-founder of the avant-jazz-oriented AACM, has tapped him consistently for projects. He worked in the late clarinet great John Carter's thoughtfully probing octet. Last year, he toured here and Europe with a mainstream group with jazz stars Don Grolnick and Michael and Randy Brecker. Then he came back to the Knitting Factory to fill the front line of a quartet led by MacArthur "genius" award winner Anthony Braxton, a fierce multireed wielder himself, for a typically quirky gig: Braxton put together a quartet to play standards, with himself on highly eccentric piano.

Ehrlich's own music mingles widely disparate musical elements within an accessible, seamless, melodically oriented frame. "I became a leader," he remarks dryly, "because I found myself more and more playing devil's advocate in sideman situations: I'd bring mainstream elements to outside gigs, and vice versa. I thought I should find out more about what I could do with that." No jolting jumpcuts for Ehrlich: he's more interested in playing out difference at length, searching for understanding, shades of resonance and difference, possible juxtapositions and reconciliations. In the process, more often than not he weaves a bittersweet, blues-based atmosphere that, as it winds through shades and highlights, acknowledges the outer darkness but lights a candle rather than cursing.

"As I move from town to town," he says with a wry grin, "I hear the stories." In this case, "town to town" means across the jazz world's subcultures, racial and stylistic. Ehrlich is one of the few white players on steady call from black avant-garde leaders. Along with bassist Mark Helias, he's one of a handful of white downtowners who consistently leads racially mixed groups. The mutual hesitations, anxieties, fears, and resentments go back to Paul Whiteman ("King of Jazz"). "The first time I met one famous black horn player," says Ehrlich, "he said, 'So, are you gonna rip us off like Stan Getz and Benny Goodman?' I was stunned; I was 17, and didn't know enough about jazz history yet to have anything to say." As everywhere in American culture, racism has left unavoidable historical scars in jazz—which, outside of the army, remains one of this country's most significant experiments in integration.

Integration—of languages, people, possibilities—is at the heart of Marty Ehrlich's music and life. Born in Kentucky, Ehrlich was in fifth grade when his social-worker parents moved to St. Louis. "University

City," he recalls, "was maybe the closest thing in the Midwest to the Village or Upper West Side. I was surrounded by poets and artists. It was the first St. Louis suburb to be integrated. It was very much a mix—very progressive, lots of white flight. My high school there had a good music program. It was integrated, which was very much an issue in University City. The community was very middle class and very political. We sent forty students to the Moratorium in Washington when I was in ninth grade. The black student union went on strike when I was in tenth grade."

Ehrlich started on clarinet at age 7, then picked up the sax in junior high school, playing in the band. A weekend arts program introduced the eighth-grader to poet Malinke Elliot—who, along with saxists Julius Hemphill and Oliver Lake (both later of the World Saxophone Quartet), was a founder of the Black Artists Group (BAG), an AACM-like multimedia-oriented cooperative that encouraged and presented avant-garde poetry, theater, music. Elliot gave him records by Ornette Coleman and Albert Ayler. His sister brought home Eric Dolphy's *Alone Together*. The boy got hooked on the local poetry scene, and listened to KDNA, St. Louis's Pacifica station. Live, Hemphill and Lake electrified him; Hemphill would later become a mentor. Soon jazz overwhelmed his classical training, and Ehrlich went from being a key member of the school orchestra to being asked to leave rehearsal after making three mistakes in a row. "I was spending every night playing jazz and listening to Coltrane," he laughs. He jammed with BAG members regularly, and made his first record in high school. Characteristically, he was also woodshedding in bop, sitting in at clubs.

College for Ehrlich was Boston's New England Conservatory. Rejected as a jazz student, he entered the classical department as a clarinetist. "That was awkward for me," he reflects. "The ideology of the period didn't permit white players to choose to go in and out of jazz. Either you committed to jazz, or not." After a year of intensive prep, he auditioned again and got into the jazz department, where he studied with brilliant composer-players like George Russell and Jaki Byard. "I was pulled into jazz by the music I heard in St. Louis, because it spoke to my time," he explains, "so then I delved back into the history. I'd made a record with Oliver and Lester Bowie, but that new music from the Midwest hadn't made it to Boston yet. The school had great beboppers teaching. That's why I went there—to learn to play changes."

Among his classmates: pianist Fred Hersch and composer-pianist Anthony Coleman.

By his third year, he was working in both Russell's and Byard's big bands, as well as Gunther Schuller and Ran Blake's Third Stream department. Within six months of graduation, he was in New York. "A friend helped me move my stuff down here on Christmas Eve. I'd met Tim (Berne) already; he was studying with Julius. Tim had this loft in Brooklyn he shared with four guys. He called me and offered me a room." He pauses, then smiles. "When I got there, Tim wasn't there, and there was no heat. I sat there with my bags and shivered." Welcome to jazz's Big Apple.

Ehrlich's first New York gig was with Hemphill and St. Louis-born pianist John Hicks, for family day at Hicks's father's church in Harlem. He worked with Chico Hamilton and George Russell. "I must've played the Village Vanguard 30 times with those guys the first year or so I was here," he recalls. (His own groups have never played that venerable mainstream jazz mecca.) He hit Europe for the first time with Braxton's big band, in 1979. With Bowie, he opened the Antibes Jazz Festival for Cecil Taylor and Ornette Coleman. He played in Hemphill's unfortunately short-lived big band and sextets, and Lake's big band. He worked with Anthony Davis and Leroy Jenkins, with John Lindberg and Wayne Horvitz and Bobby Previte. "I was doing the cutting-edge stuff I wanted to do," he says. "But nothing was really a working band. I didn't survive off that. I accompanied dance classes for 25 to 30 hours a week, I taught private lessons, did weddings and parties. I had one of the few apprenticeships in the new jazz of the time. It was very exciting. That scene was getting a lot of critical and business attention then."

In 1985, he made his debut as a leader, *The Welcome*. The title track can still surface during his shows. Next he recorded *Pliant Plaint*, his first quartet disc, on his own dime, and shopped it to 15 labels before one snapped it up in 1987. Its opening cut: "Celebration in Capetown (Strangers No More)," in which Ehrlich's quartet works through tension into hope, with Strickland on flute and the leader on the ax Dolphy reclaimed for jazz, bass clarinet. The title cut features fierce collective soloing. "After After All" is a glowing, through-composed chamber piece. Each of the pieces, in short, has a distinct character, yet they are also clearly various sides of a coherent musical personality.

The range on *Pliant Plaint* is typical of Ehrlich's recordings. *The Traveller's Tale* boasts a charged rendition of Mingus's dirge, "Alice's Wonderland" and Trane's explosive "Connie's Lament." *Can You Hear a Motion?* serves up Byard's lovely "Ode to Charlie Parker," with Ehrlich's clarinet and Strickland's flute dancing in strikingly voiced *schadenfreude*, then opening into contrapuntal exchanges. Two Ehrlich originals are dedicated to John Carter, one ("The Black Hat") a noir soundscape, the other ("Reading the River") a perky flow. In his liner notes, Ehrlich writes of his former boss: "He was passionate about his music being rich in historical continuity while sounding new in ways that are revelatory. In this current period of jazz, when originality, always difficult, is rarely even attempted, John's musical vision stands in high relief." He could be describing where he's headed himself.

Ehrlich has tested other formats. *Side by Side* sports a bristling quintet: trombonist Frank Lacy, keyboardist Wayne Horvitz, bassist Anthony Cox, and drummer Andrew Cyrille. *Falling Man* is a duo disc with Ehrlich and Cox inspired largely by Dolphy's *Alone Together*, and among the evocative originals nestles Byard's "Bird's Mother." And his *Dark Woods* (named for the clarinet) *Ensemble* finds the leader overdubbing woodwinds to trio and quartet settings, for more of a chamber-jazz hue.

But no matter what the medium, Ehrlich's vision is consistent, and consistently engaging. "What unifies my different groups," he explains, "is that I use a lot of different styles to make the point that style isn't the point. I've always felt strongly that the connections between the languages are more important than the differences. I'm concerned with creating a shape for each piece, but I'm still concerned with creating spontaneous melodies, à la the great tradition from Armstrong through Ornette. I'm willing to do solos that don't totally succeed because they express something. I'm looking for a place beyond self-consciousness. I'm writing from someplace deeper than just a style." [1996]

La Cucaracha
A Survey of Cuban Music

Mention Cuba to most Americans, and the associations are predictable: Fidel Castro, Desi Arnaz, Celia Cruz (if the kids watch *Sesame Street*), and Oscar Hijuelos. But the ties between Cuban and American culture, especially in music, are historic, deeply rooted, and ongoing. They're so strong, in fact, that they've survived the 32-year rupture in normal relations between the two countries. Kids in Havana watch MTV and hunger for the latest names in sneakers and jeans. Kids here dancing to disco divas like Gloria Estefan are probably unaware that their steps derive from the hustle, the 1960s Cuban-based dance.

It's impossible to tell the story of Cuban or U.S. music without constantly referring from one to the other. Take an example: Mambo, one of Cuba's prides, is largely a Cuban-American invention out of New York. Take another: when Jelly Roll Morton, jazz's self-described founder, spoke of that quintessentially American music's "Spanish tinge," he probably meant the Afro-Cuban dance rhythms that helped bind marching band music and blues into early jazz.

If the New World has been this century's major source of popular music, it's due largely to the rich mixture that historically horrifying situations like conquest and slavery left as their loamy residue. In the United States, the collision of African and European sensibilities, musical forms, instruments, and techniques gave rise to work songs, minstrel shows, blues, jazz, and rock. Brazil boasts related hybrids like samba, bossa nova, and tropicalia. From Jamaican reggae to Trinidadian calypso and soca, the Caribbean teems with offshoots of the same roots.

That, of course, includes Cuba. For four centuries after the conquistadors, the island was aswirl with European dances and beats brought by the West and Central African slaves working the sugar plantations. Underlying their buoyant polyrhythms was clave—the two-bar pattern with a three-two or two-three beat that American rocker Bo Diddley gave his name to here. Then around the First World War, son—a raw-edged song form that relied on characteristic West-African devices like call-and-response vocals and cyclical backing riffs—migrated westward to Havana from Oriente province. Culturally speaking, Oriente was a heavily African part of Cuba; its U.S. counterparts are the Mississippi Delta, cradle of the blues, and Louisiana, especially New Orleans, with its Mardi Gras, second-line struts, and jazz.

Early son sounds like blues set to clave—perhaps not surprisingly, given its origins and guitar-plus-vocal instrumentation. But though the anthology *Cuban Counterpoint: The History of Son Montuno* begins its fine survey with 1950s field recordings of songs in that vein, it goes back in time to trace the rapid evolution of son in Havana. Like the blues in late-nineteenth-century New Orleans, son accreted bands. Sextetos—usually two vocalists, two guitars, claves, maracas, a bongo, and a marimbula (a large version of the West-African mbira or thumb piano) or string bass—became the urban vehicle for son. When, in the late 1920s, the sexteto added a cornet (later a trumpet) that played flowing embellishments, the septeto became the unit favored by pivotal giants like singer-composer Ignacio Pineiro. (A recent recording of the Septeto Nacional, which Pineiro originally formed, can be found on *Cuban Dance Party*.)

One of Pineiro's melodies was lifted by George Gershwin, who befriended the Cuban on a trip to Havana, for his "Cuban Overture." (Gershwin, of course, was one of countless Americans who made Havana a thriving tourist stop that became overrun with prostitutes and Mafiosi—a situation dependent on the racism and exploitation abolished only with Castro's revolution.) Gershwin was hardly the first composer to borrow from Cuba. Musicologist John Storm Roberts points out in *The Latin Tinge* that New Orleans composer Louis Gottschalk went to Havana in 1854 and returned with Cuban-inflected pieces that became popular. And W. C. Handy visited Havana with his orchestra in 1900 and noted confluences between Cuban rhythms and ragtime he later drew on.

With their suggestive beats and double entendres and improvised flights, early soneros were restricted to entertaining Havana's segregated black neighborhoods. Still some, like Pineiro, managed to attract

American record-company attention. By 1926, for example, the Sexteto Boloña was recording in New York, which had become a mecca for Cuban as well as American jazz musicians. The city drew Cubans not just for its better studios but also for the creative ferment called the Harlem Renaissance. Duke Ellington, among others, was introducing Latin rhythms into his pieces, the Harlem Opera House staged Cuban shows, and Cuban composer Ernesto Lecuona penned hits for mainstream U.S. popularizers like Xavier Cugat. The two cultures were meshing more closely.

Meanwhile, white Havana was dancing to charanga—a style performed by ballroom groups that deemphasized percussion and replaced the septeto's horns with smoother flute and violin. As with nearly all Cuban popular music, dance shaped the form. The music charanga groups played was built on danzon, a syncopated Creole version of the eighteenth-century French contradanse invented in late 1800s Oriente.) Charangas aspired to the kind of elegance that characterized Antonio Maria Romeu's group, which sported white gloves and touches of Liszt.

By the late 1920s, Cuban emigration to New York had spawned El Barrio—the East Harlem enclave that remains home to Latinos today. El Barrio was soon a market: U.S. record companies stepped up recording Latin sounds to sell there and in Latin America. But El Barrio also provided a base for the growing network of Cuban and jazz musicians. Cuban flautist Alberto Socarras, for instance, did session work for Columbia, performed in Benny Carter's jazz band, and led his own orchestra, which blended Cuban, jazz, and classical idioms.

From the turn-of-the-century cakewalk on, American music history can be viewed as a series of successive dance crazes, often based on imported rhythms. In late 1930, "El Manicero" (The Peanut Vendor) launched the rumba in the U.S. An outgrowth of son, rumba soon kicked the Argentine tango (the previous craze) out of its way to introduce Cuban rhythms to a mass American audience. Throughout 1930, Dom Aspiazu—who'd recorded "The Peanut Vendor" with RCA Victor but then had to work for six months to get it released—was percolating rumba at the New York Palace, the first lengthy engagement a Cuban band had outside El Barrio. A year later, manufacturers like Gretsch advertised a full line of "rumba instruments." Soon conga lines—a commercial dilution with a heavier, less subtle beat of

Cuban carnival street dance that Desi Arnaz claimed (falsely) he introduced at a Miami nightclub—swept the nation until the Second World War. (Aspiazu's recording and other tasty morsels like Bing Crosby's version of Lecuona's "Siboney" with Cugat and Perez Prado's "Mambo #8" are part of the solid survey *A Carnival of Cuban Music*.)

While Americans were doing the conga, the late 1930s in Cuba brought a rage for conjuntos. Derived from black carnival parade bands in roughly the same ways that New Orleans jazz bands had emerged from marching bands four decades earlier, conjuntos consisted of one or two vocalists, two or three trumpets, a bass, various drums, and a piano. Adding the conga, which offered a looser, improvised commentary on the underlying clave, and deepened the fierce rhythmic and thematic crosstalk, is attributed to Arsenio Rodriguez, a blind guitar-playing sonero. (His music is on *Counterpoint* and *Carnival*.) Rodriguez played with the beats—sometimes leaving them implicit, sometimes staggering or disguising their starting points. Along with multi-instrumentalist Mario Bauza and vocalist Machito, Rodriguez and bassist Israel "Cachao" Lopez, who adapted elements of proto-mambo for a famous 1930s Havana charanga, were precursors heralding what would, at the war's end, become mambo mania.

When Oscar Hijuelos was looking for an overarching metaphor reflecting the deep intimacies and inevitable frictions between Cuban and American cultures, he didn't pull mambo out of a hat. Mambo yearns to carry that symbolic weight. A descendant of Congolese cult-music, born in Cuba, raised in New York, mambo circled back to Cuba fully grown via the Mexican-based dance band of Perez Prado, its most successful popularizer.

As a teenaged veteran of Romeu's orchestra, Mario Bauza emigrated from Havana to Harlem's Sugar Hill; soon he was playing with Chick Webb, Fletcher Henderson, Don Redman, and Cab Calloway. In 1937, he wrote his brother-in-law Frank Grillo to "come and starve with me." Grillo, better known as Machito, had apprenticed with Pineiro in Havana, but New York was, as jazzers said, "the big apple." So there he went, and there the duo founded the Afro-Cubans, a seminal band that overrode musical and racial barriers by mingling Cuban, Puerto Rican, and American personnel.

The genius of Machito's Afro-Cubans lay in recognizing the affinity between swing-era jazz and their own tradition. Though the rhythms of the two idioms were radically different, they shared key aspects— they were about dancing to improvised solos over cyclic backing riffs. But Cubop, as their powerful and captivating hybrid came to be called, presented rhythmic difficulties to American jazzers; clave threw musicians used to playing 4/4 time. From the other side, the convoluted harmonies boppers like Charlie Parker and Dizzy Gillespie soloed over were far removed from mambo's improvising section, montuno, which favors simple repeated figures over two or three chords.

Some of these divergences were bridged by tunes like the Afro-Cubans' 1940s hit, "Tanga" (on *The Original Mambo Kings*). A bit later, "Manteca" (on *Carnival*) teamed Gillespie's blistering trumpet with the fiery improvisations of Chano Pozo's conga, which drew on the Cuban's training in Abakwa—a cult with roots in Nigeria. By the late 1940s, Cuboppers were experimenting with extended forms like "Afro-Cuban Suite" by Gillespie and Pozo, and "Cubana Be" and "Cubana Bop" by George Russell, a leading bop composer (on *Dizziest*). After Gillespie's big band with Pozo appeared at Carnegie Hall in September 1947, Cubop's role in the bebop era was clinched. At the instigation of promoter Norman Granz, Bird himself in the early 1950s hitched his mercurial alto to Cubop, with mixed results. Stan Kenton's big band recorded "Machito." And Machito's own group performed with Dexter Gordon, Johnny Griffin, Stan Getz, and Zoot Sims.

Mambo took the U.S. pop world by storm. In 1947, Bing Crosby recorded "Quizas Quizas Quizas"; Nat King Cole and Rosemary Clooney sang hit mambos as well. Nor was rhythm and blues immune to mambo's allure: it absorbed the latest Spanish Tinge via New Orleans, where Professor Longhair and Fats Domino adapted mambo. In New York the Palladium, the "Temple of the Mambo" on Broadway and 53rd Street, attracted high-voltage fans like Gillespie and Marlon Brando. Jazzers working down the street at Birdland ran up in between their sets to check the Cuboppers out, and the Latin musicians eagerly returned the favor.

In popular culture as in all aesthetic realms, innovation and expansion usually lead to consolidation and retrenchment, and the 1950s mambo explosion was no exception. Even as mambo held sway, classic charanga was being revived and adapted by Johnny Pacheco and the Joe Cuba Sextet, which had a million-selling crossover hit with 1966's

"Bang Bang." (The charanga revival was reinforced when Castro took power, and hundreds of thousands of Cubans, among them many charangistas, fled to the U.S.) Facing competition from new pop styles like rock and roll, the mambo big bands died out. And so, paralleling the earlier shift in jazz from swing bands to bop combos, as big bands like Machito's became less economically viable, smaller Latin-jazz combos whose instrumentation was closer to jazz than charanga (trombones replaced violins, for instance) took their place. Key pioneers were Mongo Santamaria (*Afro-Roots*) and Cal Tjader (*Latino*). By the 1960s the cha-cha-cha, a simplified mambo, had pushed its once-regal predecessor off the charts.

From this stew of pop hybrids in 1970s New York came salsa. Originally a word Cuban musicians used the way jazzers use swing, salsa now refers to a fusion of son vocals, jazz improvisation and voicings, Cuban rhythms, and rock chord sequences and electric instruments. Over the last two decades it's developed into a lingua franca for musicians, like Panamanian Ruben Blades, from all over the Hispanic diaspora—including, naturally, Cuba, despite the isolation the U.S. has tried to impose on it. First among Cuban salseros is the fifteen-strong Los Van Van, which mixes trombones and violins with synthesizers, shimmering beats with unison vocals and call-and-response and jazzy solos. (Besides *Cuban Dance Party*, they can be heard on *Songo* and *Dancing Wet*.) Next is NG (Nueva Generación) La Banda, led by a Los Van Van veteran, composer/flautist Jose Luis Cortes; their taut, whipsaw rhythms and ensemble work and snaky vocals by Isaac Delgado sparkle on *En La Calle*.

Like prewar U.S. blues, son demands that singers improvise. Nueva trova, an urban folk music, extends that tradition. The idolized singer-songwriters Silvio Rodriguez (*Canciones Urgentes*) and Pablo Milanes (*Cancionero*) combine bittersweet romance and sharp sociopolitical insights as they move from acoustic guitar to furious salsa.

Modern Cuban jazz finds its foremost exponent in pianist Gonzalo Rubalcaba. Classically trained from childhood, Rubalcaba flourishes expansive Romantic lyricism spiced with Cuban rhythms and hurtling improvisation. After bassist Charlie Haden jammed with him in 1986, he suggested to Blue Note that they sign the Cuban. Treasury Department rulings forbade that, so Rubalcaba signed with Japan's Toshiba-EMI, and Blue Note licensed his albums for release. *The Blessing*, which teams him with Haden and drummer Jack DeJohnette, is a good introduction.

In early April, Rubalcaba was granted a U.S. visa to perform at Lincoln Center—the first time he'll appear here. Since Los Munequitos de Matanzas, a folkloric group, got visas earlier this year, and since record companies are growing increasingly interested in this potential market, this may signal that U.S. cultural sanctions against Cuba are winding down. Once the two soul mates can rejoin in free exchange, wait for the fireworks. [1994]

Stir It Up
Bob Marley

More than a decade after his untimely death at 36 of cancer, a few things remain certain about the wide-ranging musical legacy of Robert Nesta Marley. First and foremost is its durability. Its continuing impact around the globe guarantees this most prominent of Jamaica's Rastafarian songsters—who rose from abject poverty to worldwide fame and fortune, and, with those, considerable political and cultural clout—his place in history as the James Brown of the Caribbean, the godfather of international rock hybrids. Underlining that is the joint release of a four-CD overview of his work, *Songs Of Freedom*, and a new feature-length video biography, *Time Will Tell*, underline how secure that place is.

Ironically but not unexpectedly, the second sure thing is that the fruits of that legacy will continue to be disputed in the courts. The recent settlement of one set of disputes, between Rita Marley, his widow, and his longtime record company, Island, is what allowed these retrospective tributes to appear at all. But now two more suits, one in Jamaica and one in New York, have been brought by Marley's estate against Ms. Marley and the lawyer and accountant who worked with Marley before his death and continued to guide her after it. At issue: the ownership of Marley's music companies and some $20 million.

It's the kind of irony Marley would probably have relished. Raised in the squalor of a government yard (ghetto slum) in the section of Kingston called Trenchtown, Marley in his thirties became one of the most audible voices in popular culture. While he was calling for change and threatening revolution as an alternative, gradually amassing audiences around the globe with his winning combination of socially conscious lyrics, lovers-rock seductions, and lusciously grinding reggae riddims, he was also amassing the money and status and accompanying symbols of the pop star. One of my favorite stories about him has an observer who's visiting his Jamaican estate asking why he, with his political and spiritual convictions, drives a BMW. The answer: "BMW stands for Bob Marley and the Wailers."

The son of an white Englishman and a black Jamaican, Marley embodied the wondrous flow of crosscultural pop energy that began percolating during the 1950s. Not coincidentally, his career also spanned the development of Jamaican music into reggae. Like countless other teen islanders, the young Marley was transfixed by New Orleans-based radio that wafted the U.S. r&b sounds of folks like Fats Domino and Ray Charles across the Caribbean. So his first band, the Wailing Wailers, formed with neighbors Neville Livingston (later Bunny Wailer) and Peter McIntosh (later Peter Tosh), was a sweet-voiced harmony group that, like the many similar Jamaican outfits during the ska era of the early 1960s, followed in the doowop/soul-music vein of American stars like the Impressions.

Marley and his cohorts, however, wrote lyrics out of their own experiences, identifying with the Rude Boys, the gangs of the Kingston slums, and their revolt against the crush of their surroundings. ("Simmer Down," the first hit single by the Wailing Wailers, was about gang violence.) It would become Marley's musical mission to shape that instinctive rebellion into a coherent social and religious framework.

Ska—a frenetic, uptempo dance beat punctuated by stabbing, sweet-and-sour horns that dominated Jamaica when the Wailing Wailers started out—turned rock's backbeat around, using Fats Domino's Crescent City shuffles as a model. Rock-steady, a slower, steadier form of proto-reggae, had replaced ska as Jamaica's prime sound by the time Marley returned from a few months's stay in the U.S. in 1966. (This period of the group's career is well-documented on the two-CD set *One Love*.) That year brought an event that, though he missed it, would prove central to his life.

In the early years of this century, the Jamaican preacher Marcus Garvey founded the United Negro Improvement Agency to advocate creation of a black-run African state with a population brought from the Americas. By 1930, when Haile Selassie was crowned Emperor of Ethiopia, he became the focus of some of Garvey's prophecies, partly because he claimed direct descent from the child of Solomon and the Queen of Sheba. So when Selassie visited Jamaica in 1966 (while Marley was in the U.S.), his presence fuelled the syncretic Rastafarian cult. Rastas looked to Selassie (whose name before his coronation was Ras Tafari) as the African king who, it was said, would lead the African diaspora out of exile and back to the lands of its origins. Like some of his fellow Rude Boys, Marley found a spiritual grounding in Rasta that redefined his life, his goals, and his music.

Like much of the 1960s black nationalism that is another of its taproots, Rastafarianism embraces two vectors, one social, the other spiritual. Rage against oppression, emphasis on self-help and nature, and a pan-African perspective point toward an apocalypse that will somehow resolve into the millennium—the Messiah myth Marxism appropriated into "materialist" terms. To the Rasta, however, spiritual and mundane elements are inextricably intertwined. "Who feels it knows it" is a Rasta proverb that denies the split between mind and body, reason and emotion, knowledge and faith that underlies most Western philosophy.

The experience of mysticism is impossible to transport. But it can be communicated, as mystical artists like King David and Dante knew. In Marley's case, the music, with its deadly seductive combination of sensual, earthy grooves and lyrics that are now transcendentally yearning, now rivetingly specific and immediate and touching and engaged, grabs audiences who can only superficially grasp its real intentions. Because reggae evolved from a collision of Rasta chants and U.S. pop, it's musically accessible. Keep in mind, too, that ganga or herb, the Rasta's sacred weed, enjoys global popularity as one of the rock culture's drugs of choice. Being stoned may not be exactly the same as being mystically entranced, but it's close enough for rock and roll. So even though its spiritual basis is essentially out of reach for non-Rastas, the music's mesmerizing effects, which are miraculously earthbound and soaring at the same time, couple with its messages of revolutionary hope and rage and "outlaw" culture to reach beyond its cult. And then there was short, wiry Marley's intoxicating personal charisma, his utterly dazzling stage persona as well as his lyrical thrust, his pan-African activism (he played at the 1980 Independence Day celebrations in Zimbabwe), his own deep-seated and often-voiced disgust at conventional politics.

In a culture like ours, art is consistently banished to the margins of daily life and pushed to become a commodity. So it's sometimes hard to remember that artists have historically spoken to their societies from a position of authority as bards. That reflected their formative contact with the inchoate realms of inspiration—the power of divine possession, in effect. Within that ancient global tradition, Marley saw himself as a messenger. "I didn't have education, I have inspiration. If I had education I would've been a damn fool," he shrugs at one point during *Time Will Tell*. His fierce presence marked him as a shamanistic figure who, leaping back against the tides of Western history, subverted the messages of Western rationalism with his music's awesome, relentless tug. No wonder Plato didn't trust musicians.

Naturally, once he became a Rastaman, Marley's lyrical emphasis changed. The Rude Boy anthems gave way to increasingly taut, angry, moving dissections of the established order. (One too-often-overlooked aspect of Marley's legacy, however, is the fabulous love songs he wrote: "Stir It Up," for example, ranks with the greatest blues songs for its insistent, congenially bawdy come-ons.) As a songwriter, Marley consistently pushed at his horizons. His diction, for instance, could move from thick patois to grammar-school-correct English without making either seem incongruous. But the shift went beyond lyrics. Even his singing adapted, dropping his early smooth-serge soul for a rawer instrument of gruff-and-ready leather, with craftily broken phrases and hanging pauses and cracked ululations.

And the music deepened too, like Coltrane's or James Brown's, under the influence of the chants. Once the fantastic Barrett brothers signed on as his anchoring rhythm section, multiple instrumental lines began to proliferate and jigsaw across the tunes. Starting from the African base of circular riff repetition and call-and-response common to all forms of rock, the Wailers mimicked, and changed in the process, the backbone-slipping work of models like Brown and the Meters. And Stevie Wonder's groundbreaking synthesizer work on albums like *Talking Book* found its way into reggae, as synths and sonically modified guitars began to gurgle squiggles in counterpoint to the bass and guitars between downbeats.

If reggae's sound propelled it into the international arena, first across the Caribbean, then to the U.K., it was due partly to a creative use of technology that coupled daring and disregard. Technology, like art, changes as it crosses geographical lines and is integrated into a different culture. Jamaicans reinvented sound because they didn't know or ignored the "rules" about mixing it. Just as reggae turned rock's backbeat around to fit the way Jamaicans heard, it radically turned around notions of sonic space in rock recordings. Hence the heavy, blooming bottom, which mimics ceremonial Rasta drums and is partly due to the way American music boomed over the Jamaican "sound systems," flatbed trucks that roamed the cities playing current chart-toppers. Hence, too, the pioneering of "dub" mixing, which became a prototype for American hip-hop, along with "toasting"—a truck-based DJ rapping over instrumental B-sides.

Although there'd long been producer-engineers in Jamaica, like Coxsone Dodd and Lee Perry, who were pioneering these kinds of effects, Marley's music gave the efforts wide currency and thus legitimacy. By then, reggae was poised to become a lingua franca of international rock, and Marley himself became the first rock superstar to hail from the Third World. Characteristically, he used his status as a platform. He tried to make peace during the politically motivated street warfare that tore Jamaica up during the 1980 elections by holding a unity concert. (Marley himself was shot two years earlier in a still-unsolved attack that seems to have had political motivations.) He traveled to Africa in the 1960s, and his example inspired others, like the Brazilian Gilberto Gil, to seek out their own Afro-roots. That further cross-pollinated emerging urban Afropop mixes both directly and via disciples. Gil became one of the founders of Brazil's Tropicalia movement, which synthesized Bahian Afro-roots with rock. Zimbabwe's Thomas Mapfumo fashioned chimurenga out of indigenous Shona and rock elements with politicized lyrics that helped rally the ongoing revolt against Ian Smith's Rhodesia. Ivory Coast's Alpha Blondy and South Africa's Lucky Dube gave reggae a few African twists. And so on.

By the time Marley died in 1981, his stature was assured. But almost immediately after began the wrangles that have lasted to this day about the control of his music. At the same time, many if not most of the musicians who saw themselves as inheritors of Marley's mantle proved far less able to transcend reggae's Rasta program. Without the magic of Marley's lyrical and musical touch and the charismatic power of his presence and voice, without the kind of ironic humor that produced lines like "Lively up yourself/And don't be no drag/Lively up yourself/ 'Cause reggae is not bad," without the kind of telling attention to concrete but archetypal details that make a song like "No Woman No Cry" brilliantly heartbreaking and affirming all at once, Rasta lyrics often degenerated into posturing and sloganeering, and the music frequently lapsed into autopilot. Of course, even on autopilot reggae's snaky throb is captivating. And there have continued to be outstanding creators in Marley's idiom, including his childhood pal Bunny Wailer and his son by Rita, Ziggy. But it's a final irony that dancehall, a form Ziggy, sounding eerily like his father, sees as transient and empty, has largely ruled Jamaica's airwaves since.

Songs of Freedom offers an solid and interesting overview of Marley's rich and rewarding achievement. Spanning the ska and reggae eras, it's shot through with alternate takes and mixes, and serves up essential classic cuts. It also boasts fine sound and an info-packed booklet that includes historical background, session details, and a passionate essay by Timothy White, author of the outstanding Marley biography *Catch a Fire*. Indispensable for the Marley fan, it can also serve as an intro that leads the neophyte back to bedrock Marley albums like *Catch a Fire, Natty Dread, Rastaman Vibration, Live!,* and *Exodus.*

Time Will Tell is more uneven. Eighty-six minutes long, its footage is so varied in quality, and its pacing is so erratic, as it switches perspectives from stage to backstage to offstage to larger social context, that the first-time viewer is likely to get rattled or bored—or both. (For pure concert footage, try *Live At The Rainbow*; for another bio-cum-social history slant check out the award-winning *The Bob Marley Story*.) But, despite its problems, *Time Will Tell* is shattering nearly every time Marley is onscreen, whether he's sitting with an acoustic guitar, doing his dance of possession onstage to overflow crowds, or just talking— ample testimony to the charismatic pull that seemed as natural to him as breathing, smoking ganga, playing soccer, or bedding women.

Natural and supernatural at once, though: Marley the shaman was both elemental and ethereal, like the Rasta cult that gave him his grounding. "So one of these days," Marley says toward the end of *Time*

Will Tell, just before his pan-African anthem "Exodus" explodes across the speakers, "I stop playing music and I go to Africa and I don't talk to nobody no more. Nor sing to nobody. Because, you know, this is not a joke." Despite the money and the power and the fame, despite the pervasively corrupting force of the entertainment-industry juggernaut his star was inevitably hitched to, Marley apparently never grew cynical about what he believed was his true mission. And he spent his life communicating it.

Politics is what we do to one another; culture is how we talk to one another. Wherever the two rub is the frisson of hope. Marley articulated hopes that reached from Jamaica to the U.S. and Europe, from Africa to the Pacific Rim. As White concludes his brief essay for *Songs of Freedom*: "Bob Marley gave the poor a voice in the international arena of ideas. . . . So when these downtrodden say, 'Send us another Bob Marley,' they are not asking for another musical superstar, or even another candidate for the Order of Merit. They are simply seeking a kindred spirit of the kind who would believe, as Bob stated, 'The most intelligent people are the poorest people.' They want a leader who needn't run for office, so long as he has the integrity to fulfill his true destiny. They need a person with the courage to act on hope, a role model whose own voice is the voice of his conscience. And if that person ever comes, he will be the next Bob Marley."

Until then, there are the memories and, more important, the music. [1992]

Voodoo Rock
Boukman Eksperyans

Since the snake and the apple in the Garden of Eden, since Hesiod's five ages of man and the death of Gilgamesh, people have recurrently revisited the roots of their cultures in search of something lost. The most recent wave of crosscultural reexamination began in the now-vilified 1960s, a worldwide explosion of artistic creativity and pancultural awareness. American and British rockers and jazzers, for instance, delved into farflung sounds for inspiration—one of the periodic odd-angled recapitulations that mark the history of world culture, like the Islamic scholars rediscovering Plato and Aristotle for Europe. The Yardbirds spewed treatments they heard as middle Eastern, the Beatles droned through sitars, John Coltrane muscled his way through extended flights called "Africa/Brass" and "Om"; Jimi Hendrix synthesized most of that with soul rhythms and blues licks and Dylanesque lyrics and the dramatically altered guitar sounds he first imagined as a paratrooper into a vision that literally rocked the planet. For many African-American artists of the time (as now), this delving was framed by a post-civil rights consciousness, the pan-African push coming from the likes of Marcus Garvey via Malcolm X and Rastafarianism. The musical results were far-reaching, global, riding the airwaves and the trade routes, with ripples reaching to today.

Much of that is due to Bob Marley, the first Third World roots-rock superstar. (To date, he's sold 30 million records worldwide.) Marley wasn't some pristine throwback to ersatz primitivism. He absorbed not only the dances and chant-induced trances of Rasta sacred drumming but U.S. radio hits from Fats Domino to Frank Sinatra to George Jones to Bob Dylan. But his chosen role as cultural emissary to his own people gave him a legitimacy that clearly fit the kind of cultural politics born in the 1960s. And his singing in English, albeit Jamaican patois, made him more easily saleable in the U.S. and U.K. markets—the bulk of the world's music-industry retail dollars by far, then and now. The profitable results led to a continuing search for the next Marley that recalls the decades-long look for a new Dylan.

Without Marley, the rediscovery of local roots simultaneously developing, then flowering in culturally driven opposition movements of the 1970s might well have had a very different shape. The stylistic multiplication across the planet's face might not have been heard by the multinational major labels as having market potential, which in turn would have meant more limited international distribution. The global transmission of sound that accelerated with the evolution of international media pipelines during the 1960s might have had to find alternate, slower routes. As it undoubtedly would have: in the 1940s and 1950s, Afro-Cuban rhythms had already recycled back across the Atlantic to Africa, where they had an enormous impact on emerging African pop, an urban phenomenon that broke with rural traditionalist roots from Senegal to South Africa. But Marley's stardom made such transmissions economically tantalizing, even as he gave them a focus of cultural self-discovery that packed political import.

In terms of those he directly inspired, the non-Marley scenario's implications roll out of Philip K. Dick and Stanislaw Lem. No Thomas Mapfumo to forge chimurenga from the plunking rhythms of Zimbabwe's mbira, chimurenga that became the soundtrack for anti-Rhodesian forces. No Gilberto Gil to help shape Tropicalia and be exiled from his native Brazil by the period's military junta for seditious songs outlawed for their countercultural lyrics. No Ruben Blades to reimagine salsa as dance music with a social conscience and consider running for Panama's presidency. No Jamaican toasters to improvise to the instrumental B-sides of reggae hits on the back of touring sound trucks, hence no dancehall rappers, and maybe no hiphop; no Afro-pop scene exploding out of Paris and across the planet.

And no Boukman Eksperyans to mix Haitian vodou beats and chants with elements of rara carnival, Afropop, and Anglo-American rock into a new style that won the annual contest in Haiti for best song in 1989 and the carnival competition a year later with "Ke-m Pa Sote" ("My Heart Doesn't Leap/I'm Not Afraid"); to live through the last bloody spasms of the Duvalier regime; to be nominated for a 1992 Grammy for *Kalfou Danjere*, a sonically denser album that topped Billboard's then-nascent World Music charts for four weeks; to survive supporting Aristide despite his subsequent overthrow; to survive both the Haitian junta and the U.S. embargo that forced them into temporary exile, to deliver *Libete (Pran Pou Pran!)* and tour the U.S. with the Africa Fete Summer Tour 1995.

Libete is Boukman's third release in the U.S., and continues the trajectory of exploratory development the band started nearly two decades ago. *Vodou Adjae,* featuring former singer Eddy Francois, is a blend of sloganeering lyrics, pan-African rhythms, and American pop chord progressions with samba and disco inflections. It's more roughly analogous to the earlier reggae-inflected hits of Jimmy Cliff than to the deep Rasta reggae Marley pushed to the fore. *Kalfou* enhances Boukman's roots orientation, with three traditional vodou chants that sound like ethnomusicographical field recordings. But it also rocks hard with echoes of the buoyant vocals and brightly bouncy beats of South African mbaqanga. Lyrically, *Libete* is if anything more mystical, even misty, as the band deploys vodou imagery to interconnect inner and outer life and freedom in ways that can recall neoplatonists like John Lennon: "It's yours for the taking."

Formed in 1978, its name a junction of the Jamaica-born vodou priest who, until his execution, helped lead the slave revolt against French colonialism that yielded Haitian independence in 1804 and, of course, Hendrix's Experience, Boukman Eksperyans is a family affair. Leader-vocalist Theodore "Lolo" Beaubrun, Jr., started the group (then a couple of guitarists, percussionists, and singers) with his wife Mimerose and his brother and sister. As he told me in late April, when he came to New York for a gig at S.O.B.'s, he was inspired by Marley's example to search out Haitian roots he could turn to similar purpose. So it's no surprise that Lolo and other band members now wear their hair in zing style—Haiti's version of Rasta dreadlocks. They sing in Creole, which was officially despised under the Duvaliers. And until recently they lived in a lakou, the rural Haitian descendent of African villages with their communal square. The lakou is now a vodou temple.

As he was growing up, though, Lolo's rock idols included Hendrix, Santana (who brought Afro-Cuban salsa into rock), Pink Floyd, Led Zeppelin, P-Funk, and radio staples of the time like the Archies' "Sugar Sugar." They all resonate across Boukman's catalog. And there was disco, whose influence (*pace* the "disco sucks" crowd) spans from India to Africa to the Caribbean, spawning soukous, soca, and a host of genres. As Lolo put it, "The lyrics were stupid, but many of the grooves were great." In fact, the drum machine around which the percussionists in Boukman weave magical polyrhythms often sets a disco beat as the heart pulse. "Jou Nou Resulte" on *Kalfou*, for instance, sounds a lot like Chic with political aphorisms for lyrics.

For the Beaubruns, unlike for many other Caribbean roots-rockers, radio was a relatively small conduit for overseas sounds. Part of the reason is their background. Theodore Beaubrun, Sr., is a nationally famed comedian, a social satirist who was also head of the National Theater, who made bourgeois (for Haiti) money but lost the rights to authorship and royalties that might have made him a member of the true elite thanks to the, uh, unique legal structures of his homeland. Nevertheless, in Haiti his status approximates Bill Cosby's here. Sophisticated urbanites in a land hulking with rural peasants, the kids who would become Boukman grew up with the perks of celebrity.

Their father traveled widely, especially to the U.S.; Lolo told me how Beaubrun, Sr., brought back James Brown's "Hot Pants" after seeing Mr. Dynamite burn up the Apollo Theater. The youngsters also came here, visiting their mother in Brooklyn, where she moved after she and her husband separated, and avidly absorbed what they heard and saw. Daniel "Dady" Beaubrun, the group's de facto music director, lived here for a decade, going to CUNY's Queens College, returning twice a year to play with the band, shuttling demo tapes back and forth as they evolved their vodou-meets-rock approach, finally returning to Haiti for good in 1987. Lolo, Boukman's often cloudily aphoristic vodou visionary, studied business administration for two years here. The Beaubruns, in short, weren't full-fledged members of the Haitian elite; their father's barbed if comic critiques of Papa Doc (he was quite possibly the only Haitian to get away with such bravado publicly) and lack of really big bucks precluded that. But they wore many of the trappings.

Not coincidentally, that also afforded them a certain aura of protection. As Jerry Rappaport, who signed them to Mango Records here in 1990, put it, "The more organized and intelligent members of the military realized that attacking them directly would probably create too much trouble. So they seemed to play a role in keeping the paramilitary elements under some control about the band." Their partial shield would come more and more into play as Boukman deviated increasingly from the accepted cultural line of the island's governing classes.

In Haiti, that means the Europeanized upper crust, the light-skinned professional elite living behind walled mansions in select districts of Port-Au-Prince, with its profound distaste for and fear of the powerful rhythms of vodou drums. Duvalier tried to appropriate the black-magic aspects of Bizango vodou to his own ends: as Graham Greene shows in *The Comedians*, the Tontons Macoutes often cloaked themselves in zombielike shadows to enhance fear. But vodou's stubbornly independent cultural life also represented a threat. Wade Davis's 1985 bestseller, *The Serpent and the Rainbow*, provided an Indiana Jones-style account of a Harvard anthropologist's investigation of vodou's power: "Vodoun is not an isolated cult; it is a complex mystical worldview, a system of beliefs concerning the relationship between man, nature, and the supernatural forces of the universe. . . . Vodoun cannot be abstracted from the day-to-day lives of the believers. In Haiti, as in Africa, there is no separation between the sacred and the secular, between the holy and the profane, between the material and the spiritual. . . . Unlike the Roman Catholic priest, the houngan does not control access into the spirit realm. Vodoun is a quintessentially democratic faith. Each believer not only has direct contact with the spirits, he actually receives them into his body. As the Haitians say, the Catholic goes to Church to speak about God, the vodounist dances in the hounfour to become God." Davis's book was just one indicator of pop-culture interest in vodou outside Haiti: William Gibson's influential cyberpunk trilogy (*Neuromancer, Count Zero,* and *Mona Lisa Overdrive*) wound vodou and Rastafarian beliefs deep into the fabric of their dystopian vision of the future.

Given vodou's cultural clout, it's easy to understand the officially sanctioned role of compas, an upbeat, bubbly style reminiscent of ca-lypso or merengue with horns and electric guitars. "The first time I saw a group with Vodou drums in it was Nemours Jean Batiste and Jazz des Jeunes," recalls Lolo. "They used to play with my father at the National Theater; I remember seeing them in the 1960s when I was small, maybe three or four years old, and being stunned by the drums they were playing. They played vodou rhythms when Duvalier came into power. But Duvalier considered Vodou rhythms danger-ous." No wonder: in a country as widely illiterate as Haiti (some 80 percent of Haitians can't read or write), music still serves one of its primordial functions—to communicate news and views, to delight and instruct. So as Boukman refined its "rasin" (roots music), as it moved to adding drum machines and electronic keyboards (a gradual shift, inspired by Dady, that brought flack from official sources and vodou traditionalists), as they fell into trances and were ridden by vodou loa during performances, they risked disfavor and danger, were seen as traitors to their class while non-elite Haitians revelled in their uses of street and vodou culture. So by the late 1980s, Boukman's songs were routinely banned from many radio and TV outlets, and even public performance. Nevertheless, the thriving if illicit cassette-duplicating distribution network in Haiti made their music widely available. And the band was spared suppression (or worse) thanks to Beaubrun, Sr.,'s celebrity as well as their own rapidly growing notoriety.

By September 1991, when Aristide was overthrown, Boukman responded by cutting "Kalfou Danjere" ("Dangerous Crossroads"), which upped the ante. The song, naturally, was banned. Translated, part of the lyrics runs, "If you're an assassin, get out of here/If you're a thief, get out of here," and then warns "you'll be in deep trouble at the crossroads." The implications, both in vodou and political terms, were clear to all, including the military junta. Still, as Lolo admits, "The military never attacked us directly, although a colonel told me never to go out at night." And the group continued to tour abroad.

In 1993, Boukman came here for what turned out to be a successful seven-month tour. It was their first experience crisscrossing the vastness of America; they had a van with two diesel-fuel tanks that let them cruise 400 miles without a stop. Now, for most world-music outfits the U.S. is a spotty and jerry-built market staffed more by well-intentioned amateurs than pros, which produces some long stretches between venues on tour. For Boukman, that led to a wondrous encounter with middle America in Luddington, Michigan, where manager Dan Behrman drove the eleven-strong troupe from Ann Arbor's Frog Island Festival for a layover.

Let Behrman tell the tale: "My wife had set up the tour, and we pulled into this Ramada Inn. Being the white guy, I went in first and paid for the rooms in cash—$1100 for five nights, four rooms, twelve people. Don't ask; that's how we did it—still do it. I say to the clerk, Do you have a lounge with a band? He says yes, but there's no one there this week. I say, Can I speak with the manager? He comes out, very nice guy, I give him a tape (we're always selling CDs and tapes on the road) and a lot of clips from Haitian newspapers (I didn't have much American press yet), and he loves what he sees and hears. So he says, I'll give you six rooms and meals and a PA if you do three nights, two sets a night. Voila, we have a place to rehearse, I tell the guys. I get the $1100 back and give it to Mimerose. A writer shows up from the local paper the first night, which is pretty crowded, and does a story. The next night the place is jammed. The police chief is wearing a Boukman T-shirt over his uniform, with his badge pinned to it. The motel manager gives us the key to the kitchen and the game room and the pool, so we can use them whenever we want."

In 1994, Boukman left Haiti again—though their sendoff was less than auspicious. For their last Port-Au-Prince concert, armed soldiers and attaches garrisoned the crowd, and teargas filled the air when the band launched into the banned "Kalfou Danjere" and the crowd, as it usually does for Boukman shows, burst into a sea of jumping bodies and waving limbs: Lolo found himself onstage faced by an attache with a gun pointed at his head. The situation intensified, thanks to the U.S.-led sanctions against Haiti. In May, one member, percussionist-bassist Michel Olicha Lynch, died of meningitis, partly because the embargo made medication difficult to get. Finishing up their European tour, the band found itself stranded. Unable to get a flight out of England for Haiti, unable to get U.S. visas because they're Haitian, Boukman went to ground in Jamaica, and spent months working at Marley's Tuff Gong studios recording *Libete*.

"When I heard *Rastaman Vibration* years ago, it changed everything for me," Dady told me. You can hear that directly on *Kalfou Dangere*'s opening cut, which echoes Marley's "Redemption Song" combined with churchy call-and response vocals and a classic American-rock progression—an aptly syncretic setting for the Dady–penned hymn of divine praise. Where *Kalfou* was rife with Afropop and starkly arranged chants, *Libete* has a physical sound that is startling, dreamy yet precise, resonant with rich depths. More than anything, it recalls Daniel Lanois-produced Neville Brothers albums like *Yellow Moon* and *My Brother's Keeper*. "I wasn't thinking about that," Dady insisted, then reminded me, "You know, the Neville Brothers' grandmother was from Haiti, and they did that movie about Haiti with Jonathan Demme." Yes, and New Orleans hoodoo comes from the same African origins as Haitian vodou and its unique pharmocology. The stubbornly recurrent resurfacings of key parts of African culture in the New World ought to lay any doubts to rest: the Africans dragooned into slavery were not blank slates for their masters to write on, did not lose everything they brought once they got here. Rather, they found methods of transmission that not only kept alive key aspects of their varied heritages, but as a result ironically played key roles in shaping the dominant cultures. The stunning palimpsest of New World cultural hybrids guarantees, above all, the regular and fruitful return of the repressed. [1995]

The Man from Bahia
Gilberto Gil

After writing songs and performing for a quarter-century, helping spearhead the late 1960s Brazilian countercultural revolution known as Tropicalia, traveling around the Caribbean and to Africa to absorb their musical, cultural, and political lessons, and becoming a voice of international conscience in the process, Bahian-born Gilberto Gil is sitting in a posh Central Park South hotel dining room. Here, the morning after a stunning concert at the New Ritz, he's discussing, with relaxed authority, topics from recent Brazilian musical history to his election to his town council, from the relationship between Afro-pop, samba, and reggae to racism in Brazil and the U.S.

In a culture like ours has become over the last twenty years, where artists are generally either fabricated into two-dimensional entertainers or else banished to the margins, it's difficult to imagine the larger clout wielded in their societies by figures like Bob Marley or Thomas Mapfumo or Gil: for in other cultures infectiously danceable music is also the vehicle through which social ideas and opinions, as well as timeless sentiments, are routinely voiced and heeded. So heeded, in fact, that just over 20 years ago Gil found himself under house arrest, then banished from his homeland for the crime of cultural radicalism, as the ruling military viewed Tropicalia.

As he himself tells the tale: "Several reasons were behind my being jailed and exiled between 1969 and 1972. The main one was the general intolerance of the recently installed military regime. In 1964, they cut the Congress's power by half and started the process of installing a dictatorship, which was completed by 1968, when they closed the Congress and imposed new laws. That was when we were in the middle of Tropicalia, so Tropicalia came in a very difficult moment, when a dictatorship was being built. So at the coup d'etat in 1968, it caught us right in the middle of our ascendance.

"Everything became a kind of clash, between whatever we were doing and their purposes. They disliked our whole thing: the attitude, the freedom, the plurality that developed in our expression that supported new youth cultural statements, like growing long hair and dressing differently and the political implications of all of that. We were very supportive of what was happening in the universities in the States and in May 1968 in Paris, for instance, and reproduced those events for Brazilian students. From any angle, it was trouble for their point of view. So there was not really anything specific about what we wrote or said, even; it was just a general attitude toward our autonomy, which interrogated their power. It was a necessary clash.

"So I wound up in jail for two months, then house arrest for six months. Then I was sent away. So I went to London, where I stayed for three years."

Growing up listening to the raw sambas of his native Bahia, the most African section of Brazil, Gil had been both energized and put off by bossa nova, that spun-sugar blend of cool-jazz chordal voicings and tamed samba rhythms that dominated the Brazilian charts during the 1950s and 1960s.

"We were impressed by [composer Antonio Carlos] Jobim and his music, because we had already built expectations of music, despite living with day-to-day street music, percussion music, carnival music, chanting, the whole thing. In Brazil, through radio, in the 1950s we had a lot of music from different fields, like the American big bands, Mexican and European and American crooners, film music, a little jazz, everything. So around the time when Jobim came on the scene, in the late 1950s and early 1960s, it seemed that we in Brazil should come up with something elegant and very absorbing of everything, the good music of the world. So when bossa nova came, we had a beautiful mixture: the basic samba rhythm behind, very smoothly done, the Debussyian and Impressionist harmonies, the flavor of the brass sections based on American cool jazz—bossa nova linked it all. And there was especially the inventiveness of the guitar player Joao Gilberto, who gave the music a different taste. So despite our coming from a different context, we were delighted with the sophistication of bossa nova and seduced by it.

"And in a way, bossa nova paved the way for all the different musical fusions that have come out of Brazil since. Being able to establish bossa nova internationally was a great help for Brazilian musical expression;

with bossa nova we had the assurance that we had a good music, rich and complex and penetrating, everything that would enable us to produce an international music.

"Also, our recognizing the various components of bossa nova, both national and international, meant we should adapt foreign elements to Brazilian music—it gave us the confidence to try and bring rock and roll and other things in. We felt that Brazilian musicality could deal with anything at all; Brazilians have the ability to absorb musical languages easily."

That ability translated into the hybrids that drove the nascent Tropicalia movement. "I started adding the music of the Beatles and the Stones into my own music when I moved to Rio in the 1960s. It's difficult to explain. Despite being influenced by them, despite wanting to bring those elements into Brazil and mix them into my music, we never quite did it in terms of copying. We just got an atmosphere, a concept. It's difficult to really find Beatles things in my music—no harmonies or anything like that. It's a cultural spirit, so it's always been difficult for me to explain how I can use elements but not have them quite present. 'Back in Bahia' is a good example, because it's got some of the country/rockabilly elements the early Beatles used, but it's really a rhythm and blues song with touches of northeast Brazil. I wrote that song when I lived in England in exile; it was my first rock and roll song."

His exile, then, had the unintended effect of heightening his musical eclecticism: "London is where I first heard reggae, which was really just beginning, with the Wailers and Bob Marley, Jimmy Cliff—they were all playing around then. The transition was just occurring then between rock steady and reggae. The connection between politics and culture was part of what attracted me to reggae, but the main thing was the sound. I really only got deeply involved with it when I was back in Brazil, in '74, when I heard 'No Woman No Cry,' which both Cliff and Marley did." And which Gil still performs.

"What impressed me about reggae," he continues, "was how it had at the same time a simplicity and a sophistication of rhythm, both drumming and guitar and keyboard lines all interlocking in a sort of pyramidal thing. But very mild: I used to say that reggae is the bossa nova of rock and roll, the way that the drum goes in a circle, the soft and tender feeling and at the same time such a heavy bottom, so full of energy. For me it was the recycling of rhythm and blues; for me, it has the same importance as bossa nova, something that created something new out of older elements. And the whole Rasta cultural thing, the hair and the colors and the communal life, the message and the fight for freedom, the need for and problems of colonization in Africa—it was quite something, the way that it followed up on the 1960s Black Power movement in the United States. I've made the links between Stevie Wonder and Miles Davis and Cliff and Marley before: people speaking out, being proud of being black, understanding the difficulties of getting black culture into Western civilization."

Those difficulties had baffled Gil for years. "I first went to Africa in 1967, just to Angola; that was a special and difficult situation, since that was the time the Portuguese army was fighting the guerrilla movement. I went in a very protected situation, representing the Brazilian government, so I was protected and didn't see much reality.

"The first substantive trip I made to Africa was in 1977, when I went to Nigeria. We had a big meeting, delegations from all over. I met Fela, Stevie Wonder—that was a moment, at Fela's shrine. King Sunny Ade was playing every night. I stayed there in Lagos for a month. That gave me the push toward blackness, toward really trying to understand the roots, the foundation, the spirit of the culture. Just being there, I used to cry when I'd see the residue of colonialism, when a black policeman would be beating someone; but at the same time there was an affability, a friendliness, an effectiveness among the people themselves. Being able to spot the original sources of things we cultivate in Bahia shook me; it was a really emotional experience. So when I got back to Brazil, I started doing music that was in a more black-oriented vein.

"Even so, my music stayed my music. My reggae, my rock and roll, my rhythm and blues—nothing is just an imitation."

As is easy enough to hear if you pick up any of his albums. Whether it's *Gilberto Gil, Um Banda Um* or *Raça Humana*, or *Soy Loco por Ti America* or *Live in Tokyo*, Gil's deft appropriation of pop sounds from around the world fuse with his native Brazil's sounds to provide a kaleidoscopic background for his fluent, sensual vocals. The mix is infectious and like little else; and armed with it and his ingratiatingly riveting stage presence, Gil hopes to conquer the U.S. market.

While Gil has been touring the U.S. regularly for a decade, he says,

"It seems to me there's been an increased capability of American audiences to understand my music. Radio and record companies are being pushed by the times: the increased Latin presence in America, the salsa thing, the durability of bossa nova. Now and then me or Milton Nascimento come and tour, and people like Sarah Vaughan and Quincy Jones record Brazilian songs, so I feel like the audiences are more into positive expectations of Brazilian music."

It's an assertion backed by his rousing show and fevered crowd reactions at the Ritz the night before. His performance mixes brief, often funny monologues on a particular topic or idea related to the song being introduced, giving the audience a context for both his music and his cultural politics. As he sees it: "Pedagogy and music are something I've always mixed onstage; now I've shifted to belonging in the institution. It's a very personal, individual, solitary choice. I mean by that that not everybody should impose a link between music and politics. That's me—my craziness, my boldness, my faith that we can contribute.

"I think that it comes from the current situation in Brazil. We're changing from a dictatorship to a potential democracy in a very difficult way; there's a lot of confusion, a lack of preparation. The military regime cut off all political action, so there's not really a new generation of politicians equipped to deal with the many problems that face our country. Our economy's in a bad way, the debt and balance of payments are awful. All those elements made me think, Let me give a hand, try to inject some new concepts and new energies into politics.

"I also think that art and culture, and those dealing with the agencies of art and culture, have become more and more influential in politics. That's international. I think that it's just natural, because we are loved and trusted by people; we are granted more and more a right to represent our people politically. Those are some of the things that made me want to find some legitimacy in my government."

With his election to his town council, Gil has taken his political involvement a few steps farther than the stage pedagogy he's so adept at. "I ran on an anti-racism platform. Racism is still a problem, a social problem that's implied in social hierarchies of class, since black people belong basically to the bottom, were slaves a hundred years ago without being totally freed, so there's a residual slavery there, there's social apartheid in employment, which means unemployment and marginality—that's what's there for the blacks, the only thing they share is the no's of the society despite being the majority of the society. That's a consequence of the black consciousness that happened in America, the nationalism and anticolonialism in Africa. Of course South Africa is the most dramatic situation, but we still have partial apartheid in the States, and in Cuba, and in Brazil. Cuba's a socialist state, but despite its considerable black population you don't see blacks running the country; their religion, santeria, was suppressed.

"So we have to regard the black situation as a social-political one that relates to the society—they are that way because they are the poor ones, for instance. But it's also because they are the black ones; there is not only class prejudice but racism. It's exactly like Jesse Jackson was talking about in your last presidential election. It's difficult to convey, but it's necessary. The situation demands a slightly different approach because it's not caused purely by economics.

"For instance, bossa nova was perceived as the music of the upper classes, who were white. It was an appropriation by the whites: they claimed it, separated the parts and took what was cool enough and clean enough to be okay. Now, cultural and social processes are always intricate and mysterious, so we can't say that that group of people did what they did intentionally. But they just represent what they are, what their backgrounds are, so they just reproduce a class concept or a racial concept that they've always known. They don't even have to be aware of it. It's clear that when bossa nova became popular it didn't really reach street people; its popularity was confined at first to the very high reaches of society. It was too mild for others; where's the energy, the life in it? Then they started absorbing it, having it naturally mix with daily sounds. So they grew to like it, but it took time.

"What bossa lacks, especially in the form of someone like Jobim, is the black component, the rhythm and blues, the rock and roll. It's not a music that rocks the house. Which is okay, it's just different. In the pedagogic thing that we do, it's important to show American society, especially blacks and young people, to tell and show them that there are other things. Bossa nova? Okay. The postcard of Carnival? Okay. But in between those two extremes there is a full range of levels and colors, from Gal Costa to the new rockers, the local music of Bahia which relates a lot to merengue and salsa, so different from Rio. There are many many different planets in Brazil, and we try to show them all when we play so that we can communicate the sense of richness and variety." [1989]

Afropop's Avatar
Manu Dibango

Without 60-year-old Emmanuel Dibango N'Djocke, aka Manu Dibango, modern Afropop might not exist.

Born in Cameroon of parents of "mixed" tribal heritages, his father a civil-service functionary, he came of age at boarding schools in the French countryside, music clubs in Brussels, the Congo on the cusp of revolution and becoming Zaire, and, of course, Paris. (Over the last 30 years Paris has become Afropop Central, thanks to France's colonial heritage, its subsidized ex-colonial-regions franc, its legendary attractiveness to expatriates, and its modern recording studios.) A multi-instrumentalist (he doubles on sax, vibes, and keyboards) with a jazzy streak, he fashioned the first worldwide African hit, "Soul Makossa," in 1973 out of an amalgam of his loves: his homeland's native makossa, a gentle but insistent driving rhythm that he used to underpin assimilated notions from his heroes like King Curtis and Stevie Wonder. And if he's incorporated synthesizers periodically into his sound since then, garnering some justified criticism in the process, he's also refreshingly uncynical about why: "You have to get people to listen."

Toward the end of summer 1994, Dibango and I spent an afternoon at a Greenwich Village cafe ("It reminds me of Paris, and also of the two years I lived here") talking about his life and music. During his sometimes pointed, always articulate reminiscing, he chainsmoked and drank cappucino despite the dripping heat and humidity, occasionally pausing to wipe the pancake makeup left from his earlier appearance on a local news show ("I usually sweat more chocolate than this"). Funny and vivid, his stories, which are further embroidered in his recently published autobiography *Three Kilos of Coffee*, were frequently punctuated by his enormous goodnatured laugh. Despite his very Parisian ease in the telling, however, his recollections paint a revealing tale of cultural rupture and dislocation, and how they coursed from alienation into art. Far from being a traditionalist, Dibango quite deliberately split with his past, paid the price in the inevitable bouts of alternating self-reproach and self-justification, and, in parallel with contemporary greats like Hugh Masekela and Fela Kuti, created something that wasn't there before—a modern African pop that reflected not just the continent's blossoming into urban areas but its increasing conjunction with the machinery that distributes popular culture around the globe.

"I was born," he began in his booming basso, "in 1933 in Cameroon. My parents were both Protestant. My father was working in the administration at that time, from the Africa of the early 1930s and 1940s. I had a correct family with no major problems. My mother was conducting the choir in church, so from age five I was singing in the choir with her. That's like most of the musicians here, in fact. What we were singing was like what they sang here, but with African lyrics. So there's a kind of link already between the melody and harmony here and there. Now, the rhythm is different because the environment is different. So if religion makes a difference between Africa and here, as many people think, it also makes a link.

"They sent me to Paris at 15 to study everything but the music," he continued, emphasizing the "but" and dropping in a huge laugh. "That's why I'm a musician. That was the only path that remained for me; they'd closed all the other ones. I was happy and lucky, because in the early 1950s in France there was a lot of jazz. I met all the exiles who were living there at the time—Sidney Bechet, Bud Powell, all of them. So I was a fan before I ever played jazz."

A student at a pricey lycee—the title of his autobiography refers to the preferred medium of exchange between his civil-servant father and his French schoolmasters—Dibango soon immersed himself in the local music scene, which was mainly smatterings of American imports, Moulin Rouge stage traditions, and of course, ubiquitous bad French pop. Soon he was gigging around.

"I took up the sax around '54. I was already playing piano—I'd had a professor in France I studied with. I studied enough classical music with him to be in love with some of the great pieces of music in that tradition. Mozart, I think, is like a cathedral. But contemporaries like Boulez—it's all about architecture, you can't dance to it, even in your head," he said, slyly slipping in a reference to another hero, Ornette Coleman. "I played with symphonic orchestras in France, for instance. There can be a meeting between the European and the African mind here too, not just in popular music. You must explore many angles in life. People say that only black people deal with rhythm well, but Tchaikovsky, after all, is one of the most interesting masters of rhythm."

When he moved to Brussels in 1956, where he soon married the Belgian woman who is still with him, Dibango was already dabbling in all kinds of music and playing behind dancers and singers. "I listened to Charlie Parker records, Johnny Hodges records—all the best saxophonists," he recalled. "So more and more I got involved in jazz, from Louis Armstrong to the Modern Jazz Quartet, many different types of jazz. Ornette, whose album *Dancing in Your Head* has a piece with African musicians in Jajouka—I still remember his beautiful 'Lonely Woman.' He's a wonderful melodist, and someday I'm going to take a chance and play my version of it. I've played with Don Cherry [a longtime Ornette sideman] for two months in France on tour; he's also very special, a student of folklore. For jazz is another meeting of Europe and Africa, after all; it's the beautiful flower that comes from a lot of bad history."

And for that reason, Dibango suggested, not without self-contradiction, not really possible for him to inhale too deeply: "I cannot be a jazz musician because I'm not American. You can learn one part of jazz in school. Everybody can go to Berklee, whether they come from Africa or Italy or France. But the real jazz in the beginning was street music, and this is a different approach. You can learn to be a technician, but to be a real jazz musician you have to be born here, I think. Take makossa: I treat makossa like people treat the blues here, or in Brazil samba. These kinds of difference are necessary. I'm not a Mississippi man. I don't drink Coca-Cola; I drink beaujolais. But in the total realm of jazz, you can bring something to it: you can be yourself. Jazz is also free, so you can do your thing within it. It's big enough to take a lot of ingredients. Bring your differences. Within jazz everything is equal, but not the same." A lesson that underlines why jazz may be the fullest realization of Jeffersonian ideals in modern American culture.

In the early 1960s, as independence erupted across the former colonies of Africa, Dibango, like many of his fellow expatriates, felt the urge to return home—which he did by a typically circuitous route. "In 1961 I went back to Zaire. I was playing in a Senegalese club, when some Zairean musicians came. For the first time in my life I met musicians who were living through their music in Africa, creating new things." At the time, a blend of Cuban rhythms and traditional Congolese materials were creating soukous, an urban dance music that would soon sweep the continent, thanks to Zaire's central location and powerful radio transmitters. "So they hired me as sax and piano player for some records, which were so successful in Africa that they invited me for one month to tour there. I spent two years. I left Africa, after all, when I was 15; I didn't really know it, except for Douala, where I was born. But when I went back, I really learned about it. Playing with African musicians in Africa—that was really important."

The disillusionment that followed the rampant disorganization and corruption he encountered, both in Zaire and later, when he returned to Cameroon and attempted to implant a fledgling modern sound and music industry there, came quickly: "A mixed marriage was pretty explosive. Soldiers wanted to buy my wife often, for example. They thought, He's a musician and he has a nice woman like that, but I'm a soldier. . . . It's like that."

Returning to Europe threw his multifaceted alienation into even sharper relief: "There were two aspects to my fight. The first was in Europe, where people knew I played saxophone and piano but would say, That's not an African instrument. To be a musician you must play balafon or tomtom. The other was in Africa, where you could not be a professional musician. Musicians were folk artists: people invite you to play and give you food and drink. Not money. In between Europe and Africa was Manu Dibango. So when I did 'Soul Makossa' in 1973, Americans said I was doing African music, and Africans said I was doing Western music, and Europeans said I was doing American music."

When the great King Curtis was killed in a street shooting in 1971, Dibango released the raunchy "Tribute to King Curtis," a single that went nowhere but pointed to future directions: "I was in love with his playing; he sang through the saxophone, like Earl Bostic, Louis Jordan—all those alto saxophonists who made David Sanborn possible.

I'd just seen him a little before in Paris, with Aretha Franklin." He followed it with the song often credited as the start of modern Afropop. As he said wryly, " 'Soul Makossa' was a huge international hit, despite everybody thinking different things about what I was playing." When he moved to New York for a two-year stay in 1973 and met Ahmet Ertegun, legendary co-founder of Atlantic Records, Dibango remembered, "He told me, Manu, African music is gonna be something, but it's going to take 20 years. He was right. It's a different flavor in the melting pot."

Dibango sampled hybrid New World flavors, especially New York's thriving Latin culture: "I toured with the Fania All Stars, where I first met Ruben Blades and Willie Colon and Johnny Pacheco and Jose Feliciano and Tito Puente—all of them. At that time, Latin musicians were looking for their African roots also, and I was a curiosity. Then in 1979 I went to Jamaica, because I wanted to see and smell this reggae atmosphere. Chris Blackwell (founder of Island Records, Bob Marley's label) wanted me to go there and find out what would happen with a meeting between Jamaica and Africa. I still love that double album, *Rasta Souvenir.*"

Some record execs, like Blackwell, had begun thinking about how to break the burgeoning sounds from around the world into their primary market, the U.S. Marley had proved not only that it could be done, but that it could become big time. The next decade saw a series of at times contorted attempts to recreate Marley's success with African musicians like Sunny Ade, Fela Kuti, and, of course, Manu Dibango.

"My problem," he said, "was typical: people have things they want to hear from you. At that time the record companies wanted only 'Soul Makossa #2.' So you must be either a fool or strong, and say, I'm a musician, it's my job to explore. I'm who I am." The ingratiating vitality of his easygoing stage show, for instance, mirrors the lessons he's learned about just that.

Now an elder statesman of Afropop, Dibango reflects on what's emerged in his wake: "There are many younger musicians I like, like Youssou N'Dour and Salif Keita, who are more roots-keepers than me. Youssou lives in Dakar, for instance. This is a necessary change; African people must live and work and stay in Africa, but the politics don't make it easy for musicians to live through their music in Africa. So most of us live outside it. But people like Youssou and Fela Kuti and Sunny Ade make it in Africa, which I respect very much. And I'm happy there are so many African musicians popular now. When I started here in the 1970s there were only people like Baba Olutunji, Hugh Masekela, Miriam Makeba, and Dollar Brand. Now there are 20 or 30 people known in America, which may not seem like that much after 20 years. But it's like a fairy tale when I come back and people in the audience tell me their parents were the ones who first played them 'Soul Makossa.'

"When I started in America, the audience was black and Latin—few white people. In the 1970s here was the Black is Beautiful and Back to the Roots idea. Now there's many more white people. Now it's World Music, which is larger than just African, and so it's a different audience. And there's a cultural problem here too. American blacks are not encouraged in these directions; outside of America, they know almost nothing. They didn't have chance in school to learn about different situations historically. So people like Spike Lee try through their movies to make people aware of Africa, which is important, because many think we're living with snakes and Tarzan. But through people like Harry Belafonte, black Americans can maybe learn about the beginnings of their culture. Don't give money; try to learn the story. It shouldn't be the whites taking care of African culture, what's gone on in Africa.

"That's why this new record, *Wakafrica*, is important for us. The problems in Africa are talked and talked and talked about. We say, People talk too much. Let's do something, take action. So to us musicians, action is to try to talk together, play together. There's a strong difference between us, because we all come from different places. But we need that. Afterwards, we can talk about unity—which is not the same thing as doing nothing. So on this record we do African standards, from 'Pata Pata' to 'Soul Makossa,' and try to sing each other's songs. Let's try to go from Senegal to Cape Town: can we do that? If we can, why can't people in other fields, like doctors, get together for a specific project that Africa needs? So this is a kind of statement that all the artists agreed on. We need to start somewhere." [1994]

The Lion of Zimbabwe
Thomas Mapfumo

S.O.B.'s usually attracts a healthy crowd; for years, it's been New York's premier space for international sounds. But November 1989 found the smallish club crammed with excited devotees of chimurenga, since the legendary Lion of Zimbabwe, Thomas Mapfumo, was making his first U.S. appearances on a one-month tour.

Though he sang almost entirely in his native Shona—only the title cut off his U.S.-label debut, *Corruption*, was in English—Mapfumo seized the crowd and held it. The roiling and pumping grooves, the glittering guitar work, the sharp-creased horns, the precision backup singers, his own deep, resonant, gravelly vocals and exuberant steps combined into a kind of musical Kabuki. The dance floor swayed beneath the packed-in, moving bodies. Some communication, at least, made it across the language barrier.

For the rest, you have to know the background. Thomas Mapfumo—like Bob Marley, Fela Anikulapo Kuti, Gilberto Gil—is an artist spurred by social concerns. As he puts it: "The type of music that I play is chimurenga. Chimurenga means 'liberation struggle.' So I've written very few love songs. Within chimurenga there is love—for peace. In every song I have written I'm always preaching about peace, equality, justice, freedom.

"During times of war, of the liberation struggle for the Zimbabwean people, my music played a very important part. It influenced a lot of youngsters to go out and get a gun and fight in the struggle against the regime which was oppressing them. Yet when we look at the music again, it is the traditional music of the people of Zimbabwe made militant, because it was born out of the liberation struggle. It became the voice of the people, because outside of music nobody had anyways to say anything against the regime. So music became the voice of struggle."

In a society as commercialized as ours, that kind of commitment, that faith in the social role of culture, can seem romantic and adolescent if not ridiculous. But that's because so much of our culture is actually a different animal, manufactured for us—by the entertainment conglomerates that market movies, TV, music, sports, books, and ads—rather than made by us for our own uses.

Other societies remain closer to their ritual traditions that made music and art part of daily life's fabric. If totalitarian and authoritarian regimes (to echo Jeane Kirkpatrick's meaningless distinction) as well as many republics and democracies routinely add censorship to their government arsenals, it's because they recognize, in a perverted way, the sheer power of art and music to speak much more than the Tin Pan Alley clichés our entertainment industry grinds out like toothpaste. Because of the conglomerates that dominate the U.S. cultural marketplace, that tunnel vision about music's function and content effectively becomes a form of corporate-exercised censorship.

Mapfumo and his rich, provocative chimurenga don't come out of a tube. Like Marley's and Fela's and Gil's, Mapfumo's music reflects the time and place of its birth, although by the alchemical process we call art it also somehow manages to be timeless and more universal than, say, a list of revolutionary demands. In Mapfumo's case, the time stretches from the late 1960s to the present, and the place is the land its colonizers called Rhodesia, after the diamond-and gold-mine magnate who "bought" its mineral rights in 1888. As Freda Troup writes in *South Africa*, "Rhodesia was founded as a speculators' El Dorado and preserve."

So Rhodesia was one of the few African colonies no European government directly controlled. Partly for that reason, the largest tribal group inhabiting the region, the Shona, was not deliberately split into smaller, weaker subgroups by European-imposed "national boundaries"—a concept that meant little to Africans organized by tribe. Instead, despite bitter and costly wars against their colonizers, despite the imposition of white minority rule and a South African-style apartheid, the Shona today still make up some 70 percent of Zimbabwe's population—a relatively rare instance in Africa of tribe and nation-state overlapping.

Born among the Shona on July 2, 1945, Mapfumo grew up hearing and playing their tribal music. At that music's center was the mbira, also sometimes called a thumb piano, which is made of metal keys mounted on a wooden frame and a resonator; its tone resembles a slightly buzzing and distorted xylophone's. Arpeggios played on the mbira structure each piece, and the various sections within each piece; the vocals tend to dart in and around the repeated instrumental lines, a bit like a dolphin playfully breaking the ocean's waves.

By the late 1960s, however, what was called Rhodesia was quite different from the open land that had spawned and supported the Shona over centuries. Industrializing and increasingly urban, the country, like most of its African neighbors, had been infiltrated by Western imports—which included the electric guitar and recordings by the Beatles, James Brown, and Bob Marley.

By the early 1960s, Mapfumo, like many other African artists of the period, was covering Western tunes by James Brown, Otis Redding, and Wilson Pickett, and even managed to get some radio play out of it. But by the mid-1960s he'd begun to write his own songs, in Shona; unfortunately, at just that point the white minority government effectively banned indigenous music from the airwaves. Undaunted, Mapfumo continued to work on what had become his long-term goal, the creation of a contemporary Shona music that would speak to his people's conditions. He was inspired by the rebel-run radio station, The Voice of Zimbabwe, which broadcast a program called "Chimurenga Requests," featuring the ZANLA choir. He summarizes his musical growth this way: "Bob Marley influenced many many African musicians whether they play reggae or not. Look at me: I've been listening to a whole lot of music since childhood. I was into rock and roll, then jazz, rhumba music, soul music, the Beatles—I love experimenting with different things to make new music. But when I was older and it came to my own music, I was able to take that experimenting and become Thomas Mapfumo—no more chasing after rainbows, it was time to become myself.

"So I looked around and I listened again to mbira music, the music of our people. I found that it was danceable but lacking something, the modern beat. I wanted to make it appeal to youngsters, to those in the cities. That's what I did. That's why the guitar and the mbira and the brass section all interact in chimurenga. We can play almost anything, even Michael Jackson, if we want, and certainly reggae. We can play better reggae than most of the reggae bands people listen to.

But we don't like to waste time on other people's music. We have our music, chimurenga, to look after. That is our identity."

So what Mapfumo did with Shona music is very like what his idol Marley did with earlier Jamaican forms: reshape them into contemporary sounds that could revive their function as social commentary. Electric guitars overlaid shimmering mbira-derived riffs on traditional dance rhythms that were updated, urbanized. Mapfumo extended and recreated his cultural heritage so successfully, in fact, that the previously dominant musical forms in his country, Western and South African pop, were soon replaced by chimurenga.

By 1973, Mapfumo had formed the Hallelujah Chicken Run Band; by the following year, he'd begun to record some of his Shona-derived compositions. Unlike the directly propagandistic music played by The Voice of Zimbabwe, Mapfumo's lyrics, like those of other chimurenga popsters, combined innuendo and traditional sayings to make anticolonialist points. Partly, of course, this was self-protective: the Rhodesian government's secret police were no kinder than South Africa's. But the messages got through; within two years Mapfumo had garnered eight gold records.

Not without consequences you'd expect: he also became a target of government surveillance and harassment. More and more isolated economically and morally, rabidly afraid of the racial "bloodbath" they insisted was the alternative to their dictatorial minority rule, the white Rhodesians, led by Prime Minister Ian Smith, were not about to tolerate the assertion of an indigenous culture they'd tried for so long to either destroy or ignore. Mapfumo and his music became a flash point.

As he himself tells it: "I got into trouble myself because of chimurenga. That's why I kept saying it was the traditional music of our people, and there was no way anyone was gonna stop me from playing that type of music: it is within me, it's my culture. If you try and tell me to do away with my culture then I have to do away with my life. That's how I see it.

"My lyrics are in Shona. When you come to Zimbabwe you find that the Shona people are the majority of the people in Zimbabwe; they have been there since the world began. Though some of our people speak different languages, all of them can speak at least a bit of Shona, and we also can speak some of their languages. So there's a lot of communication between us. When I sing in Shona, the message gets to everyone in our country—except the whites.

"I want to point out something here. When you are living with someone who speaks a different language from yours, it is up to you to try and learn his language, so there is a good method of communication between you two. I learned English; I don't speak good English, but I can understand what an Englishman is trying to say when he speaks to me, I can answer a word or two. But the whites living in Zimbabwe wasted their time, because they never saw any reason to learn Shona. So it's the white man who was foolish, not me. I accepted his language as a human being, but he didn't accept mine. Maybe he thought my language was too inferior for him to speak. Now he's regretting it, because now it's very very important for him to learn my language."

In 1977, after Mapfumo had formed the Acid Band (acid as in bitter-tasting), he released his first album with them, *Hokoya*, which means "watch out." The Rhodesians didn't need to know much Shona to get the gist. So they banned the album from the radio, tried to suppress it completely, and then tossed him in the slammer for 90 days without a trial.

Asked about it now, Mapfumo shakes his huge, sculpted head. "Yes, I stayed in detention for three months. They were actually trying to sort of scare me. They said, 'Your music is political, you are influencing a lot of youngsters to go out and get a gun and join the terrorists'—as the authorities used to call the rebels. But I always said, 'My music is the traditional music of Zimbabwe; I cannot run away from my own culture.' They sent in Special Branch men, changed them, sent in new and strange faces to question and try to scare me, but I stood by what I said. So they changed tactics. Then they considered releasing me, on condition that me and my band were to go and play in Bulawayo for a rally of Bishop Muzorewa. When we looked at the whole issue, it was a serious one—a matter of political life and death. And it was more: we had to go along with these people because we were literally afraid for our lives. Still, we utterly changed what they expected us to do."

At the time, the white Rhodesians were attempting to inflict their own version of the South African "homeland" policy on the indigenous population, uprooting entire villages to move them in the name of "internal resettlement." But because the whites didn't understand Mapfumo's language, a simple—though dangerous—sleight of hand brought their attempts to subvert his music and its message to nought. "Our music was militant and opposed to the internal settlement," he recalls. "So when we played at the rally, we sang the same songs, chimurenga, opposing the internal settlement, supporting the guerrilla movement. The next morning there was a big picture of me with Bishop Muzorewa on the front pages of the papers, to make it look like we went there willingly. But the point is what we played supported the freedom fighters.

"Some of the people at the rally were asking why we were still singing the songs of chimurenga when we were about to get our independence. I said, 'As you know, I'm just out from detention. I didn't have time enough to compose music for the celebrations.' So they left us alone. But the papers sold us out by making it look like we had sold out the struggle. To those in the bush, they knew exactly what sort of band we were, so they didn't believe that rubbish. But some people did.

"So it became a big issue, and it affected us during our independence celebrations: we were treated like the last band in the country. But we knew our position. We kept quiet, and we kept to ourselves. So the day of the celebrations, we went into the stadium. They asked us to come at 8 o'clock in the evening. And we thought we'd start after an hour or two. Then we were told that we were meant to play at 5 o'clock the next morning. So we waited. They were trying to victimize us, but we didn't care about that. Then we played our chimurenga, and to the surprise of the authorities everyone who was there jumped to their feet and started dancing. All the other bands that played, nobody danced to their music, nobody reacted like that. So we thought, 'The people in power may think we're bad, but if the people think we're all right we're okay.' "

Because of the tangled politics and economics of Zimbabwe's recent past, albums from within the country have been even more difficult to pick up than those from other African sources. But there are a couple of U.S.-released efforts that reflect why Zimbabweans think Mapfumo is okay. *The Chimurenga Singles 1976–1980* collects tracks with the Acid Band as well as Mapfumo's ongoing outfit, The Blacks Unlimited. *Ndangariro* is a 1983 Earthworks album issued here that boasts some classic Mapfumo performances, like the soulfully aching "Emma." And now, of course, there's *Corruption*, his first effort made specifically for release here.

According to Mapfumo, his working methods haven't changed over the years. "When I'm writing, I start from traditional Shona music," he explains. "Then I work on the tune, on guitar, strum a few chords on it, try it out to see if it's suitable for the Blacks Unlimited. Then I sit down and write lyrics. When I get lyrics I feel are right, I take the tune to the band, and they all concentrate to work on it. We all sit down together to bring out the tune, the arrangement. Sometimes that changes the tune completely.

"Before we record we work out the arrangements onstage, in our shows, changing them if they don't work. We record track by track. We put down the guitars and drums first, usually together. Then we put in some keyboards, maybe mbira. Then vocals, then percussion, then lead guitar. If there are other things we want to make the song sound fuller, we put them in. We recorded *Corruption* the same way we recorded everything else; we didn't change anything."

Noting that many other Afropop artists have had varying degrees of success dealing with the linguistic and cultural barriers that greet them when they arrive in the U.S., Mapfumo insists, "If we want to be honest, the music is there, it's danceable, though we might have some difficulties having the lyrics understood by our audience. But we are there to explain the meaning of these songs; now that we know what our audience is like, we know what we must do to please and reach them.

"One other thing for our black brothers and sisters living in America: I would like to assure them that we know every star in America, every black artist, and we go out and buy their records. That doesn't mean that when our brothers and sisters go out to buy these black American records they understand every single word that's sung there; it's just because the music sounds nice and they want to dance to it. The same must happen for black Americans; they must come and see us. We are from home, where they come from. We are the roots. If they can't come and see their own roots, they are lost. They have to come to us, and we can tell them exactly what is wrong. What we are bringing them is the real thing." [1990]

Lilt

A Survey of Hawaiian Music

On February 20, 1915, the Panama-Pacific International Exposition opened in San Francisco to celebrate the Panama Canal's completion. One of its main attractions was the $100,000 Hawaii Pavillion, which for seven months hosted a Hawaiian music show several times a day. It packed the crowds in. The Royal Hawaiian Quartette played songs like "Waikiki Mermaid" and "On the Beach at Waikiki" on acoustic steel guitar, ukuleles, and guitar, while singing stirring, wide-vibratoed versions of barbershop harmonies that still shape Hawaiian vocals. And folks walked away humming the catchy melodies.

Soon Tin Pan Alley joined Hawaiian composers like Johnny Noble in writing "hapa haole" (literally, half-white—a mix of English lyrics and pop-tune structures with Hawaiian themes) songs by the hundreds. The period's big three record companies—Victor, Edison, and Brunswick—began releasing hundreds of Hawaiian records. Steel guitar players abandoned their homeland to make big money in Hollywood and vaudeville. Hawaiian sounds began to outsell other forms of pop music on the mainland U.S., and had such an impact that Mexican bands added steel guitar players and masqueraded as Hawaiians to crash the lucrative U.S. vaudeville circuit. (*The Tau Moe Family with Bob Brozman* captures one of the era's typical touring groups.)

Every 20 years or so since, the mainland has fallen for the lilting lure of Hawaiian-inflected pop—whether from Bing Crosby and Elvis Presley (who both recorded "Blue Hawaii") or smooth Hawaiian pop singers like Alfred Apaka (*The Best of Alfred Apaka*) and Don Ho (*Don Ho & the Aliis*). These native matinee idols mined crossover dreams—dreams that many of today's Hawaiian traditionalists distrust.

Given Hawaii's history, the century-long embrace between mainland and Hawaiian culture could never be easy. After Captain James Cook landed there in 1778, a series of often-explosive cultural collisions created displacement and grief at the same time that they shaped a supple hybrid music in ways that parallel cultural collisions elsewhere in the New World.

Less than half a century after Cook landed on what he called the Sandwich Islands, Hawaiian civilization imploded. A feudal hierarchy supported by an elaborate system of animistic worship reinforced by *kapu*, or taboos, it was undermined by contact with Western sailors (who violated the kapu with impunity) and by the *ali'i*, or ruling class, itself. In 1819, King Kamehameha II abolished the kapu, and a young Hawaiian went to New England to study for the ministry. The next year, New England missionaries came to the islands, and became key participants in Hawaiian culture.

Pre-contact Hawaiian culture was oral. The men of the cloth chose 12 letters of the English alphabet (five vowels, seven consonants) to transliterate Hawaiian, doing at least some violence to the language in the process. (Meanwhile, diseases carried in by Europeans and Americans were devastating the native population: within 75 years of Cook's landing, it had shrunk by about 70 percent.) The missionaries' musical contribution was the book of himeni, or hymns, which they prepared in Hawaiian in 1823. The Hawaiians loved to sing, and they loved the hymns' simple yet stirring chordal movements, group harmonies, rising and falling melodies—contours that echo through much Hawaiian music.

Indigenous Hawaiian music had its own rituals unrelated to anything Western: chanting with percussion and with the dance known as hula, whose swaying, expressive movements illustrated the words of each *mele*, or chant. The chants often described the animistic deities. After 1820, however, the hula was suppressed. The ministers saw it as licentious, and the fact that the women who danced it (originally, the hula had been a male province) were topless only fueled the outsiders' religious fervor. Then, in 1874, one of Hawaii's last native rulers, King David Kalakaua, revived hula as entertainment, and set up *halau* (schools) to train students in this nuanced, difficult art from a young age. Hula's cultural symbolism is one reason for its enduring popularity: in Hawaii, even pop bands are often accompanied by dancers.

Though much of the sacred hula tradition was lost, it didn't die. Music in Hawaii is often still a family (*ohana*) affair, and acclaimed clans like the Kanaka'olas on the island of Hawaii passed down the hula tradition orally. In fact, hula played a vital role in Hawaii's post-1960s cultural reawakening and questioning—a mood that paralleled mainland developments. (Robert Mugge's fine documentary *Kumu Hula* surveys hula's history and purposes.)

The Roaring Twenties Hawaiiana wave rode to the U.S. mainland via the vocalizing instrument that became a staple first of 1930s Western swing, then of Nashville—the Hawaiian or steel guitar. According to the most widely accepted account, in the 1890s young Joseph Kekuku began imitating singers by fretting the guitar with bolts or combs or knives. Finally he fashioned a metal bar, raised the strings (to prevent fret noise), tuned them to a single chord, and, holding the guitar on his lap, fingerpicked melodies. The results have shaped pop music around the world—even to the floating juju of Nigeria's King Sunny Ade, shot through with steel guitar thanks to Ade's love for Nashville star George Jones.

After the 1915 Expo, every Hawaiian who could play steel guitar headed to the U.S. Enduring colonies of Hawaiians still dot the West Coast and now form a mini-tour circuit for Hawaiian musicians. But the king of early steel virtuosi was not Kekuku but the redoubtable Sol Hoopii, who elevated and popularized steel musicianship during his prolific recording career for Columbia and Decca, improvising deftly on jazzy numbers like "Twelfth Street Rag" (on the two-CD *Sol Hoopii Master of the Steel Guitar*). Astonishingly vocal, his playing had its vaudeville side—tapping the guitar with his picks for a syncopated "break," for instance. The flamboyant Hoopii's work intrigued Western-swing pioneers like Bob Wills, who began using Hoopii-influenced steel players. Known as "The Hollywood Hawaiian," pals with Bing Crosby and Mary Pickford, who had him play on her silent-movie sets for mood music, Hoopii recorded with trios, quartets, and quintets—until he bailed out to devote the last 15 years of his life to working with evangelist Aimee Semple McPherson.

Like other insular pasts—think of Sicily or Crete, Cuba or Jamaica—Hawaiian history can be seen as a series of invasions, each leaving in its dislocating wake a new cultural deposit. When the first Portuguese workers for the sugar-cane fields landed in 1878, they brought their mournful *fados*, songs they accompanied on *braguinhas*, guitarlike instruments that evolved into the Hawaiian ukulele. Hawaii's last queen, Liliuokalani, a scholar-composer (she wrote "Aloha Oe" before being deposed in 1893 by a Euro-American cabal for trying to restore the monarchy's powers), insisted ukulele meant "the gift that came here." But most agree it means "jumping flea." Whatever its name means, the ukulele quickly became an emblem of the islands' music. Stars like Depression-era tenor great Ray Kinney and his often risque female contemporary Lena Machado strummed ukes as they sang, at times in falsetto, a mix of traditional and hapa haole material.

Hapa haole songs can be racist, demeaning, funny, charming, silly, or lovely. Hawaiian pianist-bandleader Sonny Cunha popularized the style at the turn of the century, but his disciple Johnny Noble codified it in countless compositions like "Little Brown Gal" and "Hawaiian War Chant." In 1928 Noble, who as the Moana Hotel's band director melded swing-era rhythms, harmonies, and instrumentation with Hawaiian themes, became a talent scout, first for Brunswick Records, then for Decca. As a result, lots of Hawaiians, like Kinney and Machado, were waxed on 78s—fruitful ground for CD reissues that's yet to be broken significantly.

Among the few hapa haole composers from the period whose music is available today is Harry Owens, a Nebraskan who extended the form. (Check out *The Best of Harry Owens and His Royal Hawaiians*.) Owens, who came to Honolulu in 1934 via a three-month contract to lead the Royal Hawaiian Hotel band, stayed for life. He became dedicated to spreading Hawaiian music, publishing reams of sheet music, playing it exclusively while touring, later hosting a mainland TV show about Hawaiiana. But it was a single tune he wrote in 1934 that, after the Depression had cut back all kinds of recording severely, revived the mainland market for Hawaiiana.

When his daughter was born in Honolulu, Owens crafted a catchy little ditty for her called "Sweet Leilani." Soon afterwards, Bing Crosby arrived for a vacation before shooting a feature called *Waikiki Wedding*. Dancing at the Royal Hawaiian, Crosby was captivated by Owens's tune, and repeatedly asked the bandleader to play it. He spent the next day trying to pry it from its maker. But Owens felt uneasy about profiting from something that had so much *mana* (spiritual force). Finally, Crosby offered to set up trust funds for the Owens kids and pay any royalties from "Leilani" into them. That did it, and Crosby recorded "Leilani" in 1935. A million-seller within a few weeks, it launched Hawaiiana's second mainland wave, which hit like a tsunami.

Just one measure: the Fleischer brothers scored Betty Boop and other cartoons with Hawaiian music.

The steel guitar, beloved by Hawaiians for its ability to mimic vocals, powered the first Hawaiiana wave, but singing is Hawaiian music's heart. Hawaiian lyrics, replete with multiple meanings, are closed to nonspeakers (which includes most Hawaiians); but the sheer rippling beauty of the singing isn't. The most breathtaking technique is falsetto, used in all forms but the chants. Some say it arose from hymns, some say Mexican cowboys (about whom more later). And some point to Henry Berger, the German bandmaster who, from 1872 to 1915, was a key shaper of Hawaiian music. Berger, who trained thousands of musicians, led the Royal Hawaiian Military Band, helped establish the prestigious Kamehameha School's music department, preserved and arranged countless Hawaiian songs and chants, and was close friends with Queen Liliuokalani, with whom he wrote music. According to George Kanahele's indispensable *Hawaiian Music and Musicians*, Berger's impact on Hawaiian music "was greater and more lasting than that of any other single individual"—another mark of the music's indelibly hybrid nature. In his role as voice teacher, Berger used falsetto and yodeling. But whatever the source, falsetto and yodeling thread 150 years of Hawaiian sounds: a marvel like George Kainapau (a friend of Hoopii's who recorded thrilling 1930s duets with Kinney and sang in *Waikiki Wedding*) could swoop and flutter beyond even the limpid elasticity of Aaron Neville's reach.

Following a third, kitschy Hawaiiana wave of the 1950s and 1960s— hula hoops, Don Ho's "Tiny Bubbles," the TV show *Hawaii Calls*— the 1970s brought a renaissance of traditional Hawaiian culture. As jets began ferrying hordes of tourists to Honolulu, with effects the city's dismal skyline reflects, many Hawaiians began reexamining the history and direction of their society. Hence the reinvigoration of traditional arts that had previously been marginal folk pursuits. Hula, for example, was integral to emerging Hawaiian-nationalist movements. When Kahoolawe, an unpopulated island used by the U.S. Army for weapons testing, was occupied in 1976 by Hawaiians who demanded its return, among them were *kumu hula* (teachers) like Edith Kanaka'ole, who invoked ancient Hawaiian deities via chants and dance.

Alongside the hula arose the unlikely musical legacy of Hawaii's cows. In 1793, the explorer George Vancouver gave King Kamehameha I some longhorns, which ran wild over the island of Hawaii. And overran it, which is why in 1815 the king granted John Palmer Parker of Massachusetts the right to tend the royal herds—the foundation of the Parker Ranch, one of the largest in the U.S. The 1830s saw the importation of Mexican *vaqueros—paniolo* to the Hawaiians, who lionized them in legend and songs like the oft-recorded "Waimea Cowboy" and "Hawaiian Cowboy." The vaqueros brought with them their horses, their guitars with their Spanish tuning (an open-chord tuning that also inspired American blues players), and their propensity to yodel and falsetto—elements at the root of the slack-key idiom.

Like its mainland cousins hillbilly music and country blues, slack-key guitar is a downhome folk form that underlies much contemporary pop. Each family of slack-key players passed its own tunings from one generation to the next. The sweetly melodious and chiming effect of the fingerpicked chords, adapted by steel guitarists from Kekuku on, suits the hypnotic wash of surf and wind, and complements the barbershop harmonies with falsetto that Hawaiians entertain themselves with when they gather ohana-style.

In the 1970s, slack-key and other traditional Hawaiian forms came out of the backyard. Two 1970 events mark the shift. One was a folk-revival concert on Maui that gathered the Sons of Hawaii, a traditionalist Hawaiian folk group featuring legendary guitarist Gabby Pahinui, and other stalwarts like female falsettist Genoa Keawe and slack-key honcho Sonny Chillingworth. (Albums include *Gabby Pahinui with the Sons of Hawaii*; Keawe's *Hana Hou!*; and Chillingworth's *Sonny Solo*.) Soon afterwards, guitarist Ry Cooder helped promote *The Gabby Pahinui Hawaiian Band*, which he recorded with, to a mainland audience, thus starting a small but enthusiastic slack-key cult outside the Hawaiian community.

The second event was the brainchild of another Pahinui disciple, guitarist Peter Moon. Along with the Cazimero Brothers, now huge local stars, Moon organized the Sunday Manoa, a celebration of traditional Hawaiiana. (*The Best of the Sunday Manoa Volumes I and II* capture the feeling.) The Sunday Manoa revived traditional music and, perhaps ironically, helped spawn contemporary Hawaiian pop—including Jawaiian, a bubble-gum but at times fascinating blend of Hawaiiana, rock, and reggae by younger groups like the Hawaiian Style Band (*Vanishing Treasures*).

Older traditionalists like Pahinui, Chillingworth, and Raymond Kane (*Punahele*) were folk artists who held down day jobs and played mostly for pleasure. But a younger generation, including the stunning falsetto duo the Hoopii Brothers (*Ho Ka Oi*) and the brilliant singer-guitarist Ledward Kaapana (*Nahenahe*), a vet of the Smithsonian-sponsored Masters of the Steel String Guitar tour, are looking to turn pro. Growing mainland interest in Hawaiiana, along with the proliferation of hula halau and slack-key guitar studies on the islands, are feeding the next Hawaiian wave. Get your hula hoops and your surf board waxed and ready. [1995]

Index